Hubert Arthur Finney (1905-1991)

Out of the Shadows

The Lightbox

Chobham Road
Woking, Surrey, GU21 4AA

Saturday 9 January to Sunday 21 March 2021

An exhibition organised by LISS LLEWELLYN

Amy Finney, née Dyer (1912-1987), Design for wallpaper.

ACKNOWLEDGEMENTS

A special debt of gratitude is due to Nicholas Finney OBE
for his unstinting support for this project.

We would also like to thank :

Andrew Cormack
Daniel Dullaway
Theo Griffiths
Geoff Hassell of Artbiogs.co.uk
Mary Haynes
Ming Li
Eva Liss
Steven Maisel
Harry Moore-Gwyn
Marilyn Scott, Peter Hall, Michael Regan & Hannah Foster at The Lightbox
Peyton Skipwith
Farang Wren
Micky Wolfson

First published in 2020 by LISS LLEWELLYN

ISBN : 978-1-9993145-2-1

Photography: Pierre Emmanuel Coste, Petra van der Wal & Glynn Clarkson

Design and Typesetting by David Maes
Printed by Zenith Media, October 2020

Hubert Arthur Finney (1905-1991)

Out of the Shadows

Edited by Sacha Llewellyn & Paul Liss

For Barrie Liss

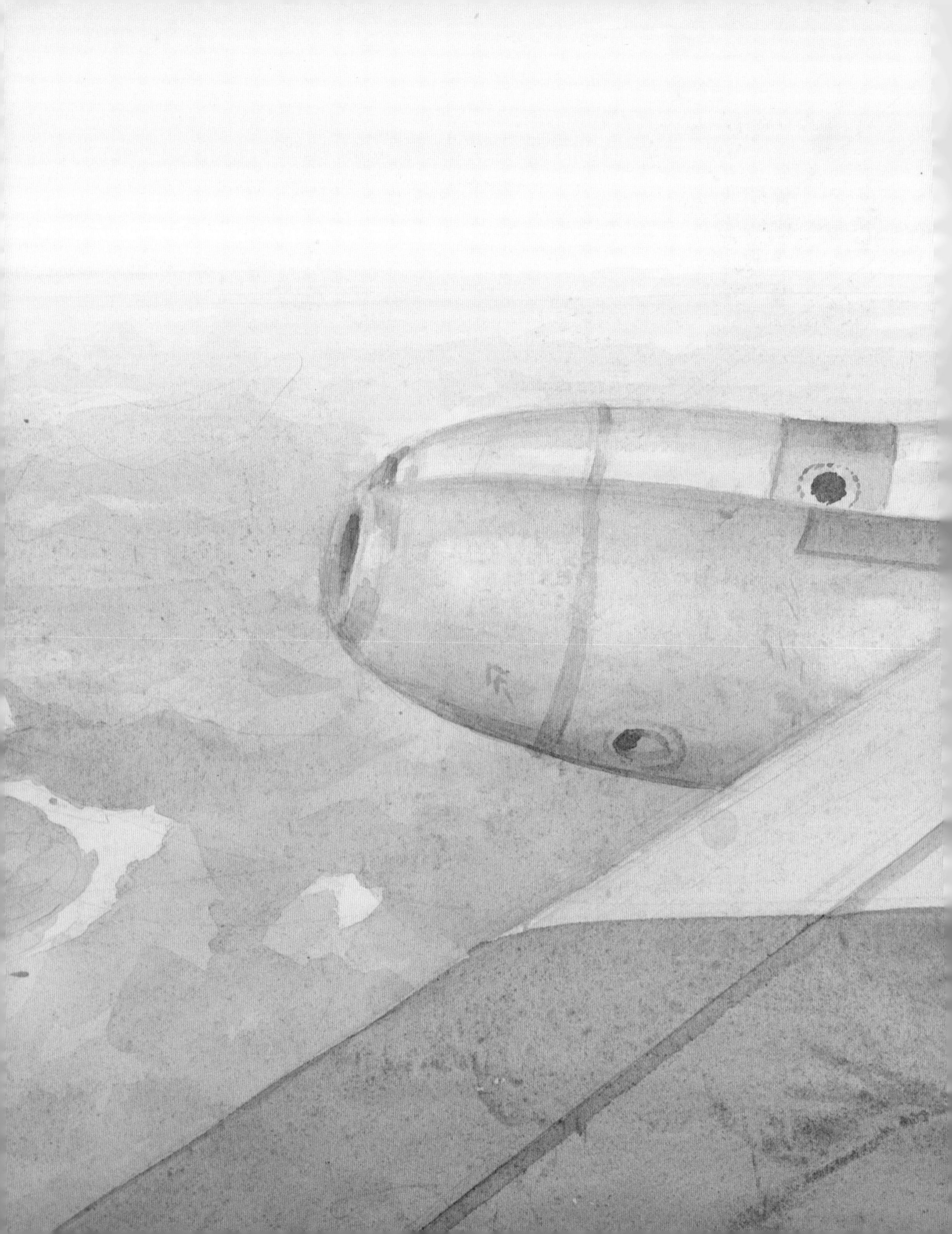

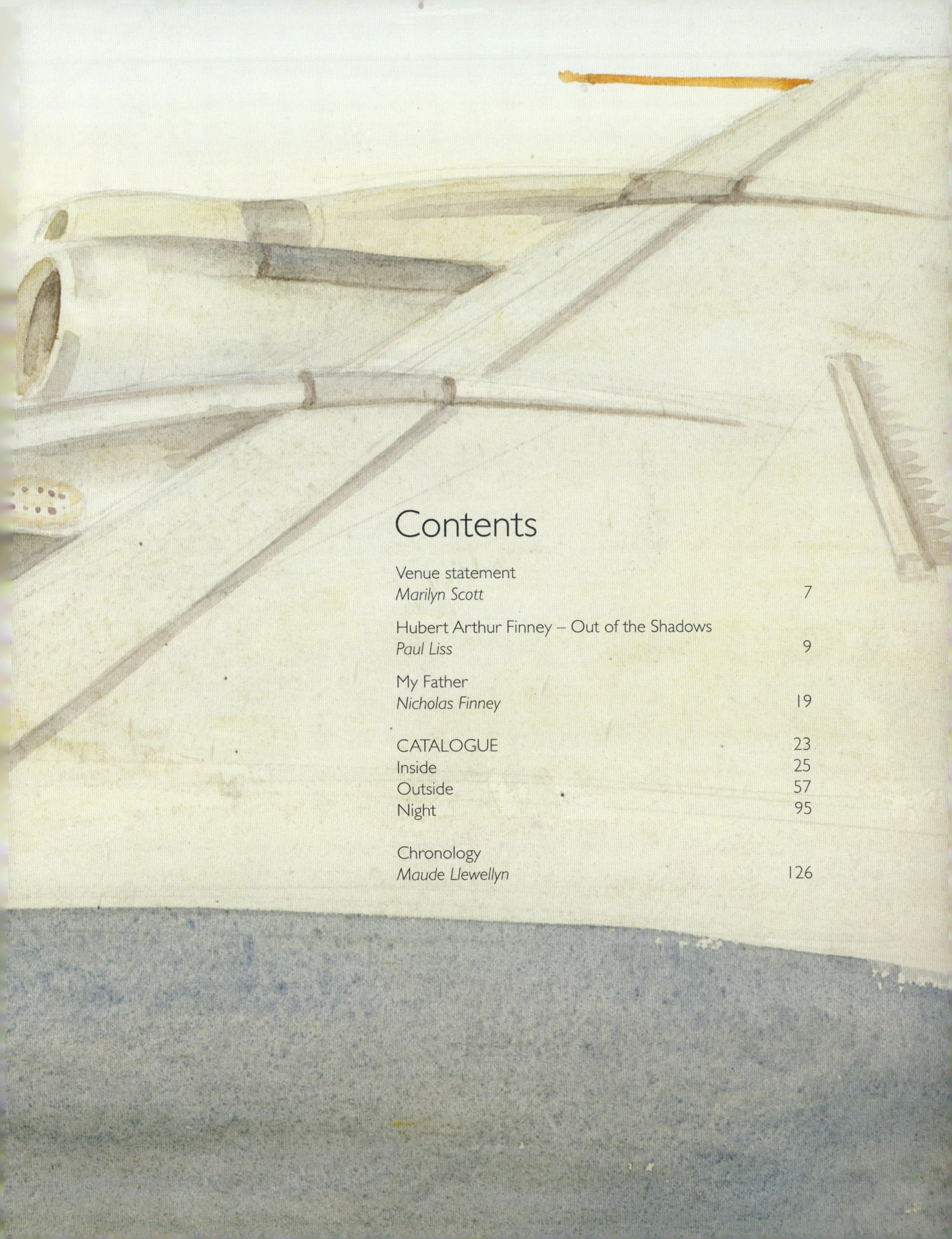

Contents

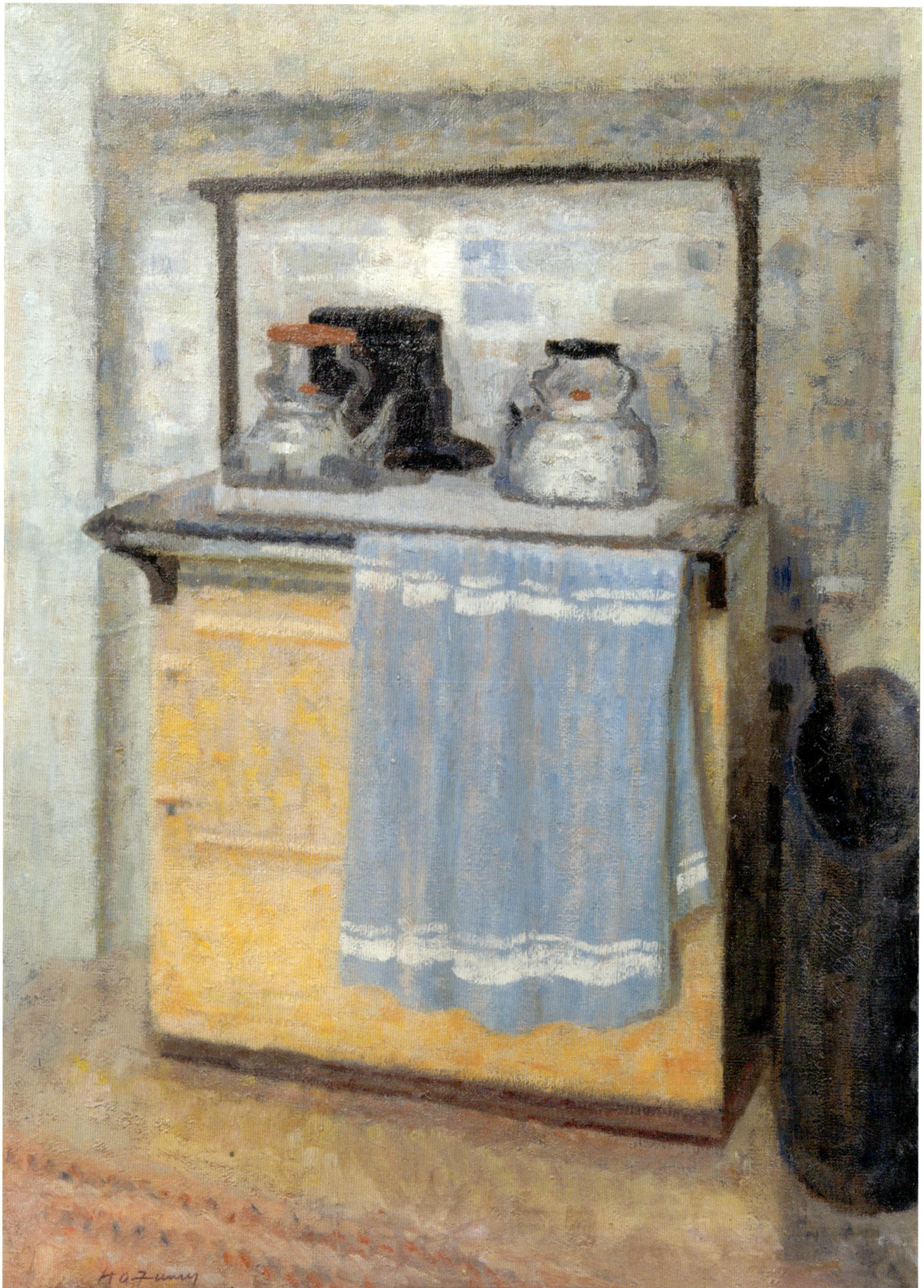

Venue Statement

There is always something exciting about discovering an artist whose work is truly striking and original and wondering why you have never heard of them before. Finney is one such artist – and a perfect candidate for The Lightbox to bring back to the public's gaze.

As an artist Finney was ambitious – he strove throughout his career to create a vision that would be enduring. His decade long apprenticeship at art school connected him with the aesthetic sensibility of the most celebrated masters of the past – and whilst Finney would never have any illusion that he was their equal, there is a touch of a modern day Vermeer in *Amy Ironing* (the painting used as the cover image of this catalogue). And Finney's landscapes have the same graphic charge as those much loved watercolours of Ravilious which so evocatively capture the peculiarities of the different counties of Britain. In contrast to these Finney's languid nocturnes, such as *Haymarket by Night*, have all the aching loneliness of an Edward Hopper, whilst his domestic interiors have passages that resonate the same sense of intimacy as an Edward Vuillard.

We are delighted to be collaborating with Liss Llewellyn who during the last 30 years have worked in association with museums and cultural institutions in the United Kingdom and abroad to develop a series of in-depth exhibitions to encourage the reappraisal of some of the less well known figures of Twentieth Century British Art. I would like to extend a special thanks to Paul Liss, Sacha Llewellyn, Maude Llewellyn and George Richards for their assistance, generosity and valuable advice in bringing this exhibition to The Lightbox. I am particularly grateful to Nicholas Finney whose contribution to this project has been exceptional.

The Lightbox gallery and museum is a charitable arts and heritage organisation with a social purpose to improve the well-being and quality of life of its community. It is one of the most exciting cultural spaces in the South East. Purpose designed by architects Marks Barfield to be fully accessible to all visitors, three stunning galleries host a huge range of exhibitions, changing regularly. A diverse cultural programme ensures that art can be enjoyed by all in an environment that encompasses the philosophy that art has the power to make you feel good. As Finney himself wrote: 'art enables us to have an awareness of beauty in the world, and a greater sensitiveness to people which leads us to a richer appreciation of life.'

Marilyn Scott
Museum Director
www.thelightbox.org.uk

CAT. 1 – *Aga with Two Kettles and Blue Towel*, signed, c.1930, oil on canvas, 29 ½ x 21 in. (75 x 53.5 cm).

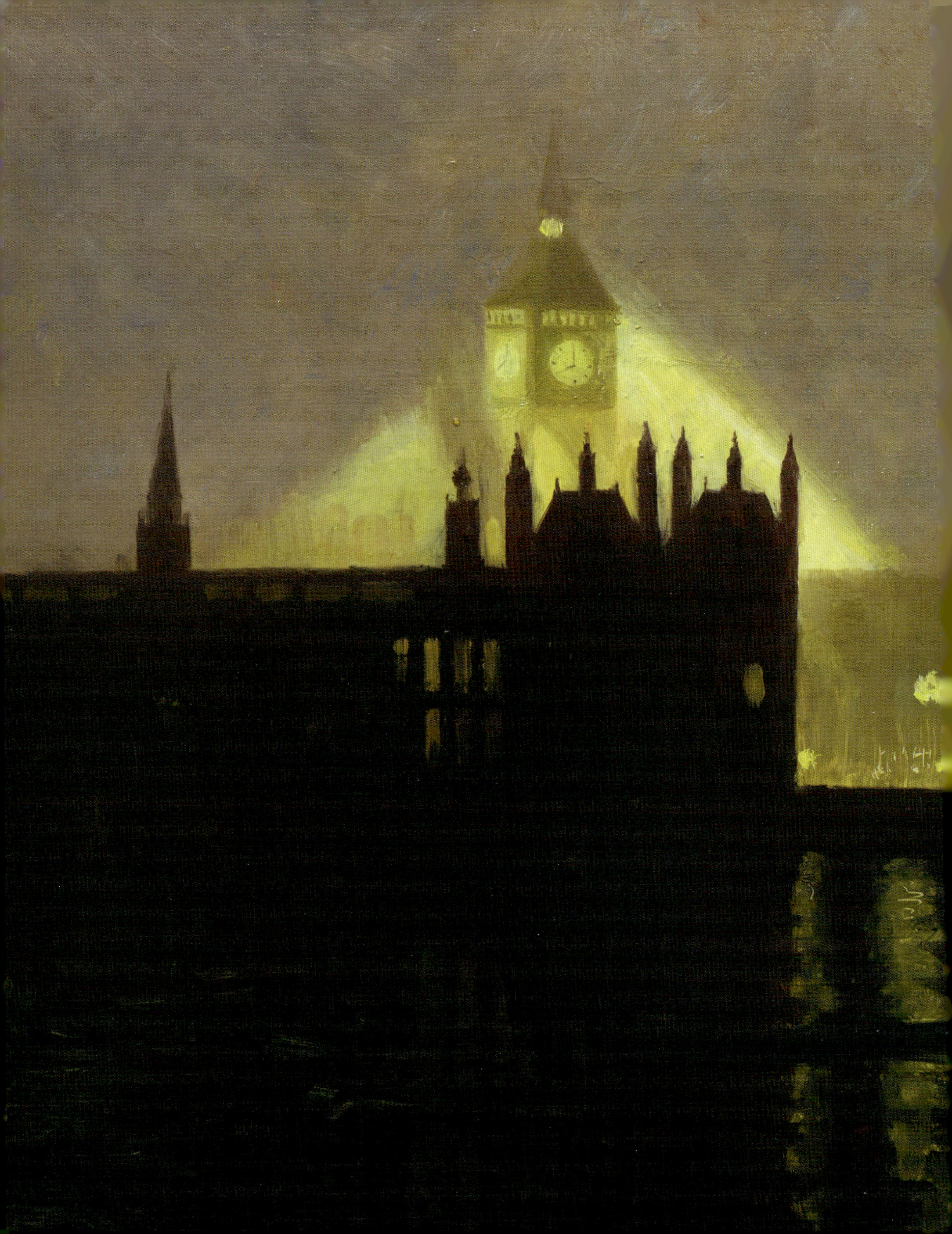

Hubert Arthur Finney (1905-1991)
Out of the Shadows

Paul Liss

The achievements of Hubert Arthur Finney (1905-1991) have been largely overshadowed. This exhibition, the first in over fifty years, presents previously unrecorded works from the artist's studio alongside the first ever publication, based on Finney's recently discovered autobiography.

Finney described himself as having "*a retiring and solitary nature, born with a consuming passion for drawing and painting.*" He saw art as a calling and strove to produce work that lived up to "*high ideals*" fearing that otherwise his "*gift as a painter, or vision, could easily deteriorate into the commonplace.*"

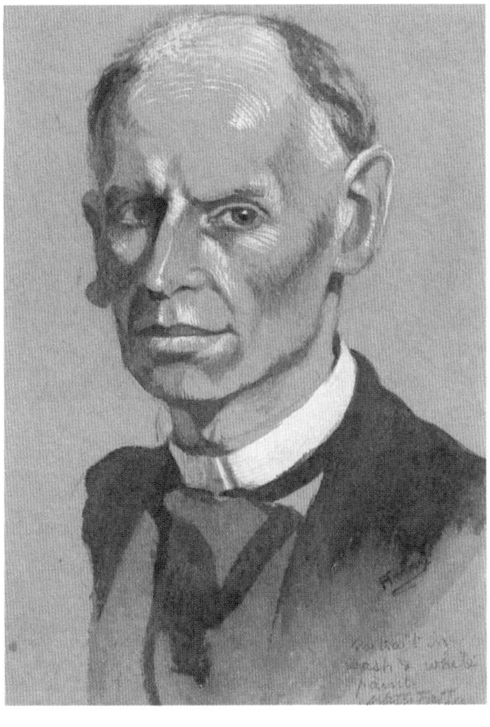

CAT. 2 – Portrait of the artist"s father, drawn at the age of 14, signed and inscribed, wash and gouache on grey paper, 6 ½ x 4 ½ in. (16.8 x 11.3 cm).

A child prodigy, Finney showed a talent for art from an early age: "*At about the age of 10 the headmaster (at Hayes school in Kent) was so impressed that he eventually put me in charge of the drawing class. My destiny as an artist had begun.*"

By the age of fourteen Finney was studying on a full-time Scholarship at Beckenham School of Art, with instruction in painting from Amy Browning (1881-1978) and Percy Jowett (1882–1955) and print making from Eric Gill (1882-1940). Jowett described Finney as 'one of the best of the younger draughtsmen that I have known.' (CAT. 2) He formed a lifelong friendship with Charles Mahoney (1903-1968), who impressed Finney with his "*gift in the field of imaginative composition*" and strong Socialist views, and with Gerald Gardiner (1902-1959), one of the most talented landscape painters of his generation.

Houses of Parliament from St Thomas Hospital at Night, DETAIL. See Cat. 72, page 99.

For all three students the countryside around Beckenham conveyed "*natures beauty in all her extended forms leading to an awareness of the metaphysical*". A search for greater meaning drove Finney throughout his life – he supported a variety of causes, including the Loyalist Faction in the Spanish Civil War and The Communist Party; later he embraced Christian Science. (FIG. 1, CAT. 3)

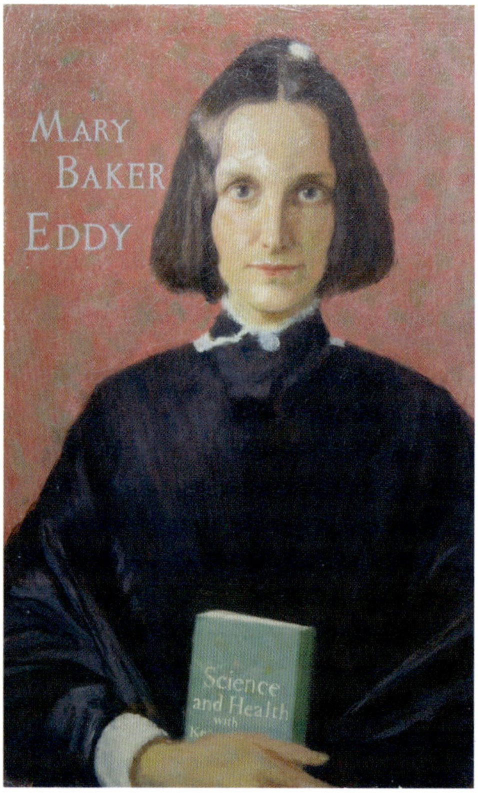

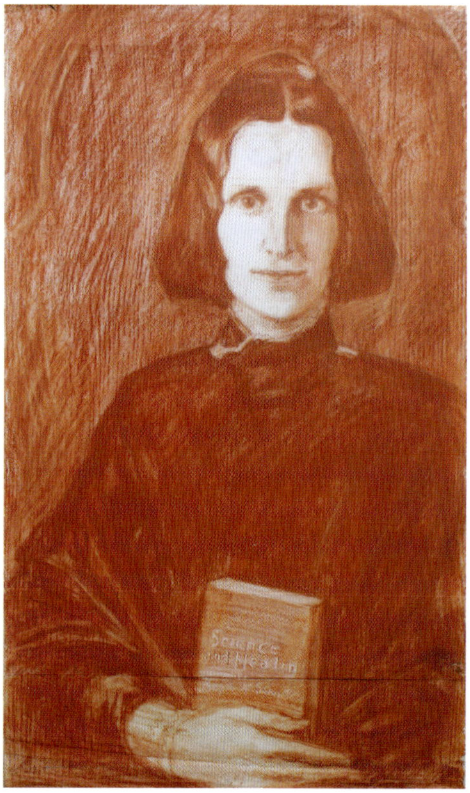

FIG. 1 — *Portrait of Mary Baker Eddy* (founder of Christian Science), c.1930, oil on board, 24 x 14 ½ in. (61 x 36.8 cm). Collection: The Wolfsonian, Miami.
CAT. 3 — Study for *Portrait of Mary Baker Eddy*, red & white chalk on paper; 25 x 14 in. (63 x 36 cm).

At the age of twenty-two Finney's talent gained him a Scholarship to the Royal College of Art. Here he was mentored by William Rothenstein (1872-1945) whose "*powerful personality infiltrated throughout the whole college and his deep belief in the significance of the Arts gave the students and most people who came in contact with him a feeling that any effort was worthwhile in finding a deeper meaning to life*". Finney was taught by Allan Gwynne-Jones (1892-1982), Professor of Painting, who described him as "*one of the best students we have had. He is very gifted as a painter and designer*". Mahoney (who had gained his Scholarship to the RCA in advance) introduced Finney to a new circle: Gerald Ososki (1903-1981), Albert Houthuesen (1903-1979),

Percy Horton (1897-1970) and Barnett Freedman (1901-1958). Inspired by his new environment – Paul Nash had referred to the extraordinary cluster of students in 1924-25 as 'an outbreak of talent' – Finney himself became one of the prodigies who helped to create a golden generation at the RCA between the wars. (FIG. 2) Nonetheless, looking back on his time as a student Finney wished "*that the RCA had been a little more open to the contemporary movements of the time.*"

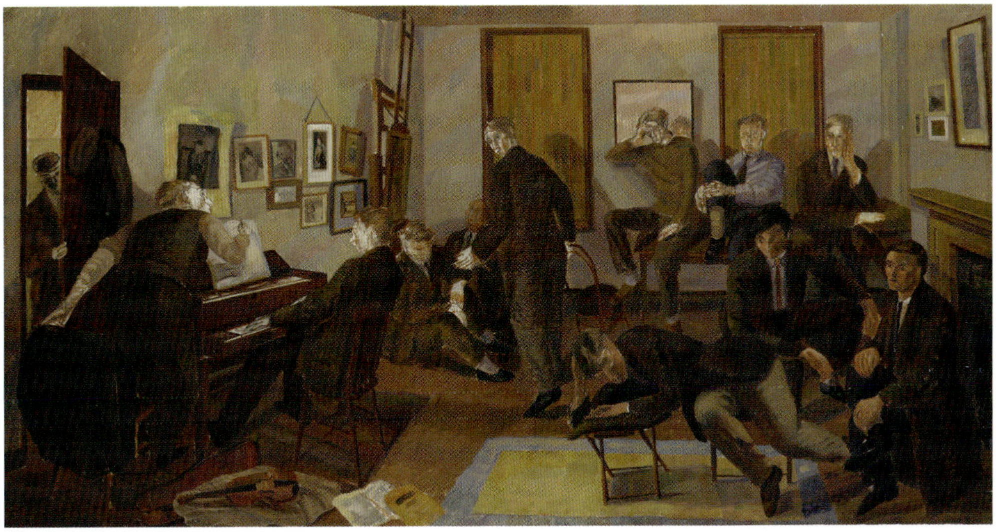

FIG. 2 – Barnett Freedman (1901-1958), *The Stanhope Street Group*, 1926, oil on canvas, 20 x 40 in. (50.8 x 101.8 cm).

Finney is seated in the foreground by the fireplace. Other figures portrayed include his friends Mahoney, Horton, Freedman, Ososki and Houthuesen.

After gaining a Travelling Scholarship to Rome, in 1929, Finney returned to London to embark on his career – but in the aftermath of the Wall Street Crash he considered himself "*lucky in obtaining a part-time teaching post at Chelsea School of Art under P. H. Jowett* (1882-1955). *This teaching post enabled me to have contact with a few of the personalities, who were ultimately to make a name for themselves in the world of the visual arts. Henry Moore* (1898-1986) *was in charge of the sculpture department and Graham Sutherland* (1903-1980) *of the department of design. After I had been there a year, Jowett resigned his post to become principal of the Royal College of Art. A most versatile personality took his place, H.S.Williamson* (1892-1978) *a considerable musician, as well as an able and vital painter*". An accomplished musician himself, Finney believed that music, along with art, had the power to elevate its audience. One of Finney's rare excursions into pure abstraction is entitled: *Visual Responses to Beethoven's Pastoral*. (CAT. 4)

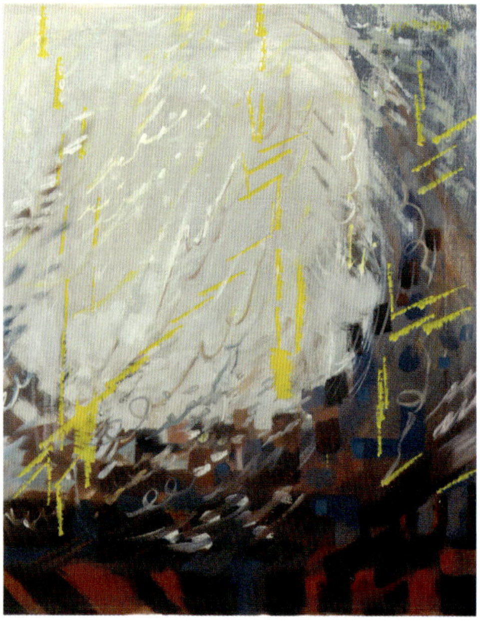

CAT. 4 – *Visual Responses to Beethoven's* Pastoral, oil on canvas, 28 x 23 in. (71 x 58.5 cm).

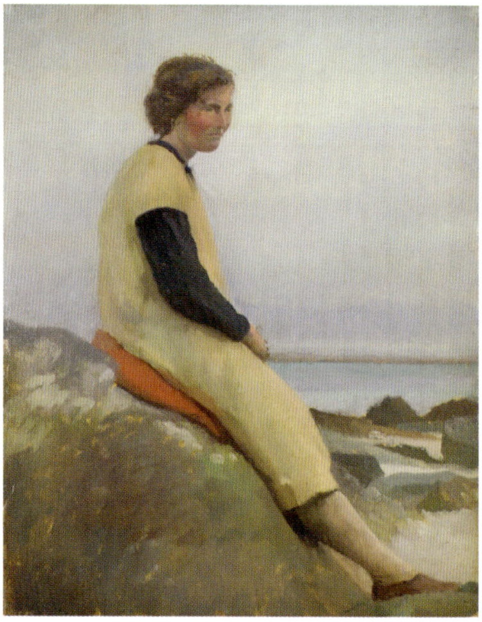

CAT. 5 – *Portrait of Nita*, 1934, oil on panel, 18 x 13 ¾ in. (45.8 x 35 cm).

In 1934 Finney married Nita Patti Hayes (CAT. 5) who "*had not only a real response to painting and a deep love of music but also because of her whole hereditary was European*". In spite of his admiration for Nita the advent marriage was not without its challenges: "*My passion for drawing and painting remained unabated, in fact I sometimes believe that the muse was jealous of any other love that might diminish my absorption with my struggles to create something worthwhile in the world of the visual arts.*"

1935 marked the birth of their son, Brian, and in 1936, Carlisle Art Gallery purchased a large painting entitled 'Mother and Child' giving Finney a little respite from continuous financial hardship. Around this time he was given his first one man show, at the Cooling Gallery; but as the decade progressed Finney struggled in both his personal and professional life: "*In an effort to try and earn more money, I completed three or four large posters of the Kent landscape and Shell* (CAT. 7) *hoping to sell one of them to the southern Railway, but there was no luck in this distinction and in a mood of despair I applied for a Steward job on board a ship at Liverpool.*"

Distraction of a kind – if not an improvement to his situation – came in the form of the war. In 1939, Finney joined the Light Rescue Service of the Civil Defence – a first hand experience that resulted in him producing a fascinating series of images of life on the Home Front. (CAT. 6 and 8) However, Finney's health suffered with "*the constant working when on duty of moving furniture and people amongst the debris and dust and hours of sleepless nights*". And when his Chiswick studio

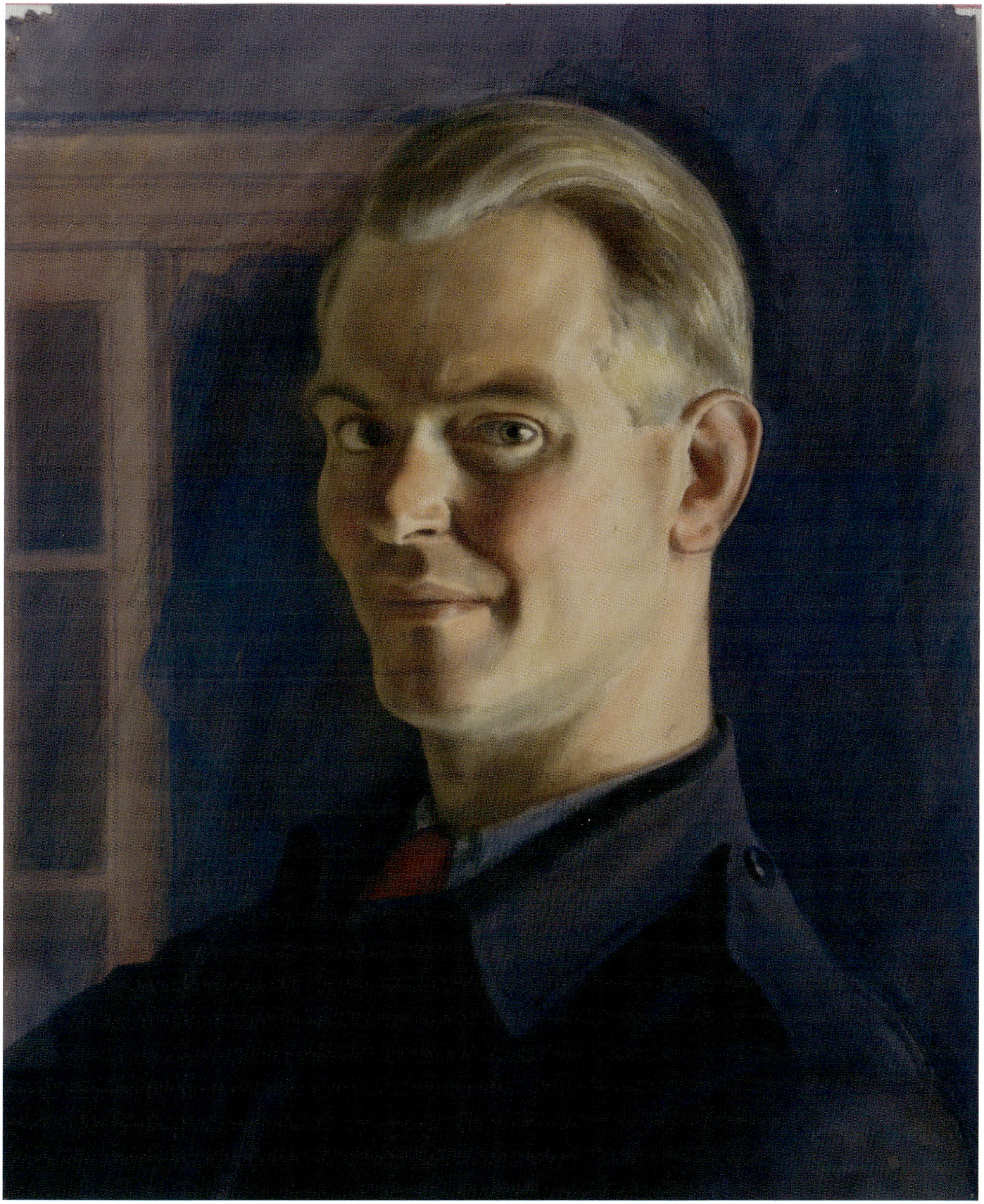

CAT. 6 – *Self Portrait in hospital clothing, convalescing,* 1945, pastel on paper, 17 ½ x 14 ¼ in. (45 x 36 cm).

"My health was beginning to show signs of breaking and I was sent to a Civil Defense Convalescent house after a serious bronchial cold. I never ceased to draw and paint ......"

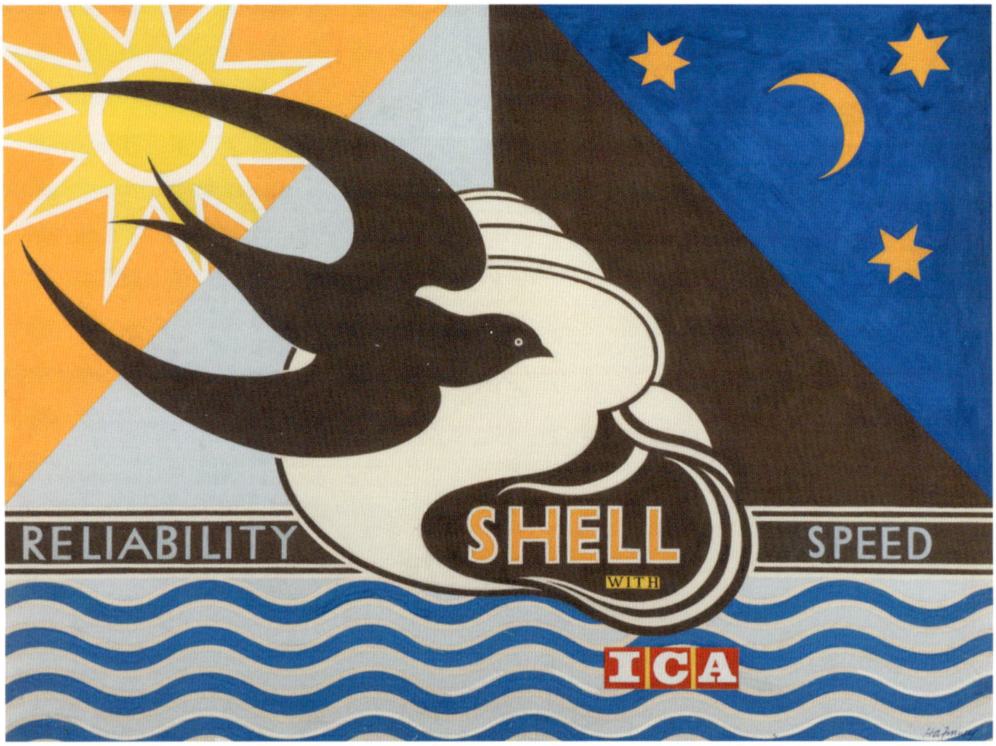

CAT. 7 – Design for Poster, signed,
pencil and gouache on paper mounted on card, 18 x 24 in. (46 x 61.2 cm).

was destroyed by bombing he lost almost all of his pre-war work: . . . "*my studio except for the wall against the railway embankment was glass, and when I returned next day it was all shattered. I can remember nights in the studio when the aircraft raids were active. The flying bombs were falling. On my nights off duty from the rescue service, playing my flute alone in the studio helped to combat my fears.*"

In 1943 Finney met Amy Dyer, his first marriage to Nita having failed. Amy was "*a lovely intelligent woman with gifts in the visual arts as a designer*" (see end papers). "*I found her intellectual vitality and extroverted personality, combined with her interest in the visual arts, an attractive and mesmeric influence in my life, and this is how the new direction in my life took place.*" After the war Finney took up a part-time teaching post at Reading University, as head of Life Drawing, a post he retained until his retirement in 1970.

In 1966 Finney spent a decisive year in America on an exchange program with the University of Wisconsin. Living in Milwaukee, he produced a vibrant body of new work (CAT. 9-11) inspired by friendships with American artists such as Joe Friebert (1908-2002) and Danny Pierce (1920-2014). Finney's striking nocturnes, glimpsed through aircraft windows, aptly record his sense of wonder as he explored new

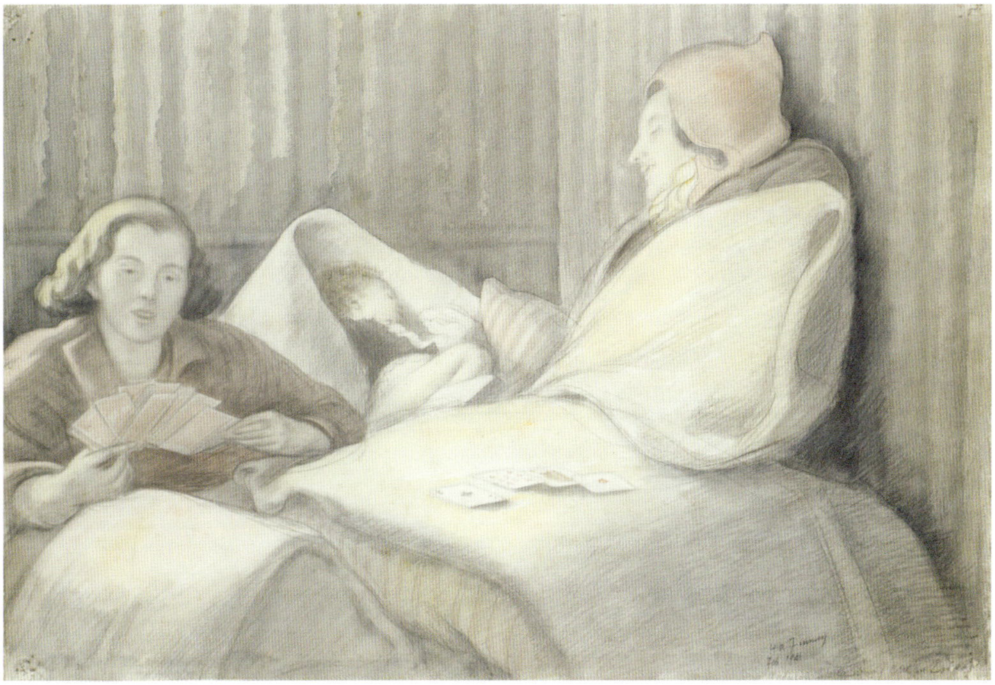

CAT. 8 – *Anderson Shelter during Blitz on London at Night, Feb. 1941*, signed, dated and inscribed with title, watercolour and pencil on paper, 15½ x 22 ½ in. (39.5 x 57 cm).

horizons. *Setting Sun*, *Dusk* and *Dawn* (CAT. 91-93) and are arguably amongst his most original works. Such overtly modern images come as a surprise when set against his gentle Kent, Berkshire and Surrey landscapes. But what all of Finney's works have in common is a fascination with tone – whether it is to be found in the landscapes (so often) painted at dawn or dusk, or in his interior and exterior views illuminated by artificial light – such as *Theatre Royal Haymarket by Night* (CAT. 84) or *Amy Ironing*, 1953, (CAT. 85) "*I have an inborn sense of tonal relationships*", Finney asserted in his autobiography, "*and even now after sixty years not much of the pleasure of painting is inseparable from beauty of tone.*"

Considering Finney's oeuvre as a whole it becomes increasingly clear that whilst he painted his surroundings with apparent ease and great facility, his pictures were a product more of personal struggle than an expression of a *joie de vivre*: work was, he said, "*a means of survival, in the battle for living*". For Finney, who had a reclusive personality, drawing and painting served both as a means to approach the world but also as a place where he could find refuge from it. His subject matter moved unconsciously between two domains – that of daylight hours, and that of the night. The former resulted in compositions capturing subtle changes in light and colour, but there is almost always a sense of light fading, dissipating into the dark.

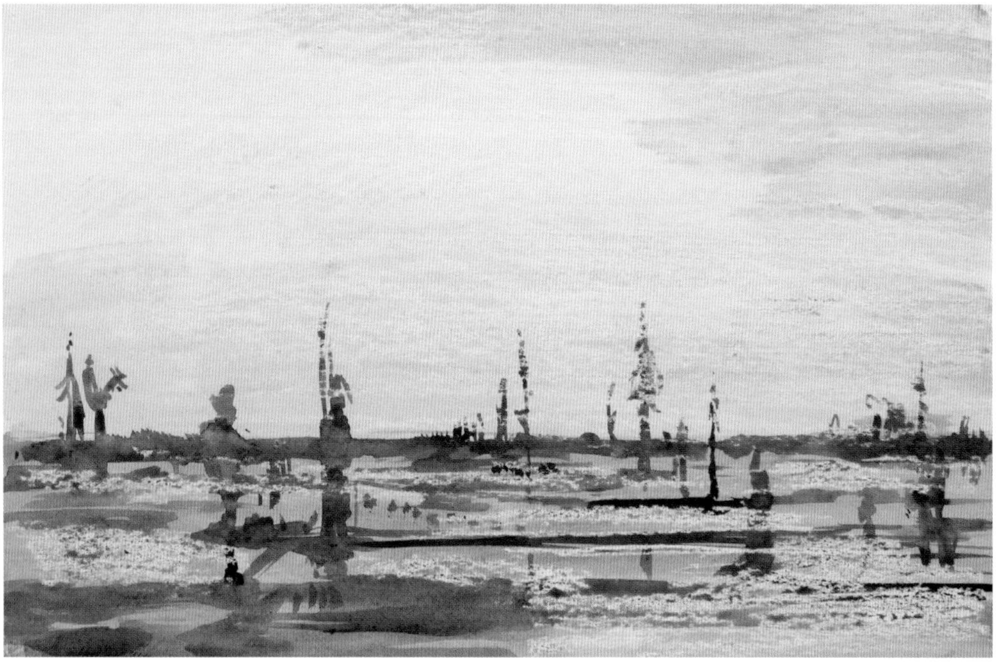

CAT. 9 – *Near New Orleans from the Train, USA,* 1966, signed, wash on paper, 12 x 18 in. (30.7 x 45.5 cm).

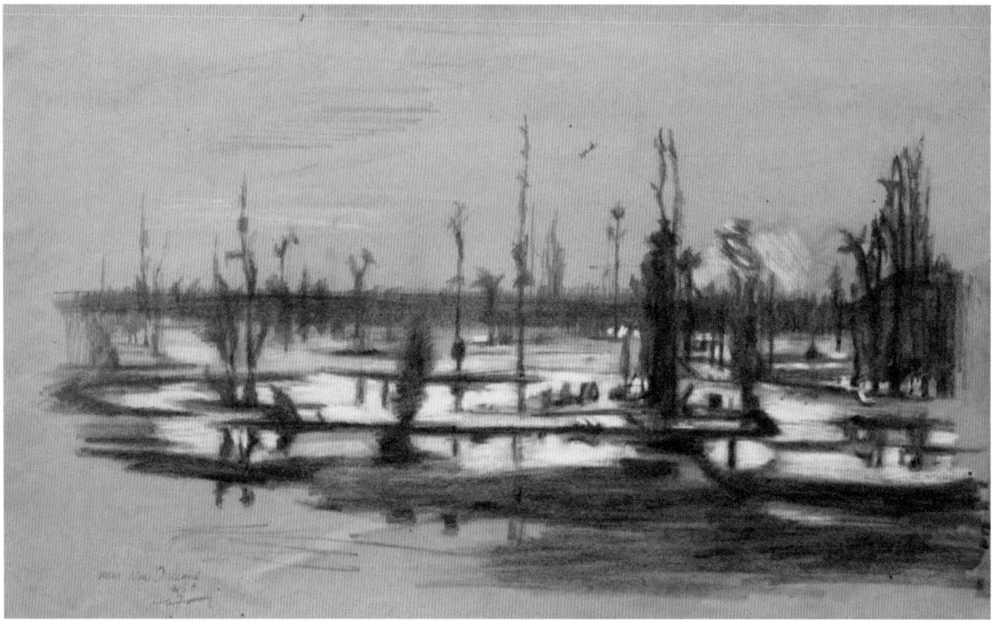

CAT. 10 – *Near New Orleans from the Train, USA,* 1966, signed and inscribed 'near New Orleans USA', pencil and white chalk on grey paper, 15 x 22 in. (38 x 55.8 cm).

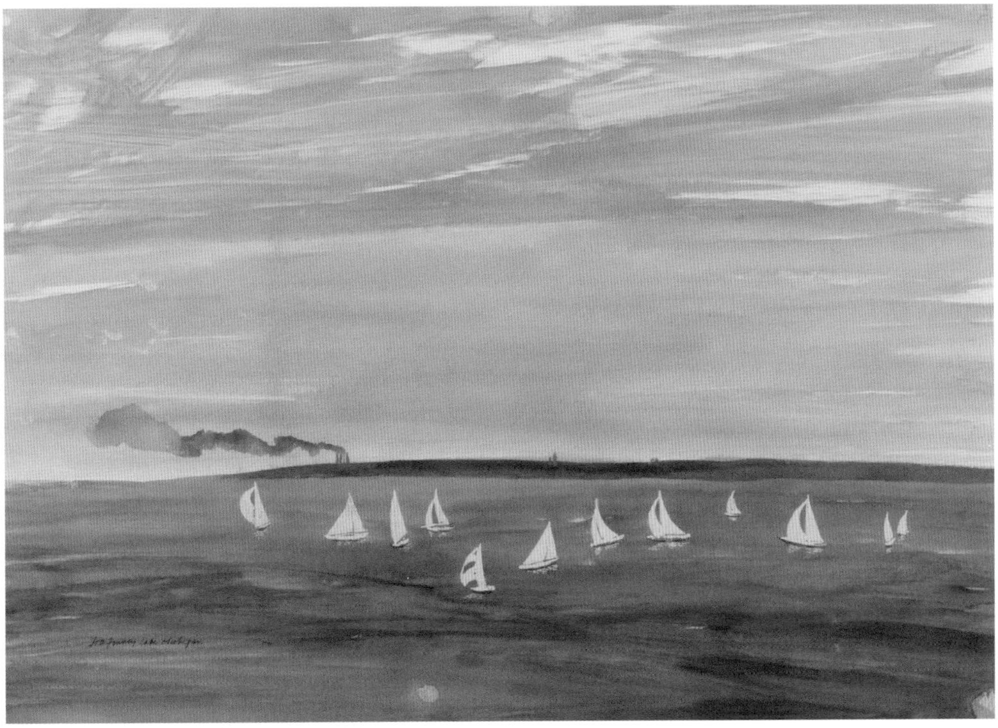

CAT. 11 – *The Yacht Race on Lake Michigan*, 1966, signed and inscribed with title, and titled to reverse, gouache over watercolour on paper, 16 ¾ x 23 in. (42.3 x 58.4 cm).

Nighttime appears to be the habitat where Finney, his compositions emerging out of the shadows, was more naturally at home.

In spite of a retrospective at the University of Oxford's Institute of Education in 1964, Finney's star, at the time barely resonant enough to leave more than a faint trace, has since all but passed into oblivion. Certainly, unlike so many of his better known contemporaries, he is rarely referenced in any art historical accounts of the period. Even with a nod in the direction of Finney's own self-effacing sense of modesty (his autobiography asserts "*I am only one of millions of humans who have passed into oblivion . . . and others might be far more worthy of commemoration*") it is surely time to bring his work back to public attention – out of the shadows and into the daylight.

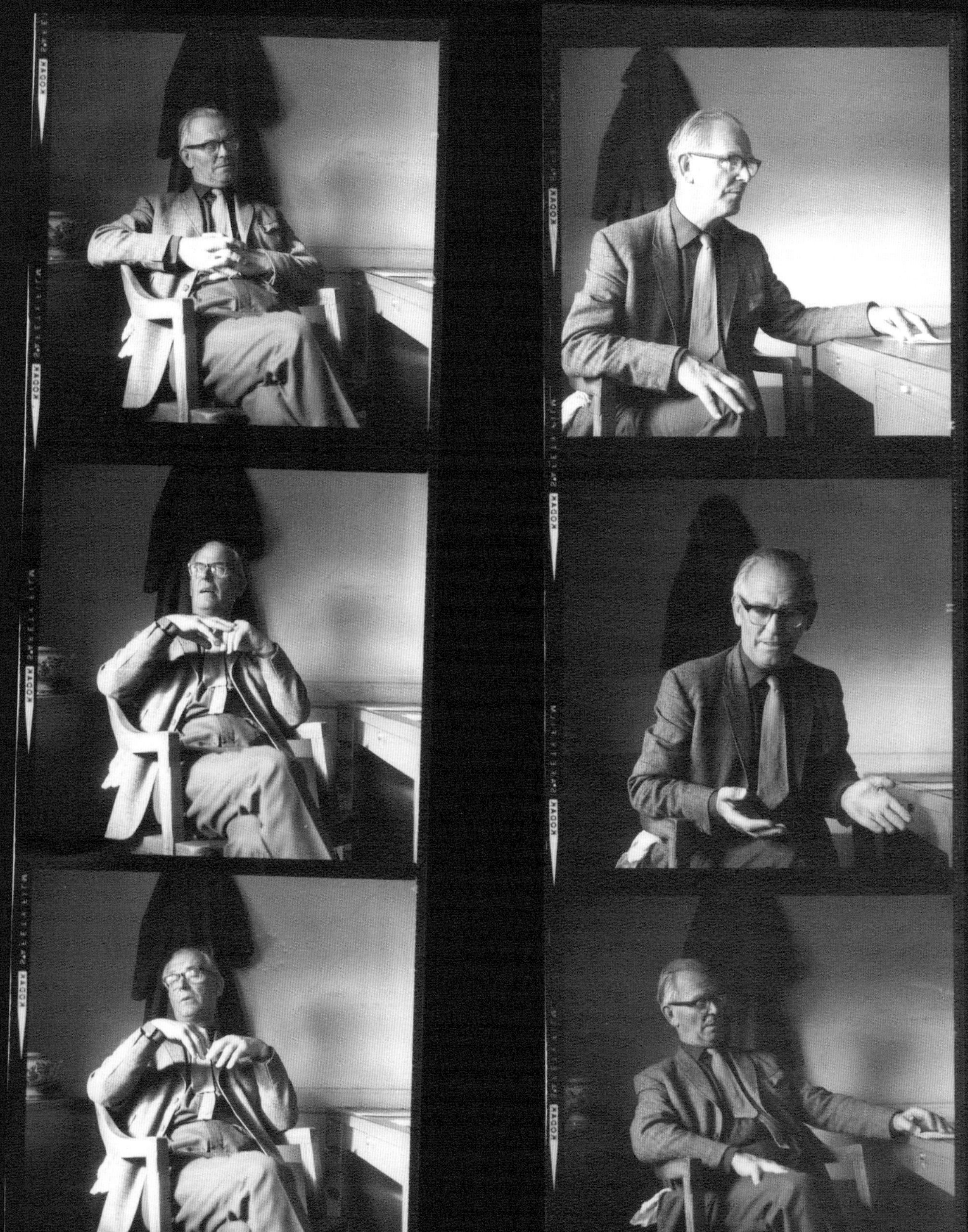

My Father

Nicholas Finney

I was born in 1946 when my father was already 41 years old. He had a rather fragile marriage to Nita Patti Hayes in the 1930s and this seems to have broken down rather quickly despite the birth of my brother Brian in 1934. My father was very restricted in his recollections and description of his marriage to Nita. My feelings regarding this matter are that Nita was a cultivated and refined individual who admired my father's work but probably despaired of his inability to look after a family and young child. Nevertheless, there are a number of moving portraits of Nita and of her early motherhood with Brian. His refusal to divorce her, even long after their complete separation, (and despite the agony which this caused my mother Amy) showed a deep affection and love for her which gives us clues to his whole approach to female love and companionship.

His character was centred around an obsessive pursuit of his art. As a child I barely remember much of a traditional father/son relationship. He was always obsessed with his painting and drawing and I was an irrelevance other than as a subject for drawing. If we ever had trips to the outside world as a family – quite a rare occurrence – my father was always sketching. If short of material on which to draw, he would use napkins or menu cards.

He was very different from my mother, Amy Dyer. It was a love match at least on my mother's side. I have a rather moving drawing she made of my father when she met him in the Royal Berkshire Hospital in Reading. He was recovering from pleurisy caused by debris dust inhaled during his service in the Ambulance Corps in London during WW2. Letters from my mother to my father showed the depth of her love for him. She was passionate and wanted to be with him always at this age. She herself had had an unhappy first marriage and had gone through a very painful divorce which saw her two sons taken away from her by her former husband Rouse. She was a practical, very hardworking lady with a Conservative party political disposition. This grew over the years and increased the chasm between herself and Hugh. She was also a very accomplished designer and artist and much of what she achieved was fuelled by the need to supplement the family's income. She taught Art at Luckley Oakfield School in Wokingham for many years after having studied at Goldsmiths College in South London. By all accounts her first marriage to David Rouse was always a source of resentment to her. She felt that her father had forced her into an unhappy and unfulfilling relationship which prevented her from pursuing her interest in the arts and crafts.

FIG. 3 — Hubert Albert Finney at the University of Wisconsin, Milwaukee, October 1966.

My father didn't know what drove him spiritually. Like many artists between the 1920s and 1940s, he took the side of the Communists during the Spanish Civil War. I found publications from the USSR which suggested that he had flirted many times with the Communist ideal. My mother probably knocked some of the idealism out of him and in his later life he became a devotee of Mary Baker Eddy, the founder of the Christian Scientist movement. He painted one or two very striking portraits of her including one which is now in the collection of the Mitchell Wolfson Collection, Miami.

My father was a very talented draughtsman and some of his portraits of his own father (CAT. x) and youngest brother, Clive, at the age of 14 are of exceptional quality. He won a scholarship to Beckenham School of Art at a very early age and then another which permitted him to go on to the Royal College of Art. His autobiography is a rich source of information regarding his friendships and work during this period of his life up to the start of WW2.

Like many of the students of that time, my father benefitted from the friendship and tutoring of William Rothenstein whom he admired greatly. He observed that Rothenstein's powerful personality infiltrated the entire college, but he tempered what could be interpreted as adulation with the remark: 'like many men of outstanding personality and force of character, he could nonetheless be a little jealous of being outshone'. Nevertheless, the warmth of the relationship can be seen in their correspondence which is part of the large collection of Rothenstein's papers held by the University of Missouri.

Towards the end of his education at the RCA my father was awarded a travelling scholarship to Italy which had an enormous impact on him and he thrived on the sensations of light and historic artistic beauty. Although few paintings of this period have survived, an exception is the exquisite copy he made of the *Circumcision of Christ* by Fra Angelico. My father told me that the Italian customs authorities believed it to be an original until he could prove otherwise.

My father didn't talk much about his war years and I'm not sure how many of his drawings and paintings survived the period. Amy fell in love with him in 1944-45 and I was born shortly afterwards. At this point Amy took charge of his fragile financial situation. They rented a house at 84 London Rd, Wokingham and my father converted the garage into a studio, though he grumbled about the poor light. My mother quickly took up a teaching post and encouraged my father to do the same. I was a frequent sitter for portraits as I grew up and both my elder brother Brian and I have many drawings and paintings chronicling our progress through childhood.

Some of my father's larger oil paintings were created between 1946 and 1954 during which he spent most of his time painting in the studio. At this time, much effort was devoted to entering paintings for the RA Summer Exhibition, with only modest success. One large formal oil painting, *Madamoiselle Alex* was exhibited in the Paris Salon and the Royal Academy.

My father eventually obtained a post teaching life drawing at Reading University. About the same time a small bequest from a distant uncle allowed Amy and him to buy the White Cottage in Winnersh which became their home for the next 20 years. A studio was built in the back garden and a plot of land was sold off to fund the purchase of a cottage in Swanage, Dorset.

Work at the university was rewarding but demanding. Judging from the many letters he received from former pupils, he was much admired and thanked for his influence on their art careers. He got on reasonably well with his colleague Professor Anthony Betts.

My father was a modest flautist and he joined the university orchestra. He was taught by a Mr Chapman, himself an accomplished flautist, who sat for one or two portraits. There are also some interesting lithographs of the university orchestra in full flight.

A one-year exchange with the University of Wisconsin in Milwaukee in 1966 provided wonderful stimulation to his artistic output and his life drawing took on a new vibrancy. He was much appreciated by the artistic community there and formed long lasting friendships with Joseph Friebert (1908-2002) and Danny Pierce (1920-2014). Two other close friends were Robert Burkert (1930-2019), professor of Fine Art at the University of Wisconsin, his wife Nancy Ekholm Burkert (b.1933) and Schomer Lichtner (1905-2006). When he returned from America Amy tried hard to interest him in applying for portrait commissions, some of which were obtained, mainly within the local Berkshire Community.

My father's introspection was both a curse and a blessing. His love of the countryside is reflected in many very sensitive watercolours and pastels of the gentle Berkshire Countryside. Holidays in Wales, Devon and the Lake District, but particularly Dorset and the Jurassic Coast, produced a remarkable collection of paintings many drawn or painted from life. I can remember camping in a rain and windswept camping plot near Lake Windermere reading the *Lords of the Ring* whilst my parents battled the elements to paint as much of the beautiful landscape as possible.

When Betts retired in 1967 Professor Claude Rogers took over and curtailed the importance of life drawing. My father found himself increasingly isolated until his retirement in 1970. At this point he moved to Bonnings cottage in Barrington, near Ilminster, Somerset, with my mother. He continued to paint and correspond with former students until his death in 1991, four years after my mother's death in 1987.

I wish that my father – who was incredibly gifted from early age – had spent more time teaching me how to draw and paint. Troubled most of his life, I came to love him increasingly as he moved quietly towards death. I can truthfully say that some of his original work, with its sensitive use of colour and form, ranks him as an equal of many of his better known contemporaries.

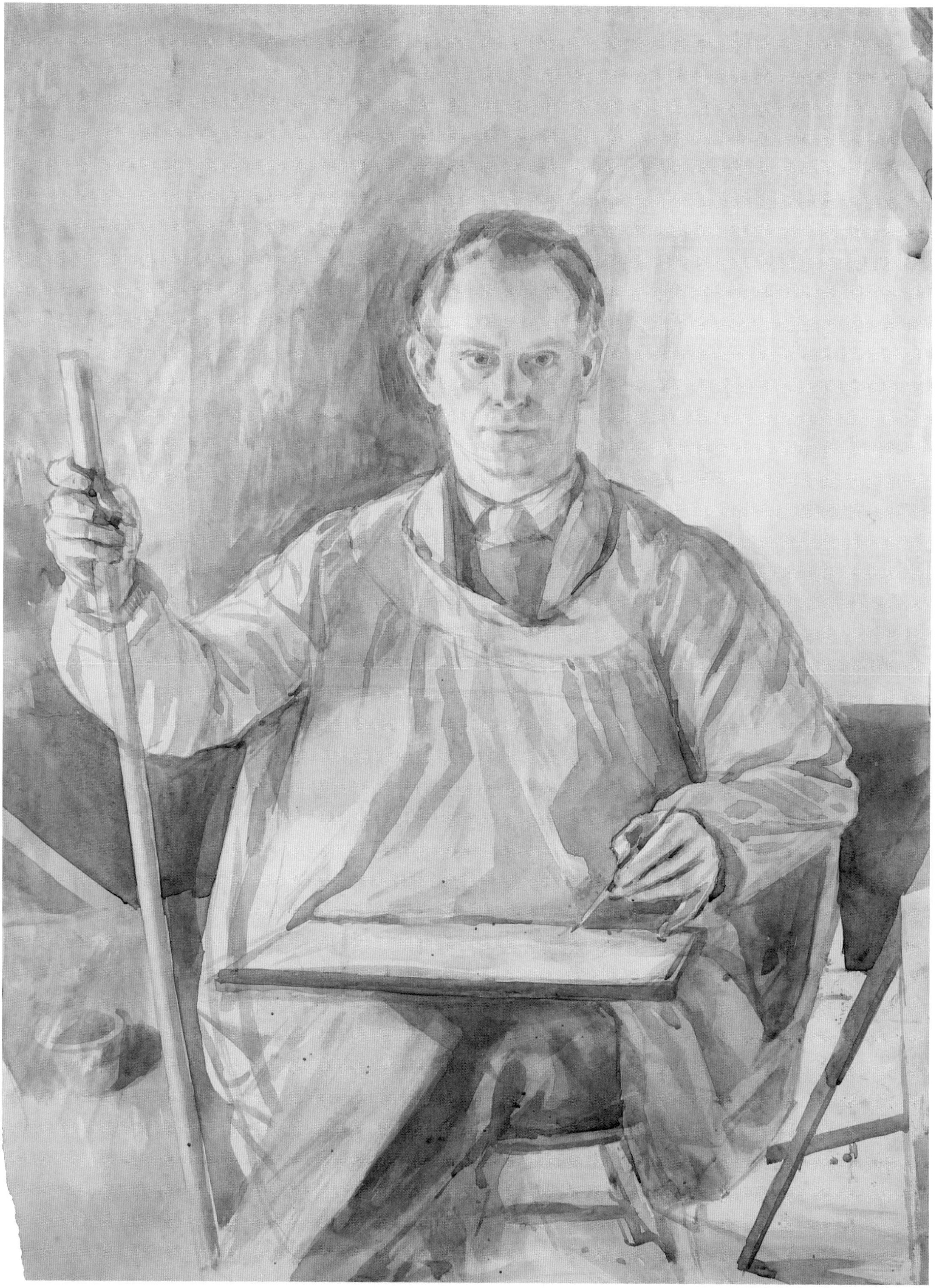

CATALOGUE

Between March 1977 and November 1978, Finney produced a 63-page memoir in which he examined his life from early childhood to the period just after the Second World War. The manuscript was destined for his two sons, Brian and Nicholas. A selection of passages from Finney's manuscript accompanies the works reproduced in this catalogue.

'It may appear conceit on my part to write down these memories as I am only one of millions of humans who have passed into oblivion, yet whose lives would have been worthy of recall. Biographies and autobiographies have been written in the hundreds by men and women who have achieved distinction and reputation during their lives. But the millions of old wary citizens have left few records of their lives yet who may have been remarkable people, such is the irony of life . . . .'

Hubert Arthur Finney

CAT. 12 – *Self Portrait*, signed and inscribed 'self portrait', mid 1930s, blue wash on paper, 22 x 14 ¾ in. (56 x 37.5 cm).

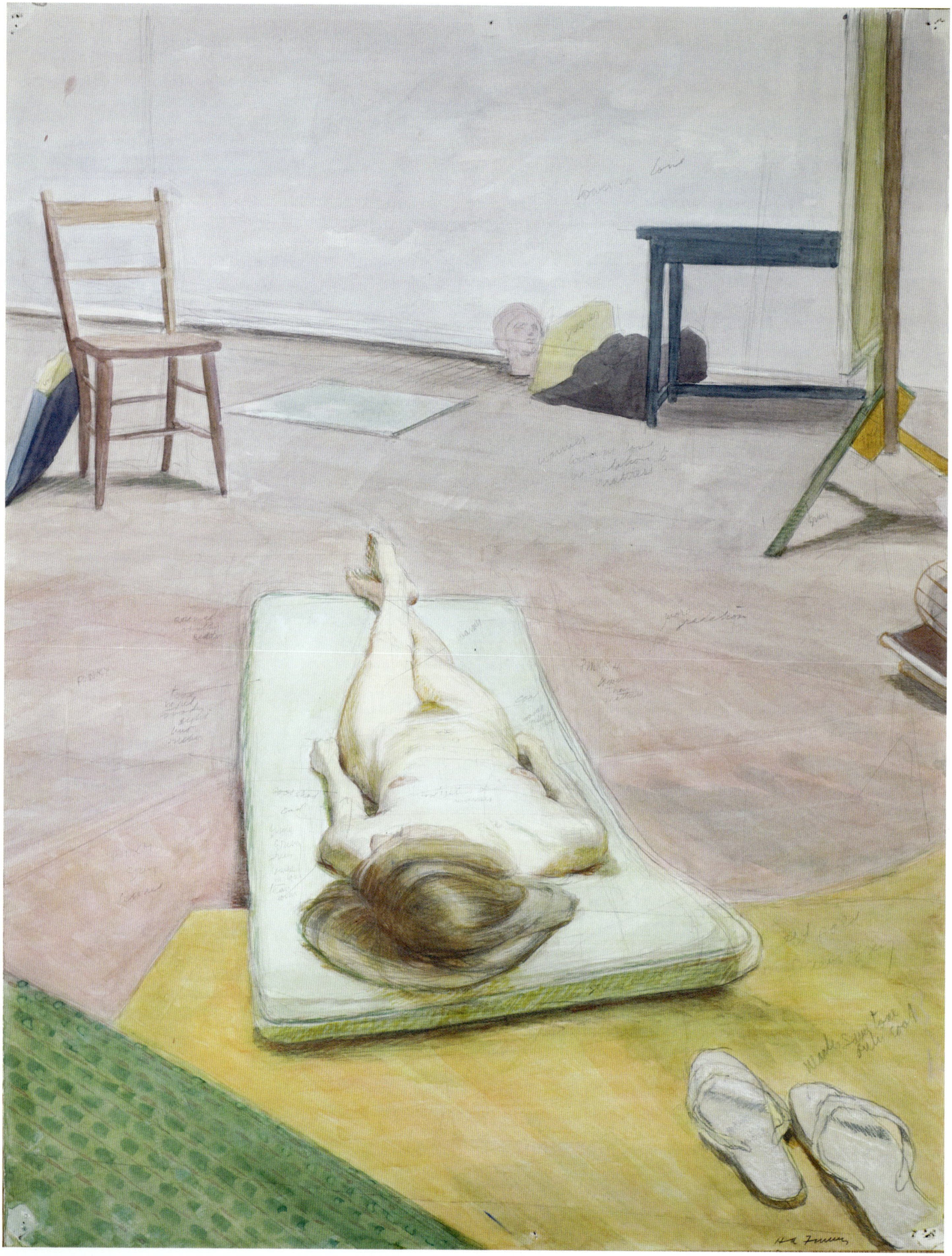

Inside

'In the year 1905, I was born of a middle-class family in a small house in Chelsea. Naturally, I do not remember the Chelsea of those days, but it must have been a fascinating part of London, very different from the Chelsea today.

My earliest memories; are of a garden somewhere in the suburbs of that now, ugly town of Reading, where I remember I used to sit happily on a swing, singing to myself, to the garden, and sky around. My father had a restless nature and was constantly changing his work and home, which accounts for my next early memory in a different environment. We were living somewhere near Notting Hill Gate, and I distinctly remember coming home from private school in a happy mood, with my hands clasped over my head singing happily in a London street, where I saw my aunt walking towards me who was rather ashamed to find me so unselfconscious, happily in my own dream world. I shocked her middle-class sense of good measures.

Although I had an elder brother and sister, I had no memories of their presence in the early years, except that my older brother who was two years older than myself, because he was first born, having a special place in my parent's affection and esteem.

The association of our home in Notting Hill as the beginning of a significant development in my childhood, was because my Father was in charge of a small post office in this district of London and an incident which happened in this house was the beginning for me of a consciousness of a choice between right or wrong. I remember I took a few pennies from the shop and hid them in a box under the wardrobe in my room. One day my mother in cleaning out the room, discovered the box and asked me if it was mine, saying that it had some money in it. I cannot remember whether I owned up to the fact that I had taken the money, but this small incident was the beginning of a moral sense awakening in me, the realisation that one had a choice between right and wrong even at this early age. . . .There are large spaces of complete black in my childhood recollections, but my father must have been on the move again because I have quite vivid visual memories of The Pantiles in Tunbridge Wells in Kent, as I became a pupil at The King Charles School in that town. There is no recollection of my older brother Noel going to this school, but for me it had pleasant memories. I can even now visualise the classrooms in which I worked and that every fortnight a pupil in the class was encouraged to make a drawing on a special board beside the door, and this privilege stands out in my mind. It must have been another exceptional old established old grammar school because encouragement in the visual arts was sadly lacking in most of them, until the Education Act forced them to have an art masters. . . .'

CAT. 13 – *Artist's model in the studio*, signed, inscribed with colour notes, watercolour on paper, 20 × 15 in. (50.8 × 38.1cm).

'My only memory of a holiday with my parents was in these early years, walking through a field of poppies on the cliffs overlooking the sea at Cliftonville near Margate. We never had family holidays like most families and it must have been a disappointment and deprivation for my mother who was a kind, loving and patient soul. My father in these early years was a good parent, but what does a child know of a parent's struggles for existence, for survival in society, its memory of father and mother image is evidently dependent on the love and affection shown to it in these early years. I would like to have known more about my father's childhood, his adolescence, his ultimate struggles to earn a living and his love for my mother. He was not trained for any profession, and his father was from his few comments about him rather a Victorian tyrant. This lack of information about my father's childhood and adolescence, is partly the reason why I am trying to recall my own memories of childhood, early life and manhood, as I think my two sons and grandchildren should know something about my background as a child and the gradual growth into a mature human being.

The clearest memories of my childhood begin when my father moved to Bromley in Kent. He had now started a photographic business in Greenwich. I must have been about nine years of age, my only brother Noel becomes a cleaner image in these memories. The house we lived in had a large garden with apple trees and Noel and myself cultivated the garden between us. We three, my brother Noel, my sister Eileen,and myself now became a more closely knit unit, which was brought about by my parents being absent during some weekends, in his business at Greenwich, we three children used to clean the house from top to basement so that it looked nice when our parents came home, a real communal effort. We were happy in this house, and I can recall it vividly even now after sixty years. It was on the outskirts of the town and one had only to walk a short distance from the main Farnborough road to be in the real country, of the lovely county of Kent. . . .'

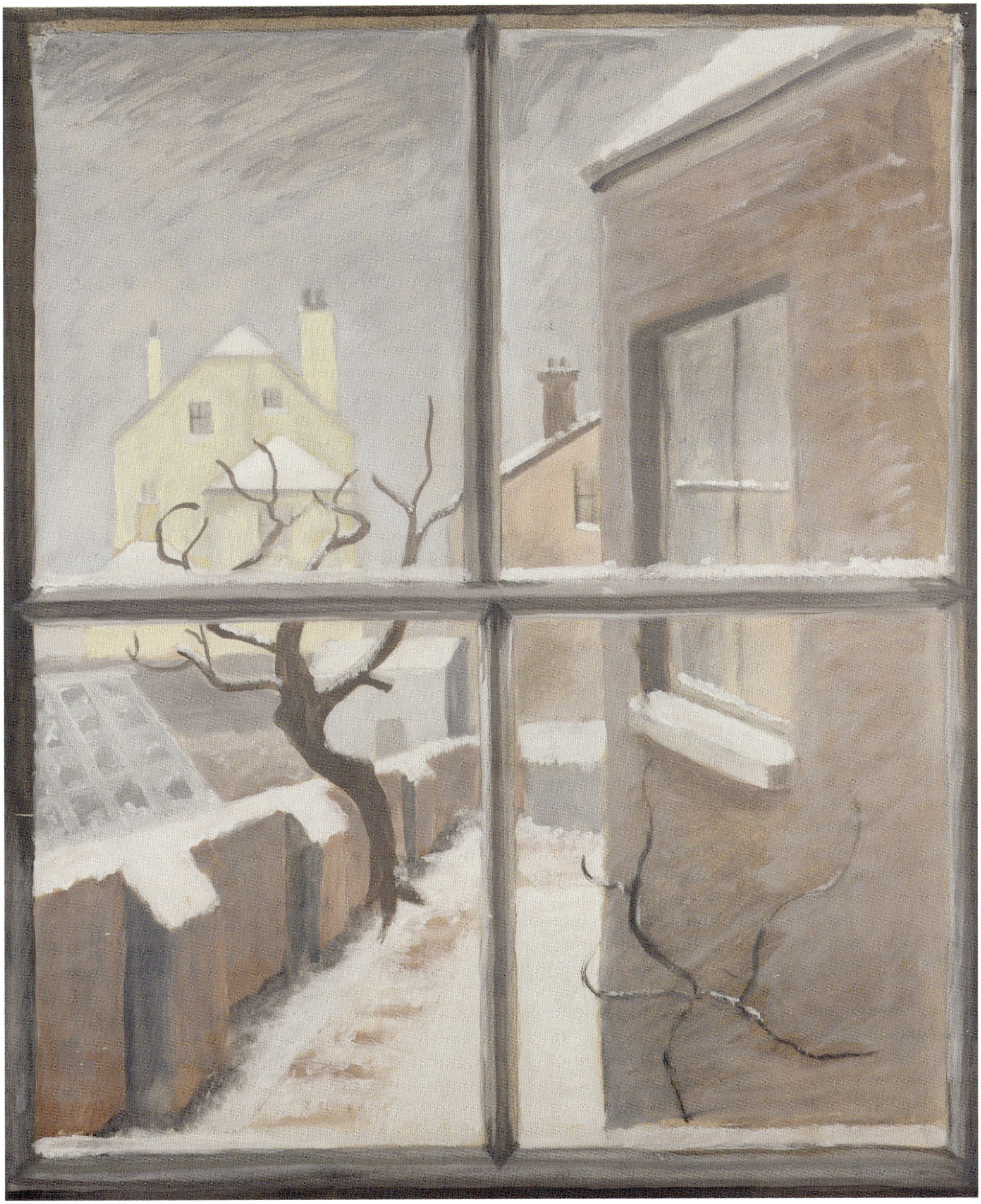

CAT. 14 – *Langford; view through a window* (second year composition), inscribed with title, gouache on paper, 18 ¼ x 14 ¾ in. (46.3 x 37.4 cm).

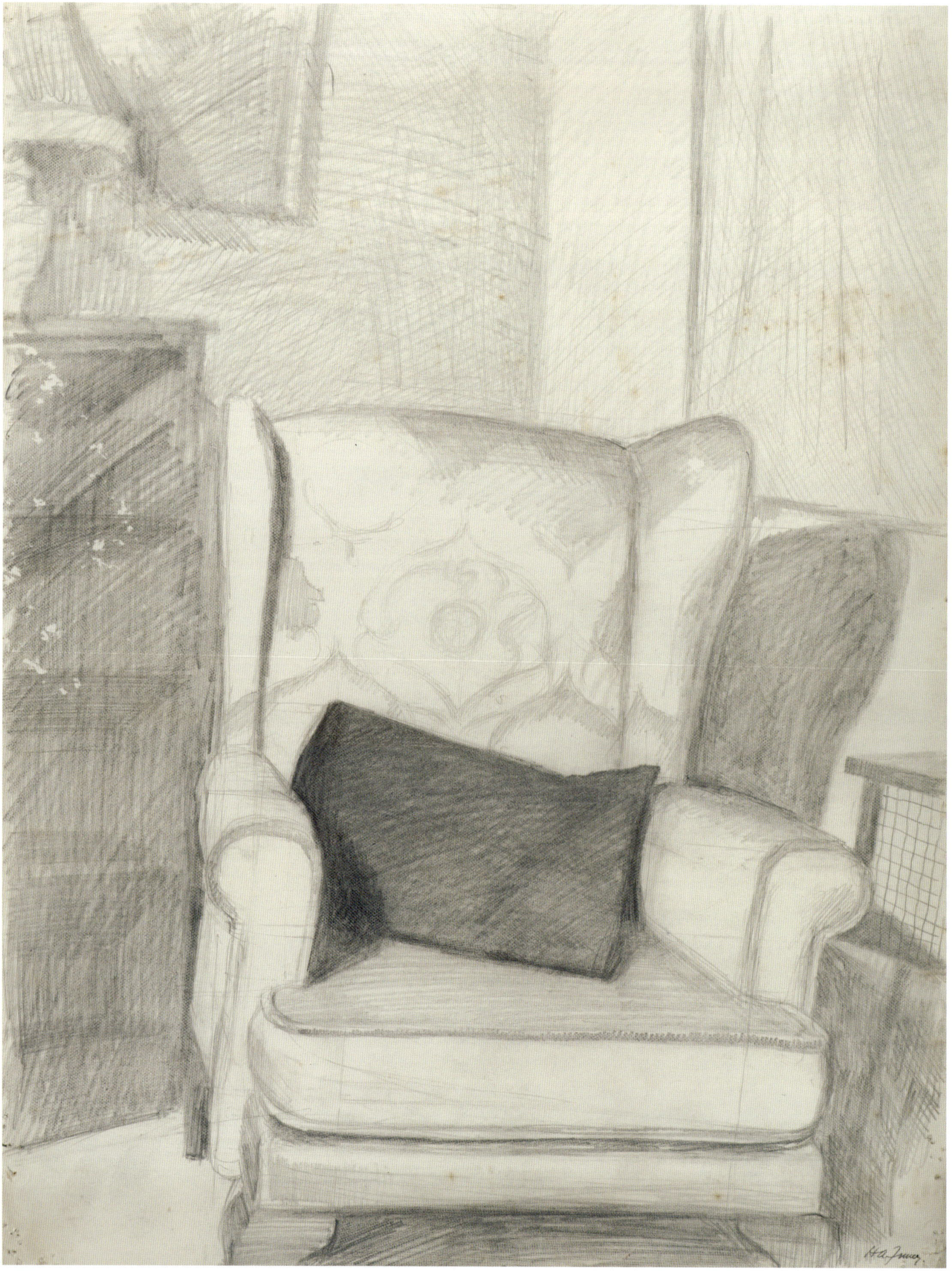

'To try to make some pattern of my father's life is difficult, I know he used to speak of his voyages to America in a sailing ship a windjammer, about the age of twelve to fourteen. He ran away to sea as a cabin boy and eventually made his way to California. This event seems to point to the fact that his home life was not a happy one and his relationships with his father strained and conflicting. His father was a bank manager and therefore it was not poverty that made him want to escape from his home. It was probably a typical middle-class Victorian home at Colwyn Bay. He also spoke of his life in California as a happy one and working on a farm built up his constitution which enabled him to withstand the strain he put his health during his later years. . . .

My father was highly intelligent with an enquiring mind and his eventual involvement into the world of miniature painting is a mystery to me. He told me that his half-sister taught him to paint miniatures and to play the piano. She must have been a cultivated woman, as I have two miniatures she painted on silk, one a portrait of Shelly and the other of a sailing vessel. On his return to England at the age of 19, which he always spoke off as the most significant event in his life, he met my mother and fell deeply in love with her which eventually ended in marriage. Her parents tried to persuade her to break off the engagement as they evidently saw the unstable qualities in his personality, but my mother told me once that he said he would commit suicide if she did not marry him, and his handsome looks, and charm made her give in. Her own character was steady, and she possessed a warm nature with a puritan tenderness. There was nothing superficial about her. I cannot remember her ever being unkind to me or giving me physical punishments and my memory of her is a kind, good, long-suffering, maternal, human being who deserved a happier life. She was not intellectual but possessed shrewd common sense and practical organising ability. She had high moral ideals and ought to have married a more steady character than my father. He was always coming up against the law, and liked to fight it, especially in the matter of paying the rates on the house. During the early part of his married life, he was commissioned to paint copies of miniatures in the famous Pierpoint collection. My father and another artist were set this task and they were paid a disgraceful wage for each copy, my father often worked until midnight, to make duplicates of the copies he made during the daytime, in order to get a collection of his own. This was, of course, an immoral thing to do, but when one balances this against the fact that this millionaire Morgan Pierpont paid a wretched sum of money to these two highly skilled miniature painters for their work, one wonders if one could call it immoral. . . .'

CAT. 15 – *The Armchair,* signed, pencil on paper, 20 ½ × 15 in. (52 × 38 cm).

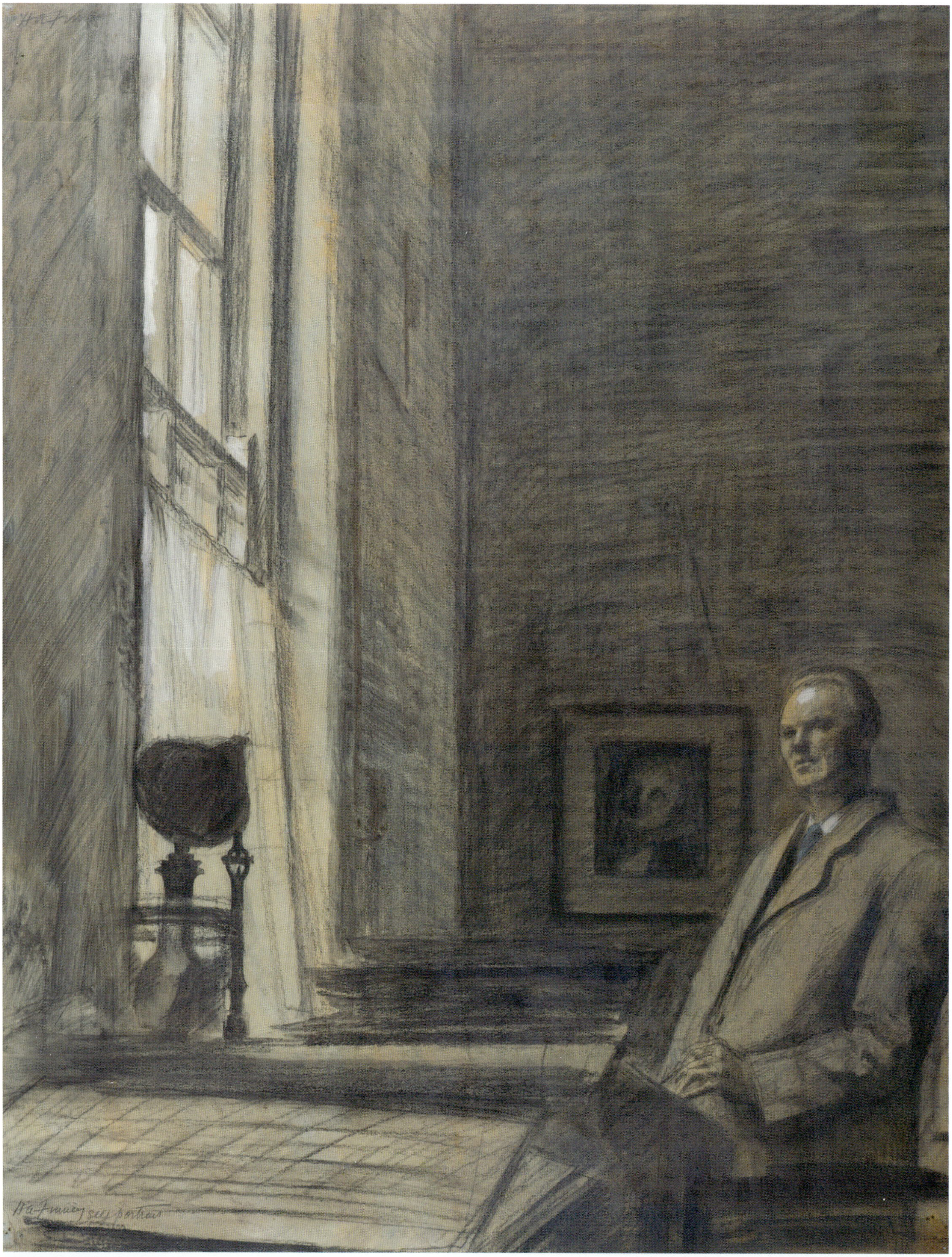

'Even silence can be either a silence of gentile thoughts or the silence of hostile thoughts.'

'After sending his family of three children to a small private school on the outskirts of the town, which turned out to be a failure, it was decided that we should attend the Village School of Hayes, about 4 miles from our house. I believe the headmaster of the school was rather flattered that parents of a middle-class home should want the children to attend his school. They could not have been more than 30 children in the boys' school and his wife was in charge of the girls in a separate building, I cannot remember ever receiving any different treatment from the village children. I have no recollection of my sister Eileen attending the school, but only my older brother and myself. The headmaster's name was Mr Plant and he deserves to be remembered for the respect he commanded. He was a strict disciplinarian, but a cultured man.

When I reflect upon these school days in the small village, which was then in the heart of Kent, I consider they were the happiest times of my childhood. The school of about 30 or 40 children, was a manageable size and we were housed in an adequate building consisting of one large room, a smaller one divided from the larger one by a sliding protection, a cooking room also used for poetry reading, a cloakroom and a concrete playground which had a fine walnut tree in one corner, and four or five lavatories. Adjourning this playground was a forge, the blacksmith was an important man in those days and was quite a character and personality. When I visited the village many years ago, a petrol pump stands in place of the forge. This village school was typical of hundreds all over the county and although the majority of the children lived in the village there was a very small minority of children from the middle class. But even the small community was not free from isolated forms of snobbiness. The policeman's daughter was rather set apart because of her father's position of management power in this village community. We walked four miles to school in the morning and took sandwiches for lunch and then walked home in the evening but occasionally one was offered a lift home in a bakers cart and sometimes allowed to hold the reins of the horse. . . .'

CAT. 16 – *Self Portrait by Window*, signed and inscribed 'self portrait', pencil, black chalk and thinned oil on paper, 20 × 14 ¾ in. (50.8 × 37.6 cm).

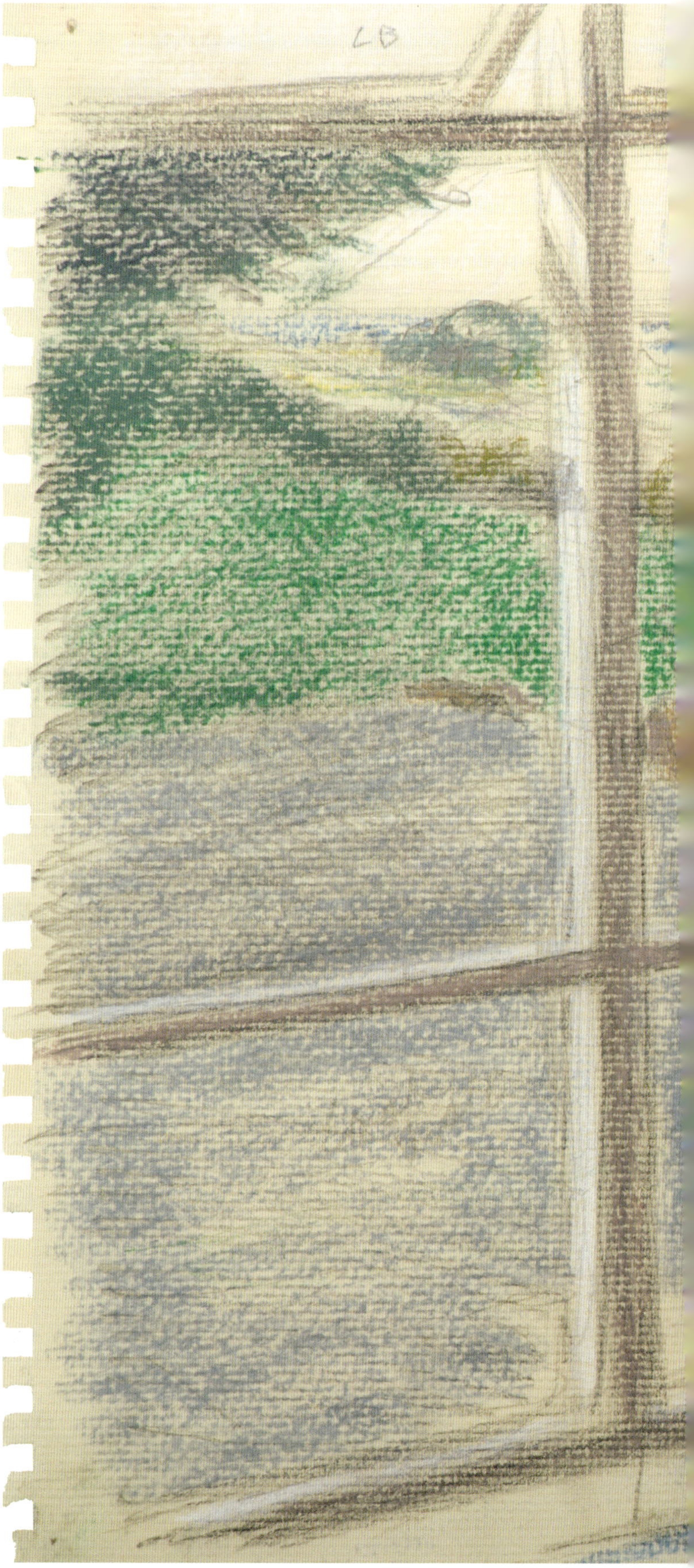

CAT. 17 – *The Window*, inscribed with notes,
pencil and pastel on paper, 9 × 12 in. (22.8 × 30.3 cm).

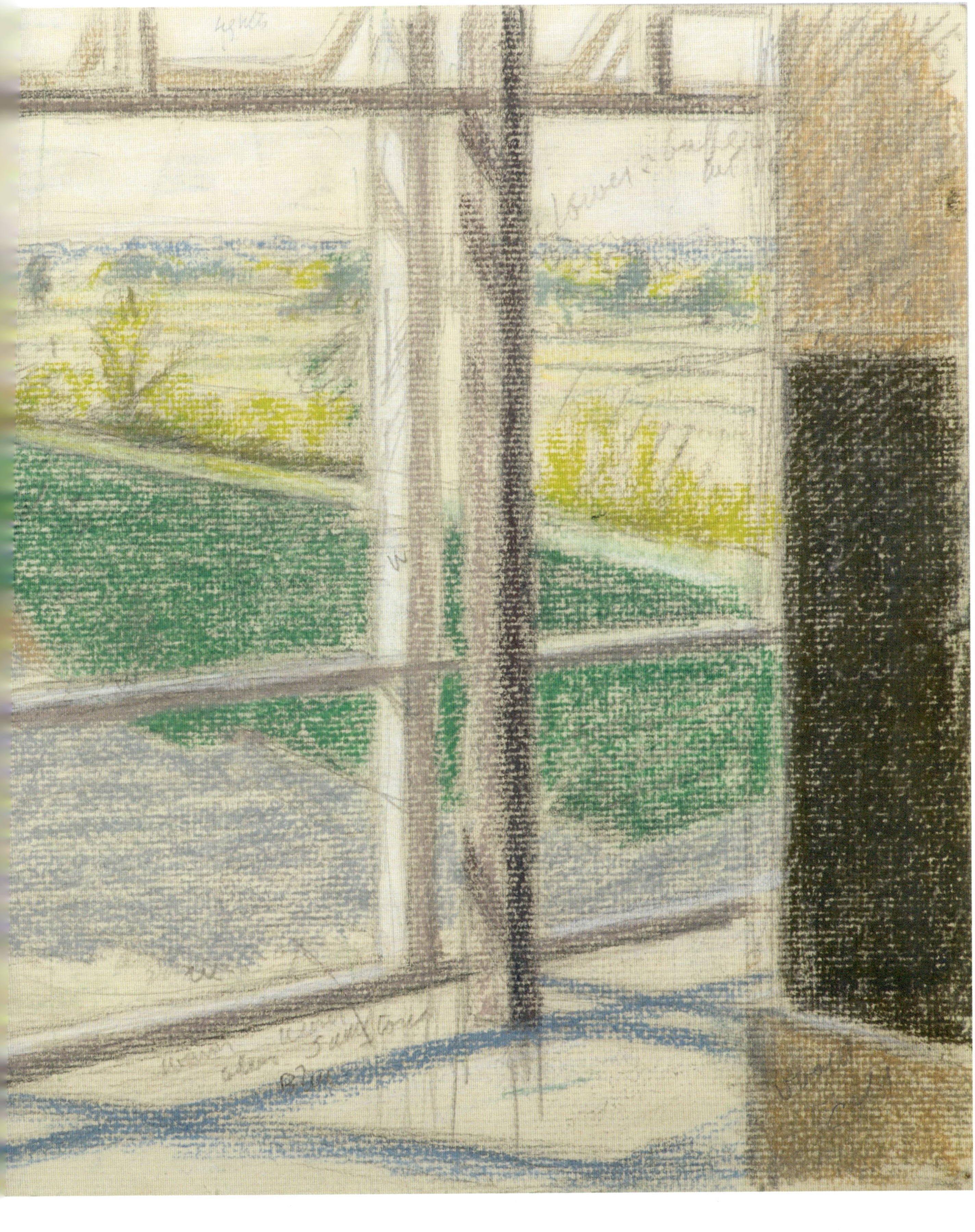

'The school days in the village school, one full of happy country memories, skating on the small pond during hard winters, but in the lessons with parties of children taken out on Hayes common by the new young teacher, when I used to disappear from the group and go off on my own which was the beginning of a sign of my desire to seek solitude with nature and like to speak to me through sky, trees and earth. The particular characters of one's personality began to appear at the age of 10 or 12 and there were already signs that I needed to remove myself from humans and be alone among nature's wonders. I have spoken of the allotments we were encouraged to cultivate every Friday afternoon, and there was an enchanting wood of small factories protecting these allotments from the north winds and it was among these woods that I picked violets and gave them to the young female teacher. . . ..

I was nine years old when the first world war was declared and I have no recollection of this great and tragic war altering my daily life at the school, we were, as the scarcity of food was beginning to be felt, sent out into the fields to pick potatoes to help with the harvest as a contribution to the war effort. About the age of 10 or 11 years, my desire to draw became an absorbing interest, it was while the young female teacher was at the village school that I made a copy of Bouguereau's "Madonna and Child" to give to her, it must've been about this time that the headmaster sitting at his desk roused pulpit above the pupils asked to see what I was hiding under my desk, only to find that it was a portrait drawing of himself. He was so impressed that he eventually put me in charge of the drawing class, such was the poverty of instructions in drawing in so many schools at that time. My destiny as an artist had begun, and my gift showed itself in portraiture. The days, weeks and months, of these unselfconscious happy days moved on and my gift and growing passion for drawing began to fill my spare time. I was too young to have any awareness of the disastrous social breakdown that was happening to the world, but as the war years developed it came closer to me, by the fear of the Zeppelin raids on moonlit nights. I remember my mother having to cook lentils to put on bread, as butter was scarce, my own little world of the mind and senses remained removed from the great events that were happening, there must've been a quick development in my mental growth between the age of 9 to 12 years of age, because about this time I was admitted to evening drawing classes at the Bromley School of Art which was only five minutes walk from our house, I was allowed to this special favour because of my promising gift for drawing. My young sister must've been born about this time but I have no recollection of her birth or a change of narrative in the house. I shared an attic room with my elder brother in this old Victorian house, we slept together. . . .'

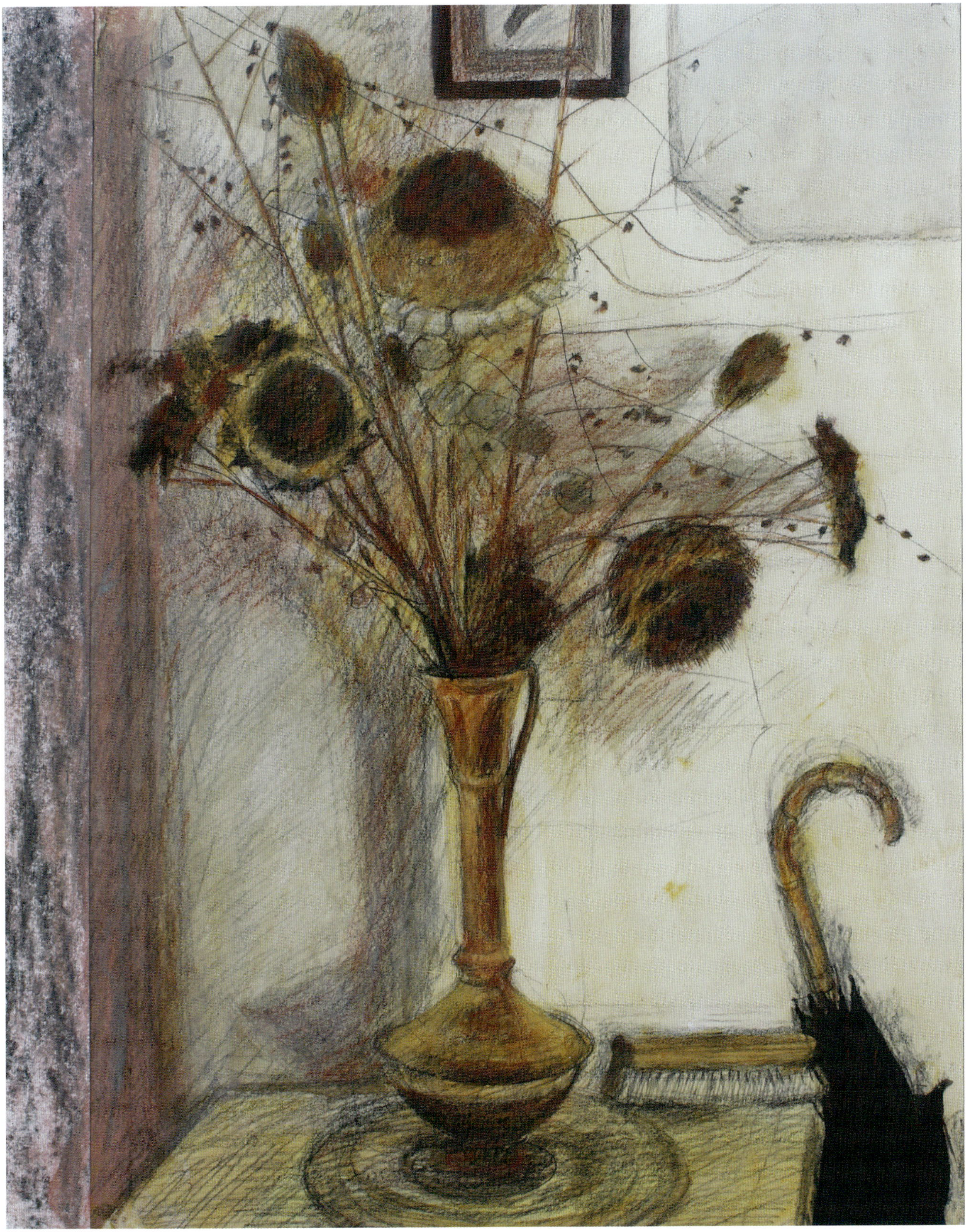

CAT. 18 – *Idea for a still life painting,*
pencil, pastel and gouache on paper, 16 ¼ × 12 ½ in. (41.3 × 32 cm).

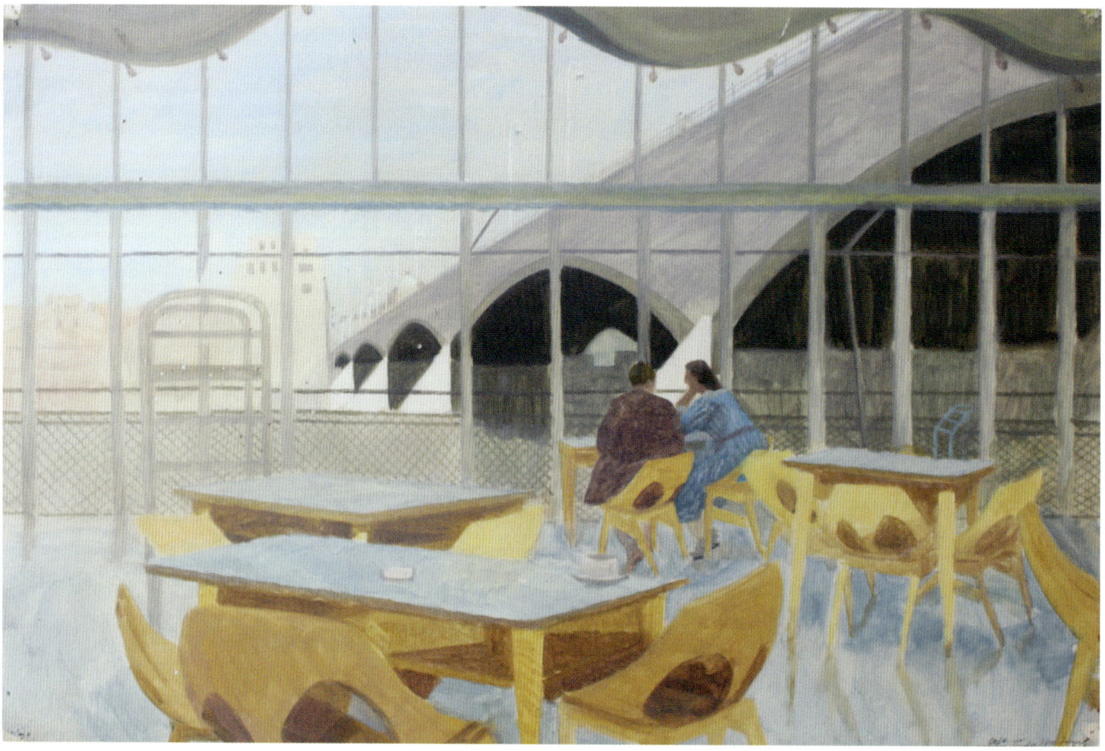

CAT. 19 – *Café Near Waterloo Bridge*, signed and inscribed with title, pencil and gouache on paper, 14 ¾ x 23 in. (37.5 x 55.7 cm).

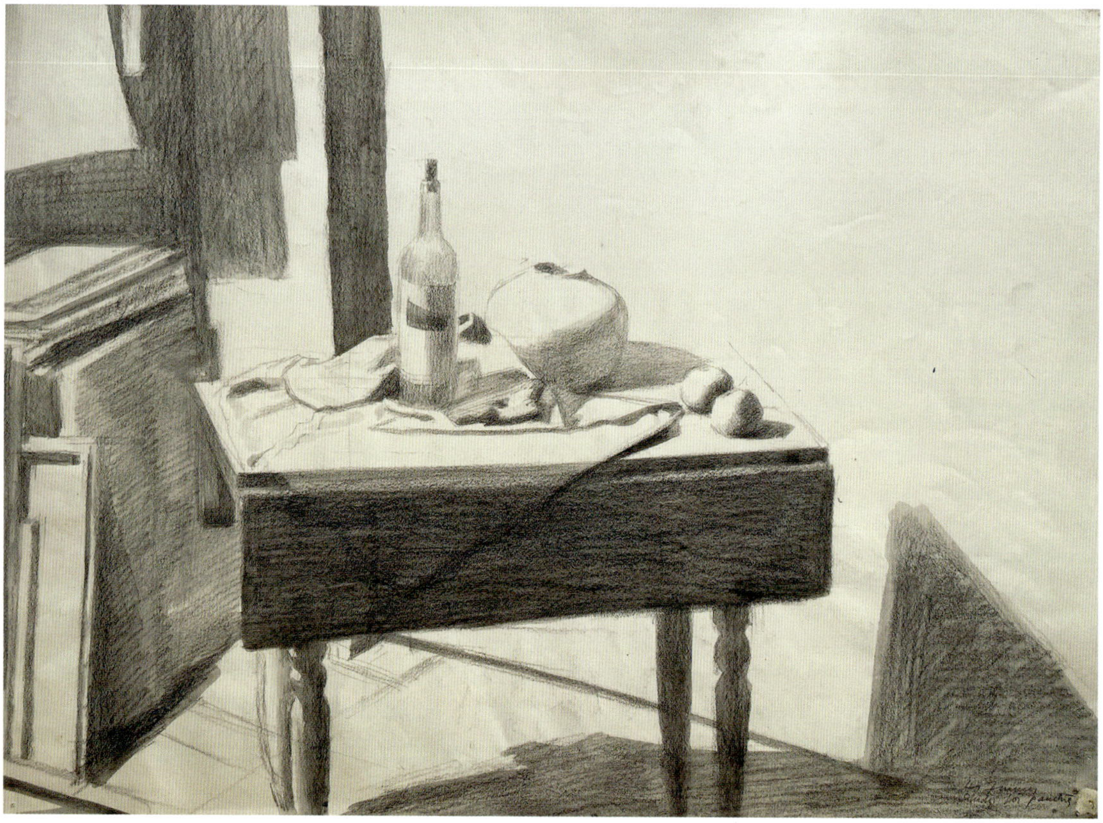

CAT. 20 – *Still Life – Study for painting*, signed and inscribed 'Study for painting', black chalk and wash on paper, 15 x 20 in. (38 x 50.5 cm).

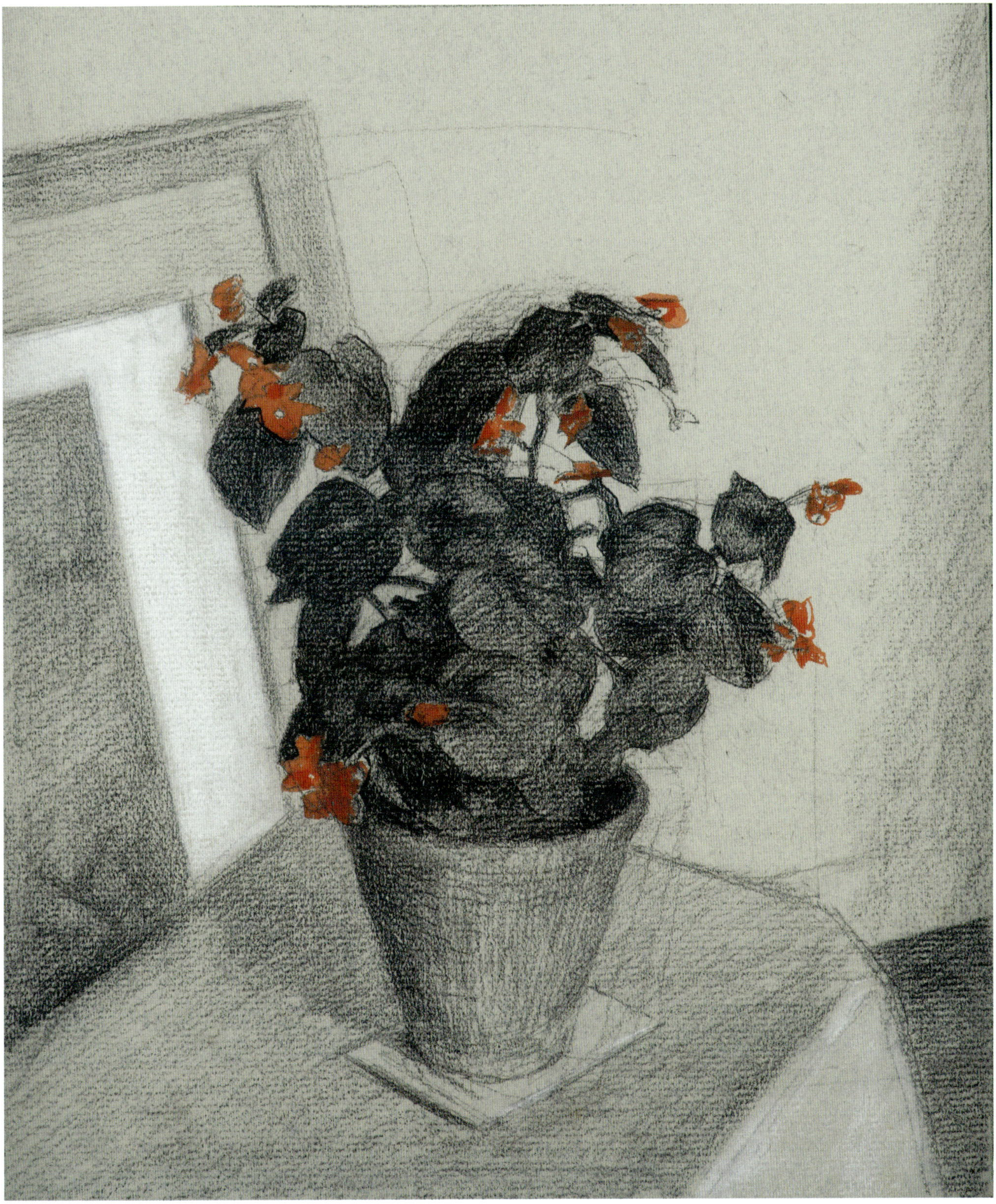

CAT. 21 – *Flowers on a Table*, black chalk and gouache on grey paper, 11 x 9 in. (27.8 x 22.8 cm).

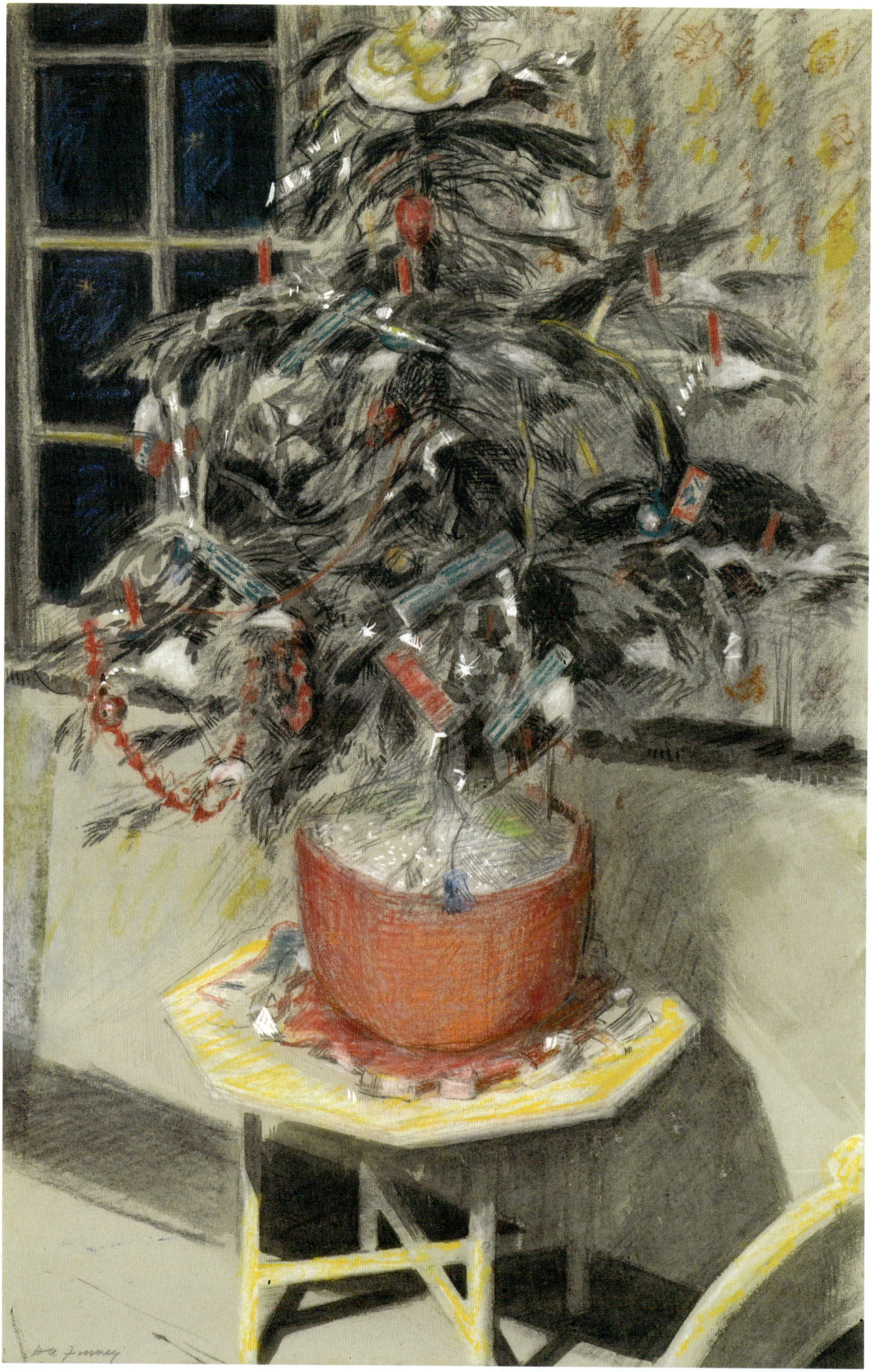

'When my father became aware of the growing gift I was showing for drawing and painting he showed greater interest in me. I was awarded a scholarship at the age of 13 to what was then called a trade school, which consisted of three days a week at Beckenham County School for boys and the rest of the week working at mechanical drawing at the Beckenham School of Art. . . .

The beginning of my life at the the Beckenham School of Art was a new experience in the forming of one or two true friends. I came in contact with a highly gifted student a year older than myself who in later life distinguished himself as a mural painter and eventually became an R.A. As well as sharing my love of drawing and painting, he helped to channel my thoughts towards socialism, as he belonged to a Socialist Sunday school. His name was Charles Mahoney. He had much force of personality, and his gift was in the field of imaginative composition. He would at the age of 14 paint imaginative pictures in gouache of the crucifixion and other biblical subjects in a Dürer like manner his gifts were so different from my own and stimulus I required from the development of my mind came from him and we used to go out painting together. Unfortunately for me a year or two later he gained a scholarship with distinction to the Royal College of Art. His influence which was free from the sentimentality, was not removed from me and was a real loss, and I think he must have been more mature for his age than I was. The new exciting life at the Royal College where he made many new and more interesting painting friends left him little time to see me at the local art school. . . .'

CAT. 22 – *The Christmas Tree*, 1952, signed and inscribed on the reverse with title, pastel on paper, 19 ½ x 12 in. (49.5 x 30.5 cm).

'My enthusiasm for drawing and painting was immense and the intensity with which I worked with at the Art School and in the holidays at home in my attic room, only leaving it for meals was unusual in so young a child. Wiser parents would and could have seen that this could lead to dangers ahead for me, if pursued without other interests, both in social activity and physical games.

After working for six months at the Beckenham School of Art studying mechanical drawing, in which my time was divided between three days at Beckenham County School in academic subjects, I was suddenly, through no effort of my own, transferred to the Beckenham School of Art as a full-time art student. I would only have been fourteen years of age. When I look back on this significant event, I think it was not a good change for the development of my whole personality, and it would have been more beneficial if my general education had proceeded for at least another two years before I was transferred to the Art School. I would have been forced to participate in outdoor games.

The Beckenham School of Art was a pleasant and well organised school and the first two years were happy ones for me. I worked hard at drawing in the Antique room which possessed a good collection of casts of classical sculpture. It was a spacious room with large windows really reached down to the floor which looked out upon a garden belonging to the school, and then to the large playing fields of the County School adjuring the Art School. The atmosphere was harmonious with male and female students working in the same rooms. . . .'

CAT. 23 – *The Sewing Machine*, signed and inscribed with notes, pencil on paper., 22 x 15 in. (55.7 x 38 cm).

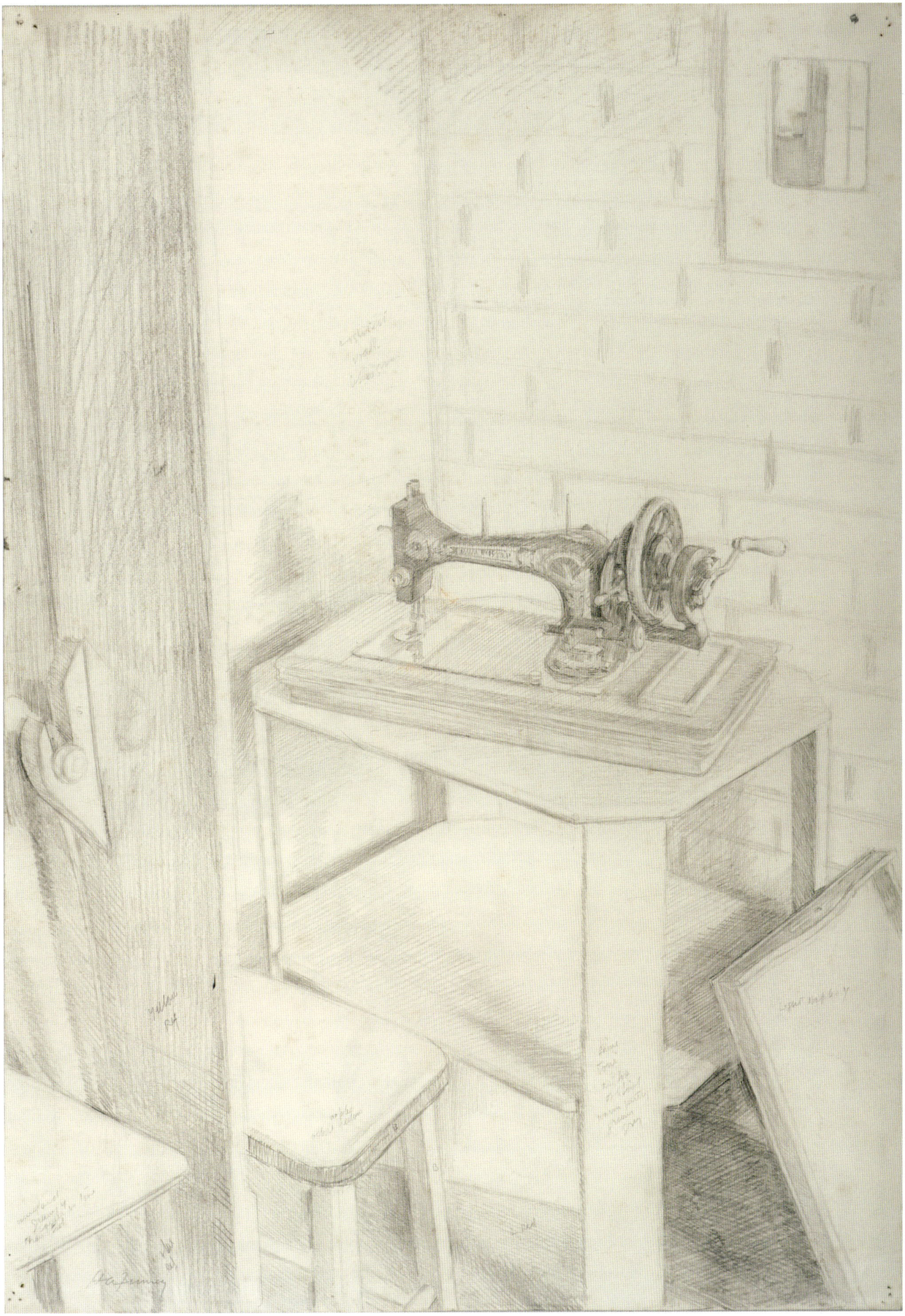

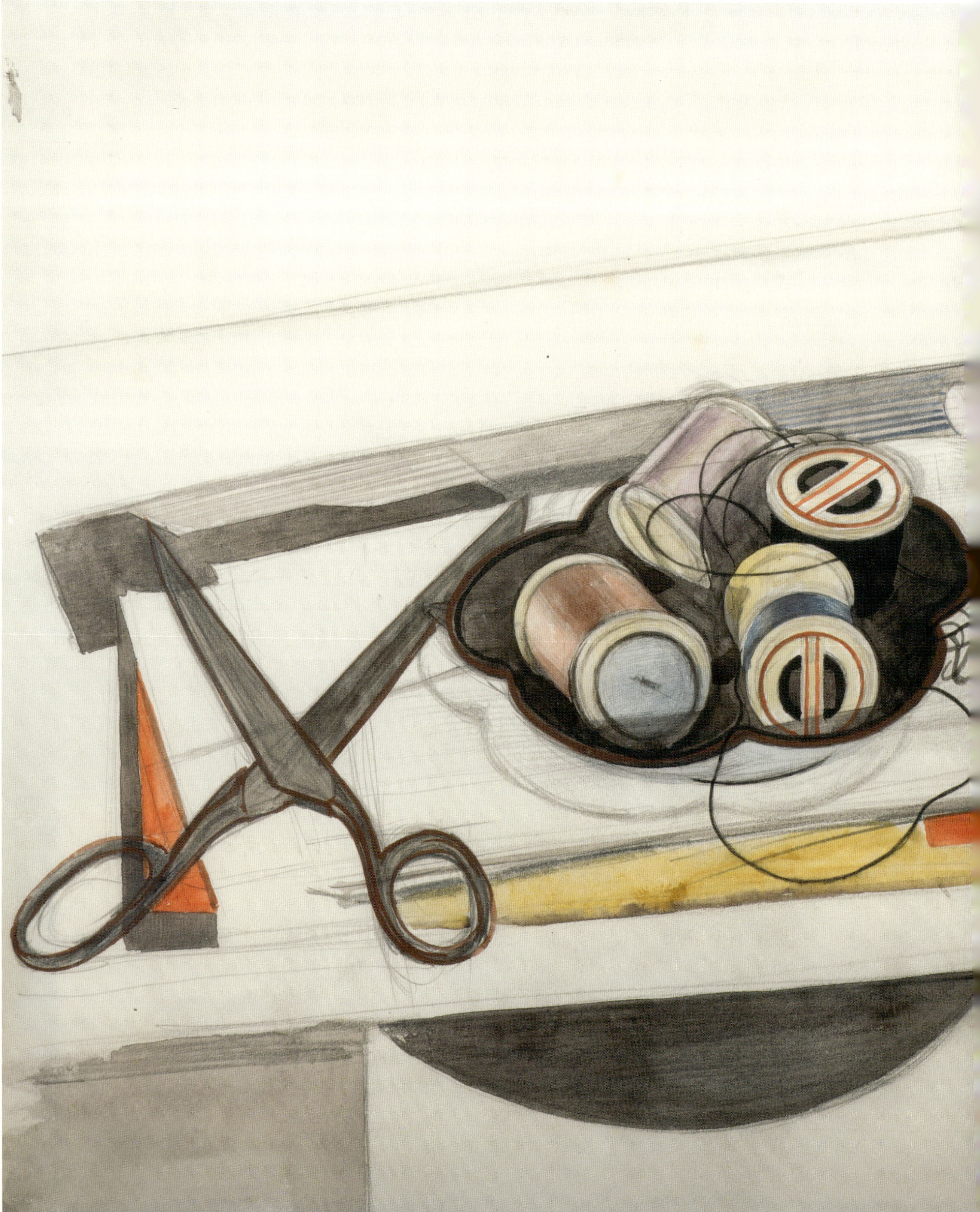

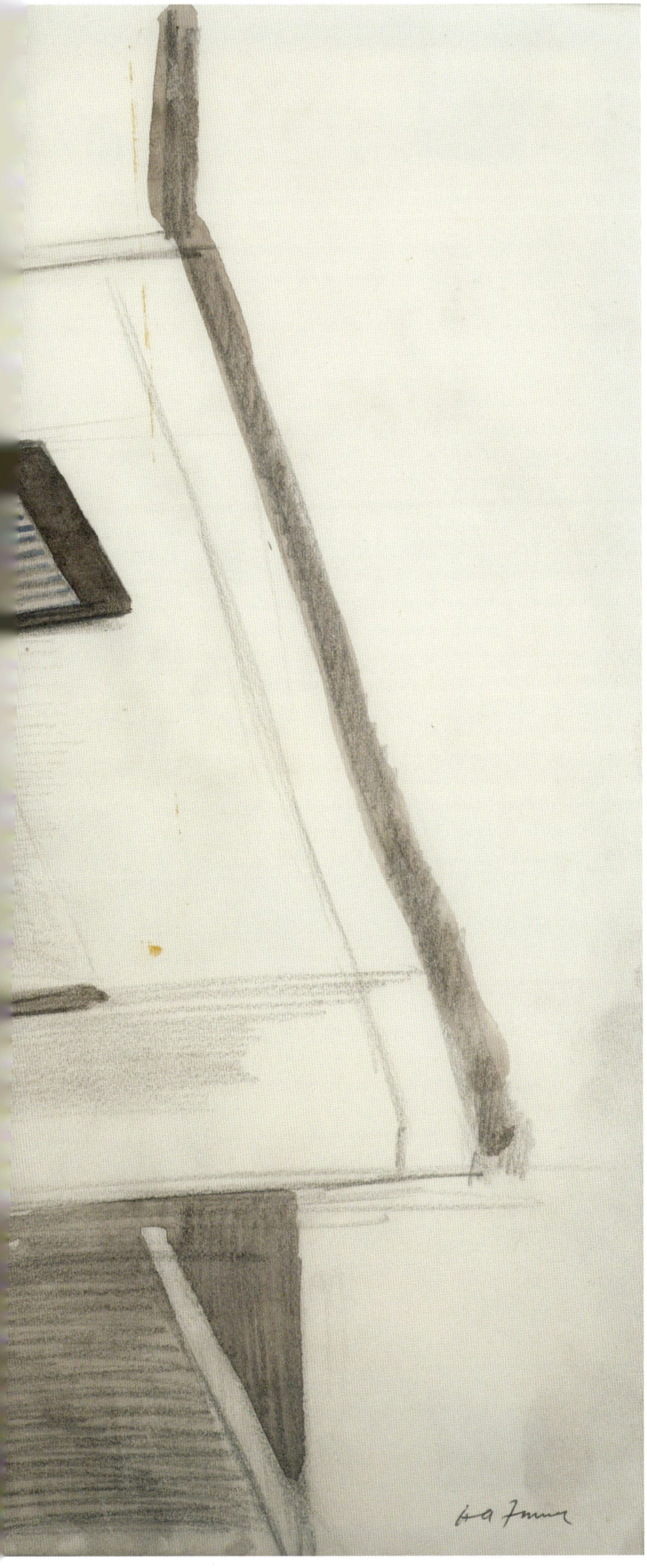

CAT. 24 – *Sewing Tools and Material*, signed,
pencil and watercolour on paper, 14 ½ x 18 ¼ in. (37 x 46.5 cm).

'The war had little impact upon me and I was 14 years old when it was over, but I do remember the Zepplin raids on the moonlit nights and one daylight raid where I was travelling on a train to Greenwich one weekend to help my father with his photographic business.

The departure of my friend Charles Mahoney for the Royal College of Art, left me with a desire to make other friends in the school, and I was lucky in making a new friend in Gerald Gardiner. He was a gifted student, and there was a healthy rivalry between us, he also had another inseparable friend in the student named on the school who I naturally became friends with, although his personality did not inspire me towards high ideals, there were quite a few gifted girl students, but although they worked with us in the classes, they kept very much to themselves in the communal life. The mixing of the sexes was not so free in my youth as it is now. Although we both attended the same new life classes. . . .

About this time the principal engaged a part-time teacher and painter who possessed a distinguished personality. This was a significant event for the school. His name was P. H. Jowett and he had returned from the war and at times suffered from shellshock. He visited the school two or three days a week, and by the inspiration of his teaching gained our confidence and almost hero worship, transferring his own enthusiasm for drawing, and the beauty of classical construction of the human figure, to all who came under his instruction. I remember still with clarity, his beautiful selective demonstration drawings on the side of our own drawings, which we eventually cut out and treasure. But like so many things in life they became lost. It became a lively little school, and it had a small garden at the back in which we had models sitting drawing, fine summer days. If my life at home had been happier and my father had been less disruptive in his influence in the home, these days could have been happy ones during my study in this school. One of my great regret is that I did not preserve or try to keep some of the drawings and paintings that I made during these formative years, when one's vision was fresh and one's emotional response to things was intense and full of excitement. . . .'

CAT. 25 – *Aga with two kettles and blue towel*, c.1930, (study for painting CAT. 1), signed and inscribed with title, pencil and pastel on paper, 21 x 15 ½ in. (53.5 x 39.4 cm).

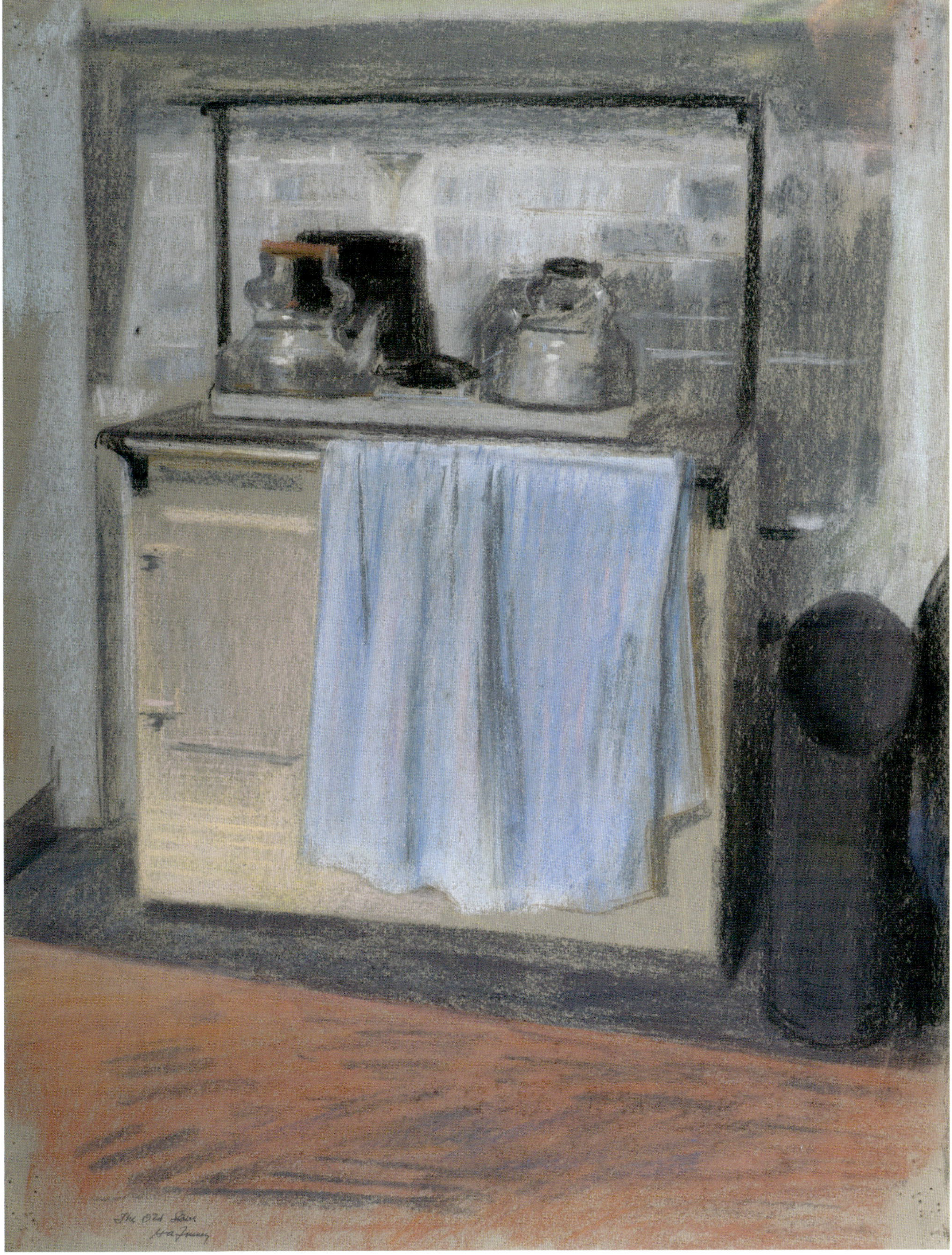

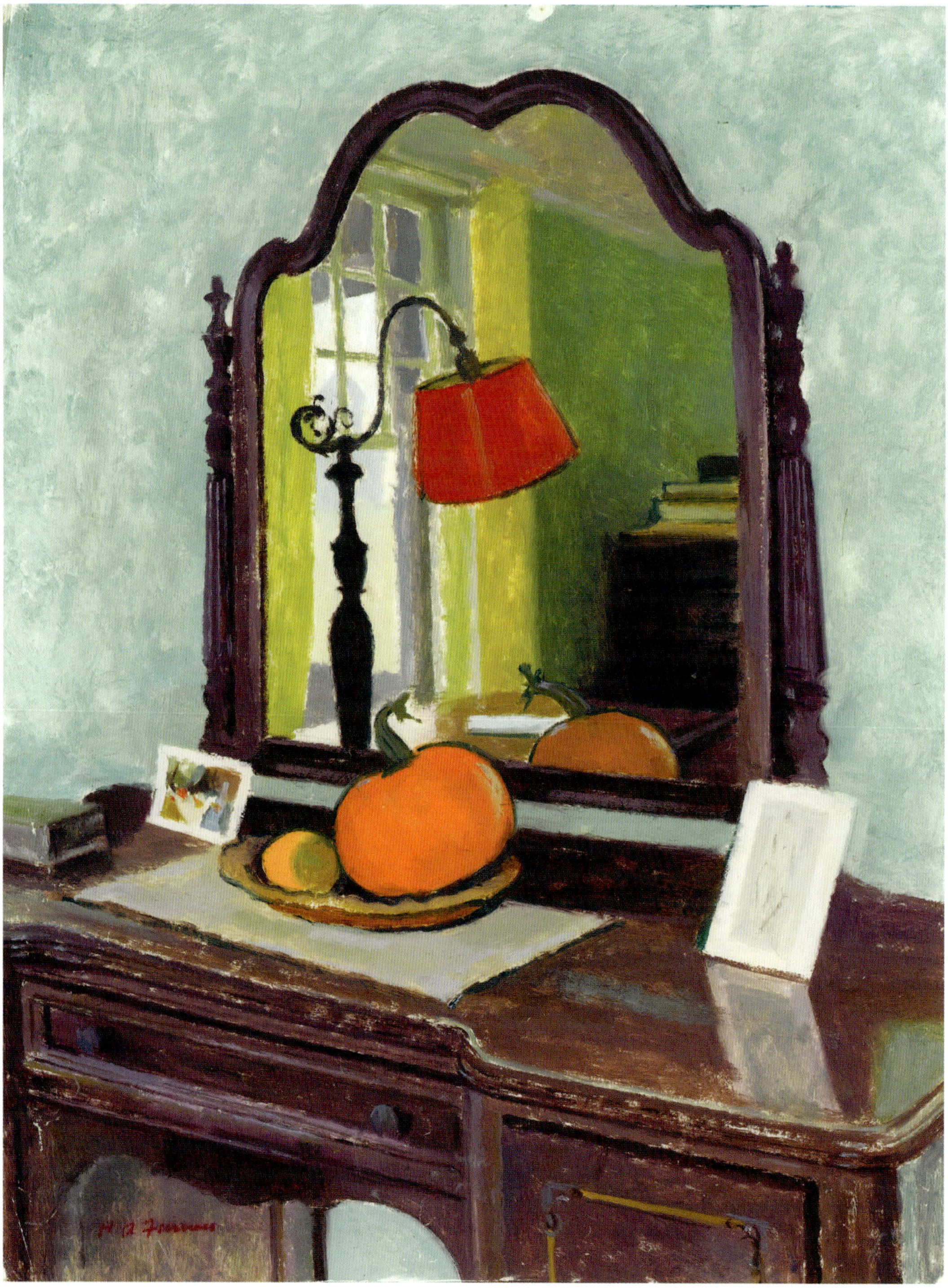

CAT. 26 – Study for *Still Life Painting, Milwaukee*, 1966, signed, oil on paper, 23 ¾ x 17 ½ in. (60.5 x 44.5 cm).

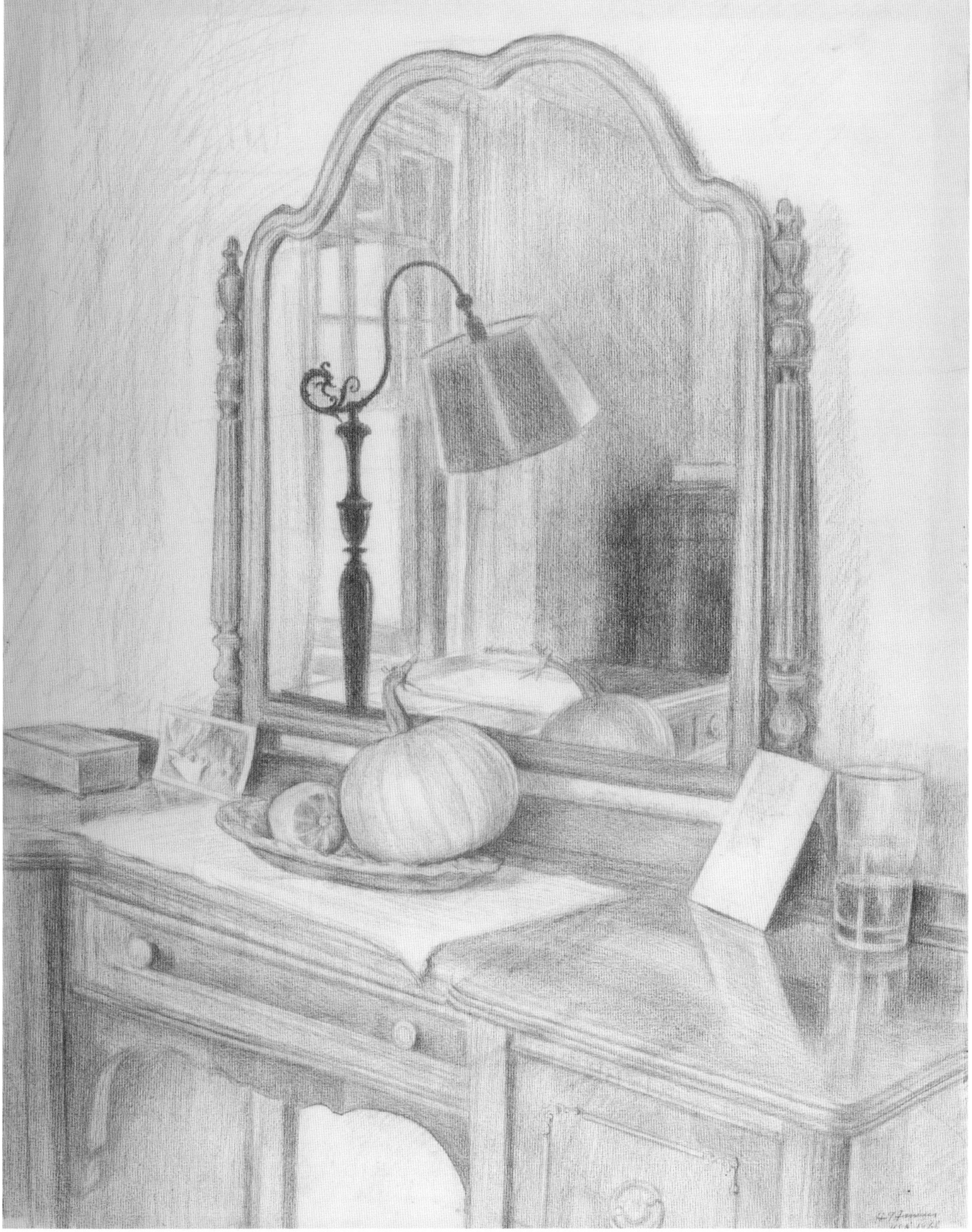

CAT. 27 – *Still Life and Mirror,* 1966, signed and inscribed 'USA 1966', pencil on paper, 23 ½ × 18 in. (60 × 45.7 cm).

'During these years of adolescence I created many drawings and paintings, having interesting and distinguished qualities. I remember painting a self portrait of myself holding a Lupin flower which was like an Antonello da Messina. I made many drawings of my mother (one or two I still have) of my young brother Clive, and my young sister Pauline. In my attic room I modelled in clay a self-portrait from a mirror drawing one summer vacation and then cast it. My industry was terrific. . . .

After the first year or two my studies in the art school were directed towards the passing of an examination called the board of education drawing examination, I remember the teaching of prospective and architecture were quite beyond my age, and the teaching of architecture on the wrong lines and in instances absurd. My first visit to the National Gallery made a great impression upon me, and I was introduced to classical music by my friend Gardiner. He was a very gifted student with much facility as draughtsman, he love to paint landscape and had a natural feeling for it, I remember many paintings he made in the country around my home of Famborough in Kent. My gift was expressed more through an emotional and sexual experience, than through an intellectual one and I was involuntarily directed towards the human head and figure. I have an inborn sense of tonal relationships and even now after sixty years not much of the pleasure of painting is inseparable from beauty of tone. . . .

I learnt the craft of etching from Mr Gill and I wish I had some examples of the work I produced under his instruction, I have observed during my own teaching life, that strong forceful personalities, cannot avoid imposing their style or manners of working upon those under their influence and this can often submerge the real personal intuitions of more sensitive personalities with creative gifts. While under the dominant teacher many be interesting works maybe produced, but removed from this influence, the hypnotised people becomes left with a sense of loss, and often takes years to find his or her true self again. . . .'

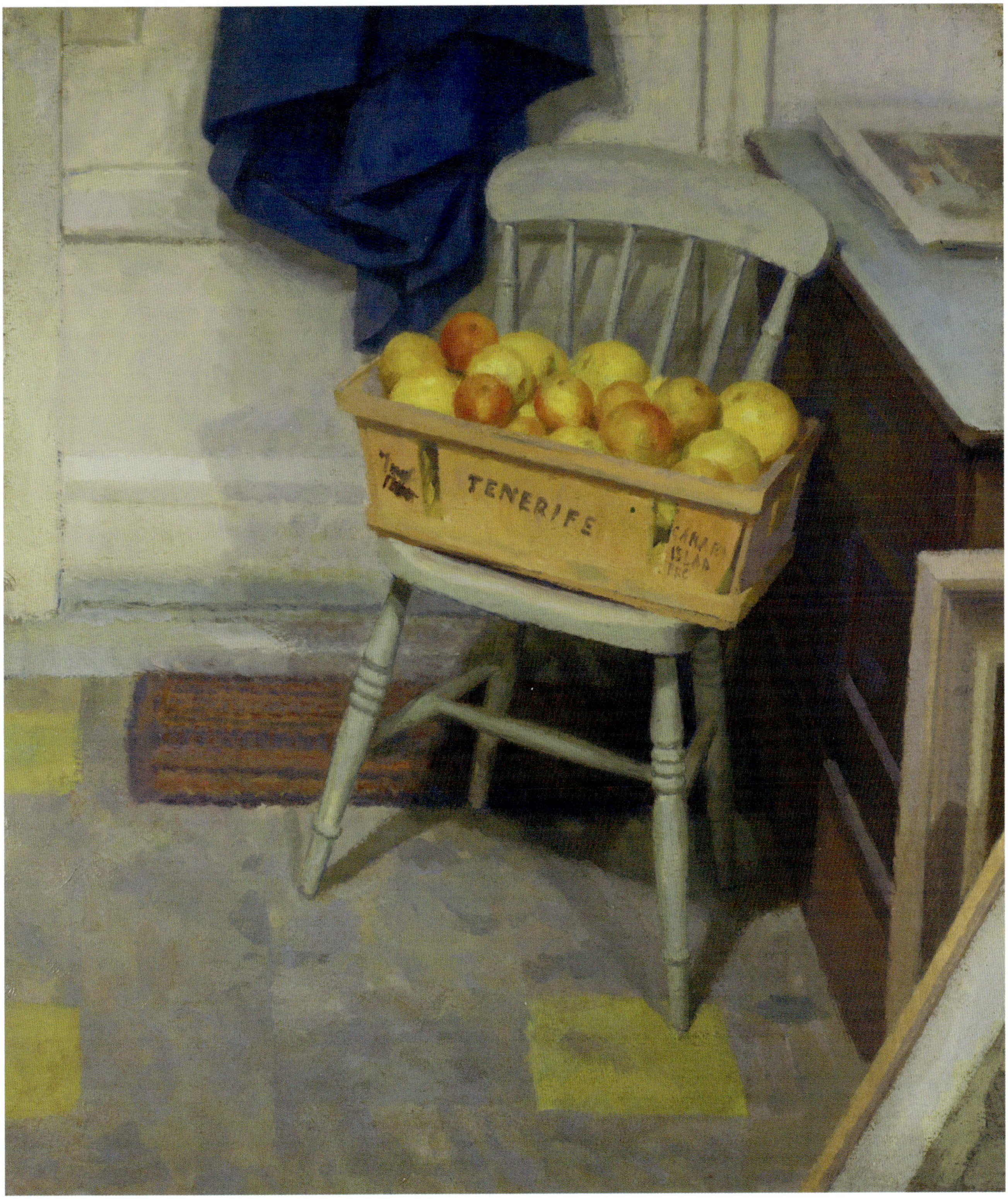

CAT. 28 – *Tenerife crate with apples on a wooden chair*, oil on panel, 24 × 20 in. (60.8 × 50.8 cm).

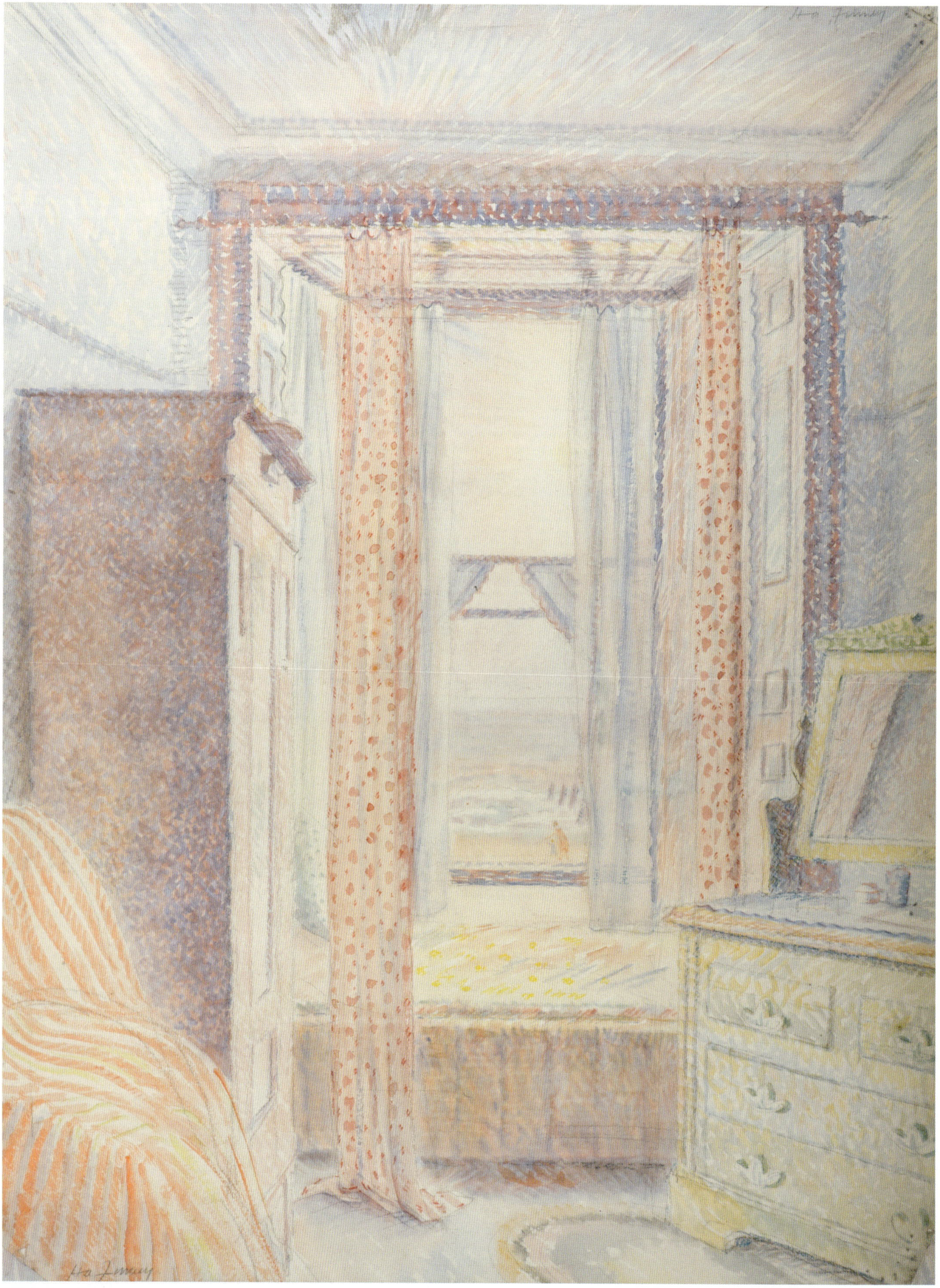

'I attended evening classes as well as day classes, therefore my creative life was very full. But now came the lightning stroke that completely changed, the interesting, if overworked life I had been leading since I entered the school. There was a girl student who I had observed with much interest, and one day I was buying some materials from the school shop which faced the entrance to the old school, when this girl Irene Turner walking up the path looks at me, and it was though something pierced through me, and from that moment I was never without constant image of her personality. Poets speak of Cupids darts and this is what they must mean. It is what is so called falling in love. It was not unlike the story of the Stigmata of Saint Francis. . . .

Encouraged by my friend Gardiner, my interest in classical music developed. The works by Schubert, Mozart, and Beethoven moved me tremendously. The emotional content of their work helped me to bear my own emotional intensity. I would wait until my parents brothers and sisters were in bed and then play my favourite records in the kitchen far into the night. The kitchen was sufficiently removed in the auditorium house from the rooms above for the sound not to disturb the sleepers in the other rooms. . . .

I have forgotten to mention that during the summer exhibition when I exhibited my picture "The Three Marys at the Sepulchre", the principle of the Royal College was invited (then Professor Rothenstein later Sir William Rothenstein) to open the summer exhibition and to present the prizes. His interest in my picture I believe, helped to lead the way to a future friendship between him and myself.

In the first year at the college I shared the studio with my old friend Charles Mahoney who introduced me to many of his friends. He never knew how for many weeks I wept at night and every night in silence my suffering was still with me. How little we know one another's lives. Waking up early one morning, I saw by his bedside a small glass with an artificial eye in it, and then for the first time I realised he had only one eye, yet I had known him for five or six years. . . .'

CAT. 29 – *Room Overlooking the Sea*, signed, pencil and watercolour on paper, 21 x 15 ½ in. (53.5 x 39 cm).

'The change from the small art school at Beckenham to the larger environment after the Royal College of art helped me in my fights to find some amusement in my emotional and mental life. Compared with the life of students at university today, my life was a frugal one on a scholarship of £90 a year, and for the first six months I went up to London by what was then called a Workmen's train which arrived in London before 8 am and I used to spend the time in Kensington Garden before the R. college opened in the morning.

Charles Mahoney introduced me to many of his friends which now, were to him, more important in his developing artistic life than I was, which was a natural process of a developing human being. A friend of his Barnett Friedman, was a personality who had great influence among the painting students at the college. He was a Jewish cockney with rich and colourful personality, and a humanism which is to be found in many Jews. He painted some remarkable paintings and was a dynamic force, also a passionate lover of music and played the violin. Sad to say, he did not fulfil this early promise, but became a successful book illustrator of distinction. . . .

There were so many personalities who possessed much creative gift and were fine human beings. Gerald Ososki, Albert Houthuesen, Percy Horton, a Russian named Mollo Kestelman and many more I was never privileged to know. It was a rich environment, even though the teaching was rather academic and unadventurous. I'm looking back at these years of tortured adolescence, my life would have been a treasure house for the experimentation of a modern psychologist, and I think perhaps I was fortunate in not being a subject to their experimentation, but having to try and heal myself I gained a self-respect, although the uphill climb to mental health has been a lifelong process. Hard work combined with the healing power of worship for Nature and the sun, and much metaphysical thinking and searching for the meaning of life enabled me to gradually find a harmony, and so became a reasonable human being in society.

These confessions and intimate revealing of my early life are for the interest and benefit of my sons and grandchildren. I know I could well be accused of an awful excess of self pity. But I believe this recalling of my other lessons will help to show the growth of human personality from a happy child with a normal sunny nature to the torturous paths of adolescence to manhood. . . .'

CAT. 30 – *Still life of a corner of the artist's studio with a broomstick,*
oil on board, 28 ¼ x 21 ¼ in. (71.5 x 53.5 cm).

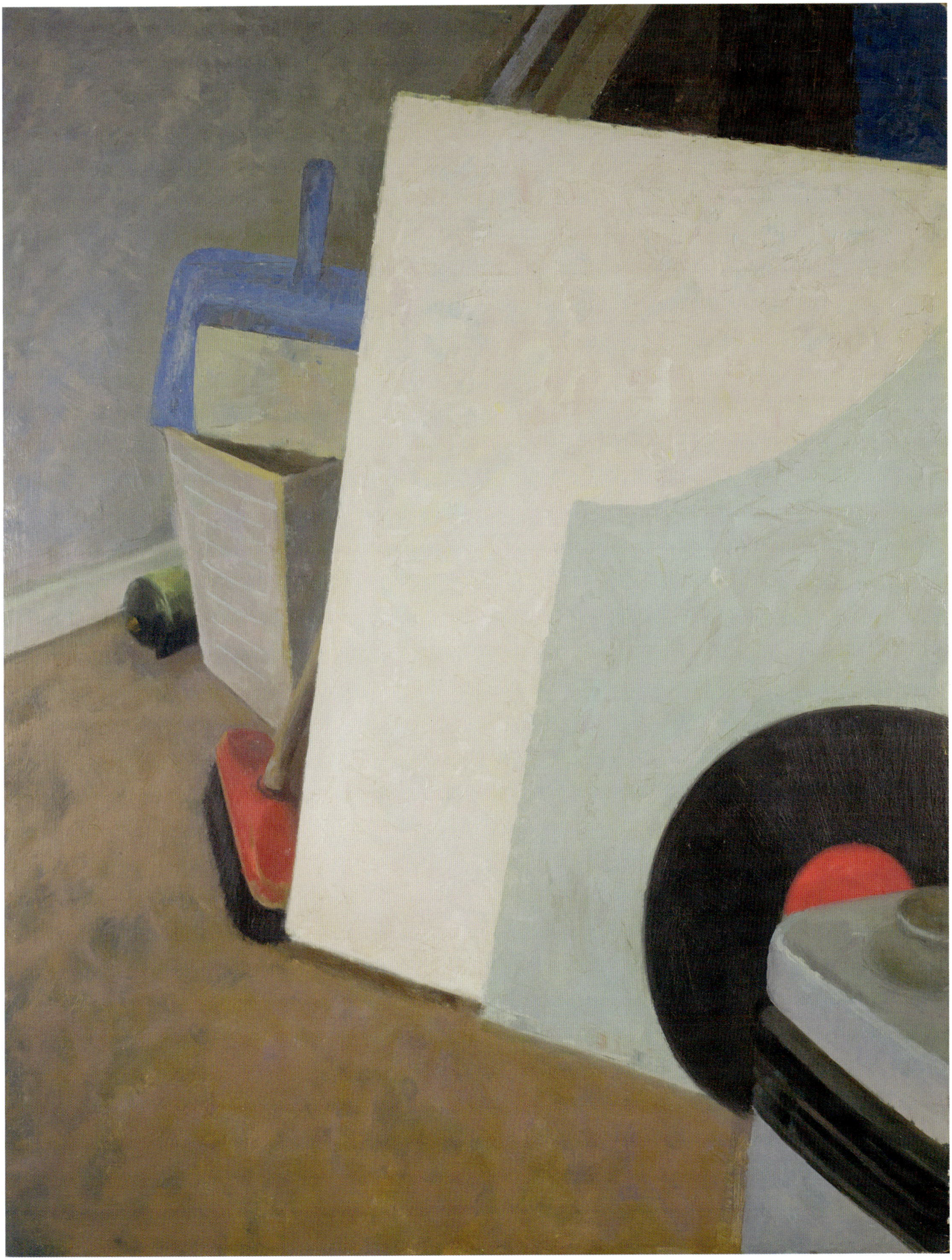

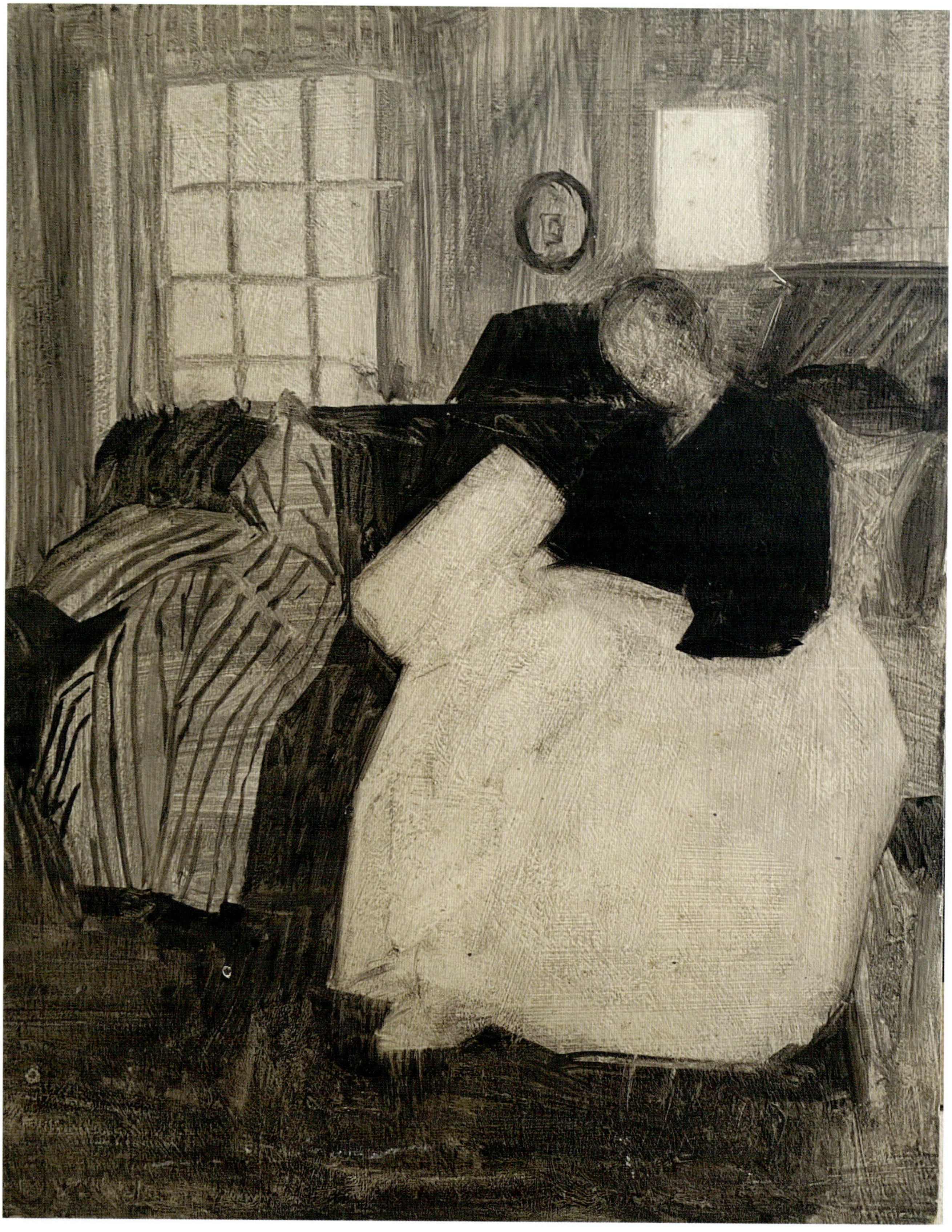

CAT. 31 – *The Artist's Wife Nita, Sewing*, c.1935, oil on panel 14 x 10 ¾ in. (35.2 x 27.2 cm).

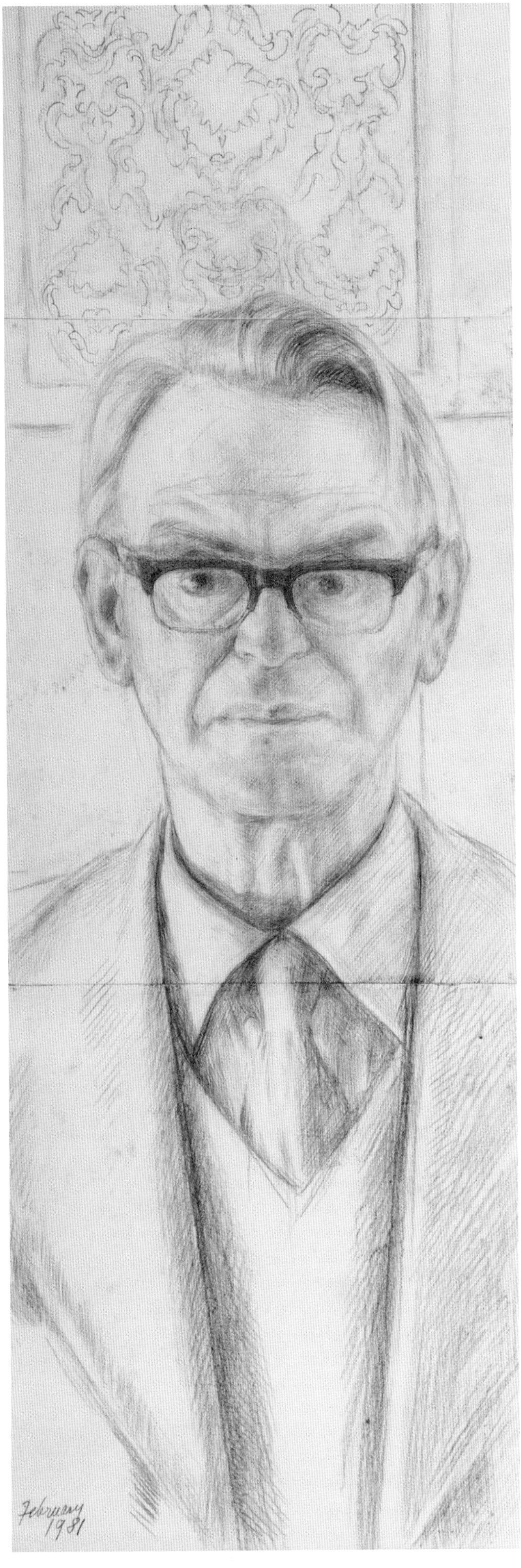

CAT. 32 – *Self Portrait, aged 76*, dated February1981, pencil on paper. 20 ¼ × 6 ½ in. (51.3 × 16.8 cm).

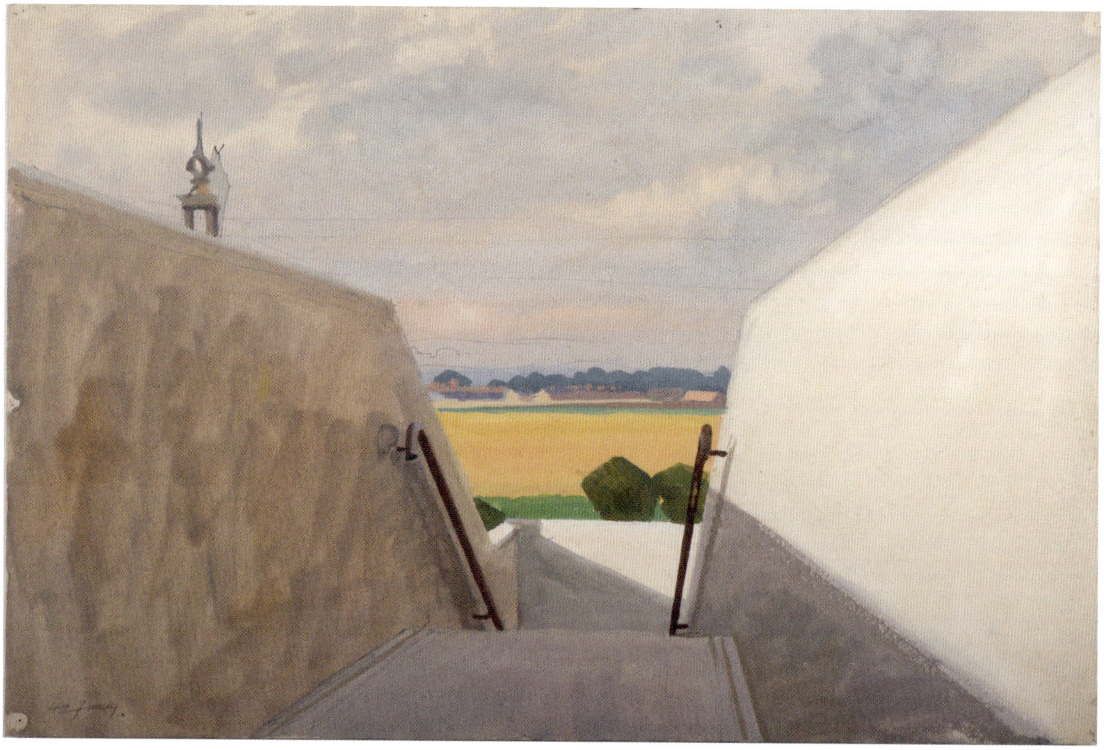

CAT. 33 – *Stairs and landscape*, signed, thinned oil on paper, 15 ¼ x 22 ½ in. (38.8 x 57.2 cm).

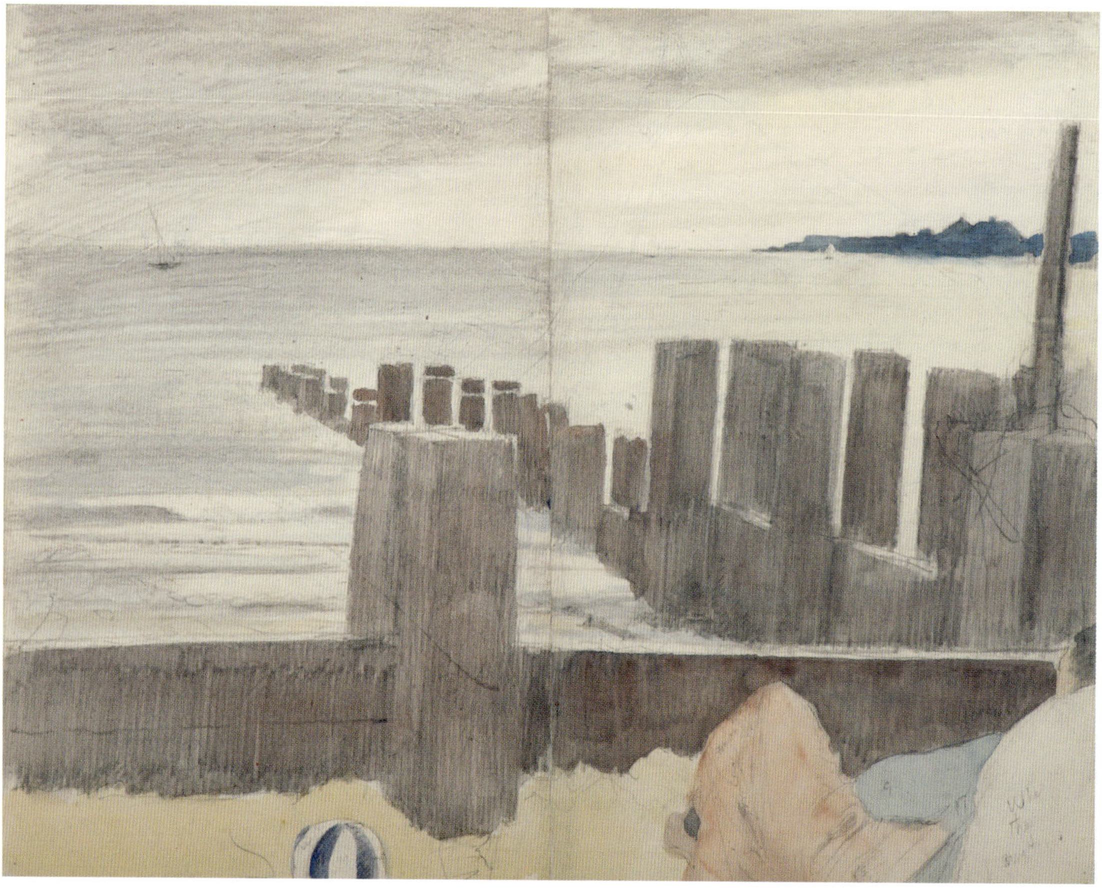

CAT. 34 – *Wooden groins on a beach*, inscribed with notes, pencil and watercolour on paper, 8 x 10 ¼ in. (20.7 x 25.8 cm).

Outside

'My change of environment to the RCA did save me from perhaps a shattered human personality and on looking back I'm grateful for all the human companionship I found there and the rich intellectual life I was exposed to.

Sir William Rothenstein showed much kindness to me and during his own illness asked me to his house to play chess with him. To form into words or written language, so much of what I thought, felt and experienced in the new environment would be like trying to make a life drawing of objects seen through drifting mists. Mental struggle, doubts, happiness, and an underlying sadness and withdrawing from life was the pattern of my life during these formative years.

Although I was an introvert by nature I made many friends, and was liked in spite of my inner struggles and secret inner life. When I think back after nearly half a century, many facts and interesting experiences, about my day-to-day living in the college are dim and misty...

As my college days were going to come to an end, my hard work and industry combined with an innate gift enabled me to gain the travelling scholarship award by the R.C.A each year. This was in 1929 after I had gained my degree A.R.C.A. which entailed working for a week or 10 days in a separate cubicle to carry out a composition in the oil medium of a given subject, "The Supper at Emmaus". My friend Houthuesen distinguished himself by painting a remarkably moving picture of the subject..

'It was during March of next year but I decided to start on my travels to Italy. I was a very inexperienced traveller having travelled little in England and never to the continent. On the sea crossing to Calais, the boat was prevented from entering the harbour because of the heavy mist, therefore my train was late on its arrival at Paris. I lost the connection for the train to Pisa and had to stay the night in Paris. My first sight of Notre Dame from a bridge over the Seine was a memorable one and I made a small drawing of it in my Italian sketchbook.

I never recaptured the emotion I felt when I saw Notre Dame for the first time. Under my calm exterior I was very nervous in the train to Pisa, and on my arrival an interpreter had to be found at the station, as my rail ticket was not an order. . . .'

'Mussolini was now in power in Italy and fascism was rearing its ugly head. One had to report as an alien to every police station at each town one resided in. Being practically ignorant of the Italian language, I was spared the humiliation of many insults told of me by officials in various police stations. The English were hated by the military authorities at this time. A student friend of mine Eric Jones who won the Prix de Rome scholarship in engraving was working in Rome. When I was in Florence, he came to see me and during our conversation, he expressed his hatred for the Italian police, saying he hoped one day he would have the chance to humble them in a likely war. Some days later he left a note in my hotel room saying, "goodbye! I am leaving for England in a few days and giving up my Rome scholarship. "...

'From Florence I moved onto Arezzo travelling by bus.

On leaving the church where the Piero Della Francesca's frescoes are to be seen, standing on the steps of the church in front of me, was an almost identical sky to the one I had observed in a fresco by Piero Della Francesca. I was much moved by his frescoes, he is one of the truly great painters of the early Renaissance. Arezzo is not a particularly interesting town, but it had an attractive small park on the top of the hill, where I used to go and sit in the evenings, and watch the circling of the swallows over the town, a beautiful memory. After about 10 days, feeling it was time to move on, I took a bus to Siena, which was an interesting ride and the landscape reminded me of the landscape in some of Piero Della Francesca's frescoes.

Siena is a beautiful city and Sienese painting moved me much, especially Duccio. I found a hotel quite close to the cathedral and I would be deafened by the deep vibrating sound of the cathedral bells. I fell in love with Siena as I had with Florence. Time passes quickly and I worked at drawing and painting with much concentration, but I was by now feeling the need of a companion, and the food, much spaghetti, and trying to live as cheaply as possible was beginning to have an effect upon my health....

Here was I, obsessed by the beauty of the external world, by the light of Italy, by the world of the Renaissance, yet completely divorced from the main movements in the world of contemporary painting, in the formative years of my life, I cannot remember visiting one exhibition of contemporary Italian painting. It was inevitable that my paintings never became lit by the influence and experimentation of contemporary painting. But I believe this travelling scholarship saved me as a human being from becoming a neurotic mental patient, in and out of hospital....'

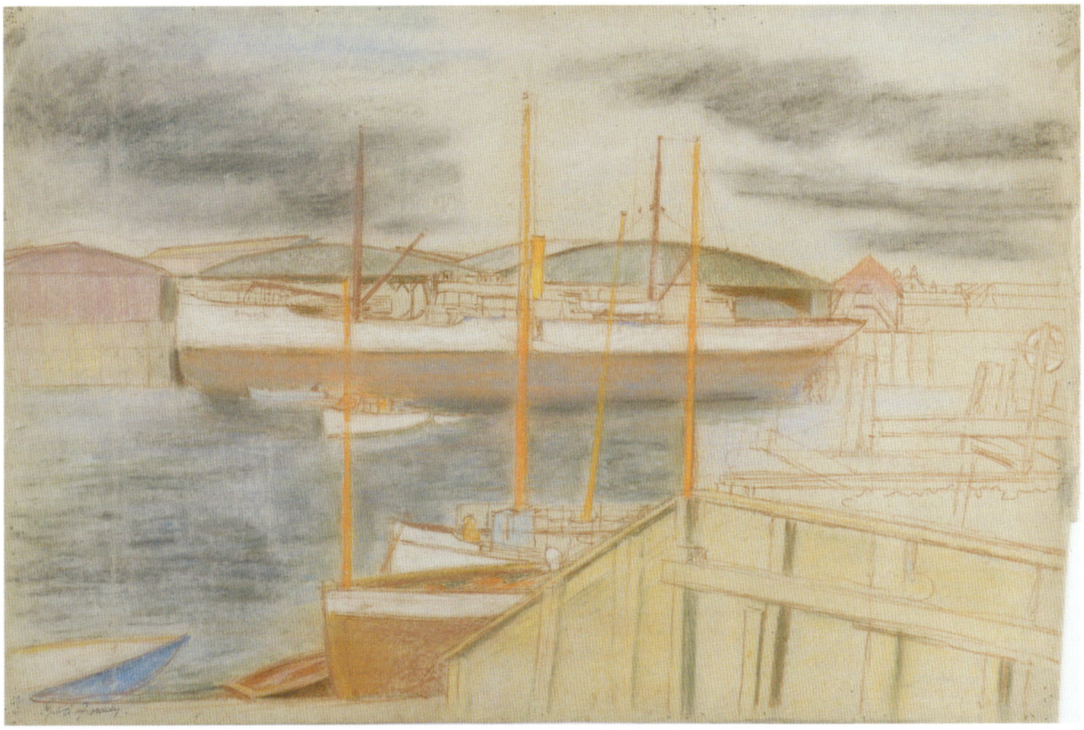

CAT. 35 – *Boats in Harbour*, signed, red pencil and pastel on paper, 15 ½ x 23 in. (39 x 57.8 cm).

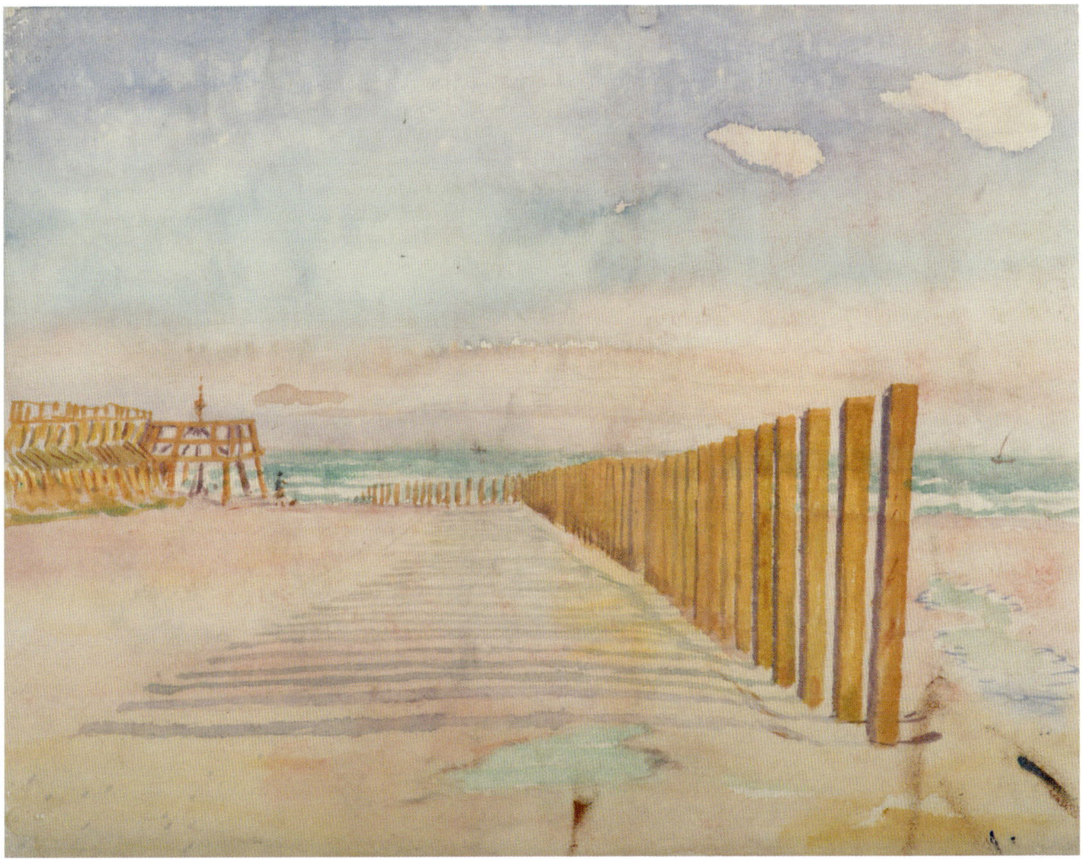

CAT. 36 – *By the Ocean*, pencil and watercolour on paper, 11 x 13 ¾ in. (28 x 34.7 cm).

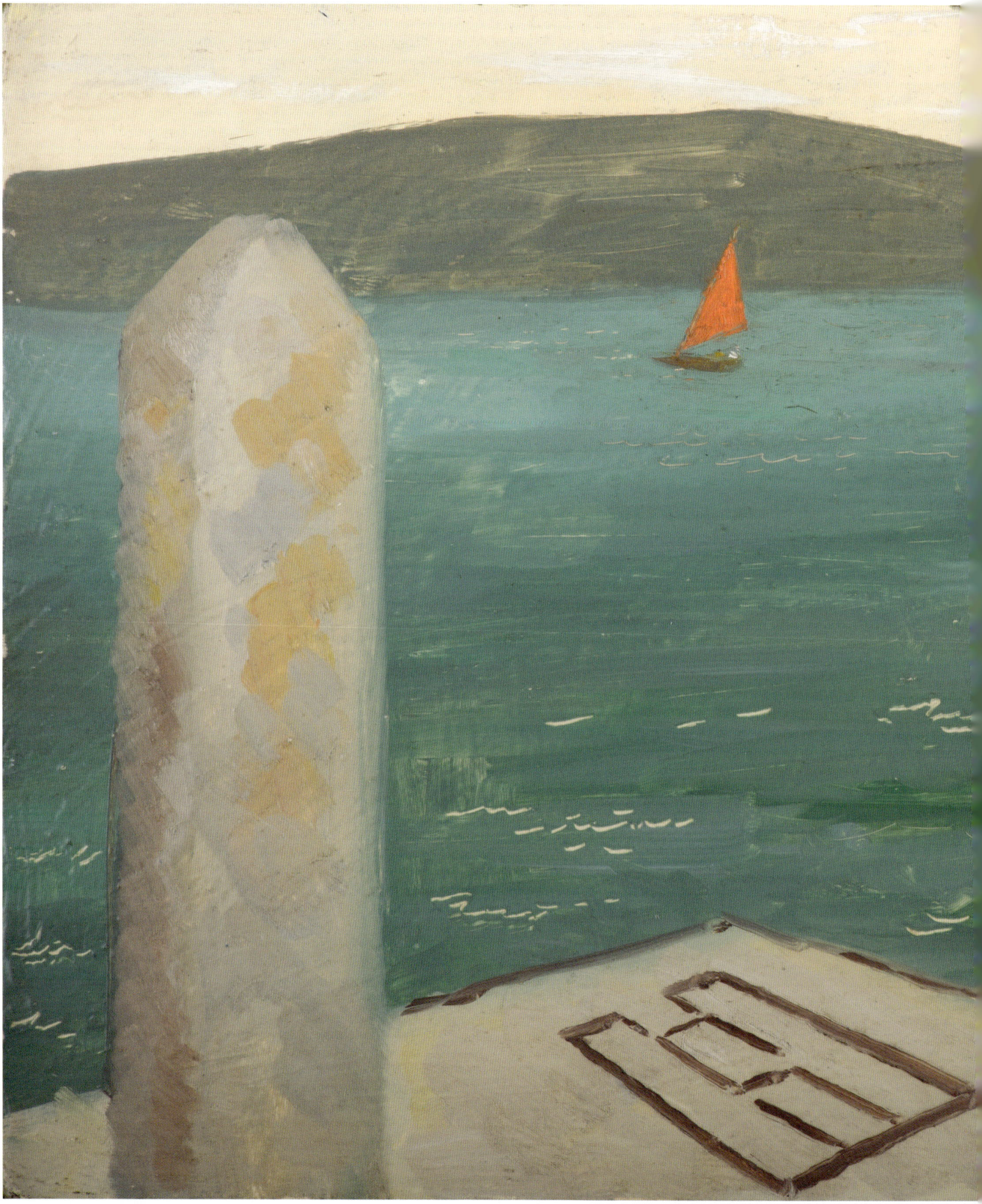

CAT. 37 – *The Red Sailboat*,
oil on panel 9 ½ x 13 in. (24 x 33 cm).

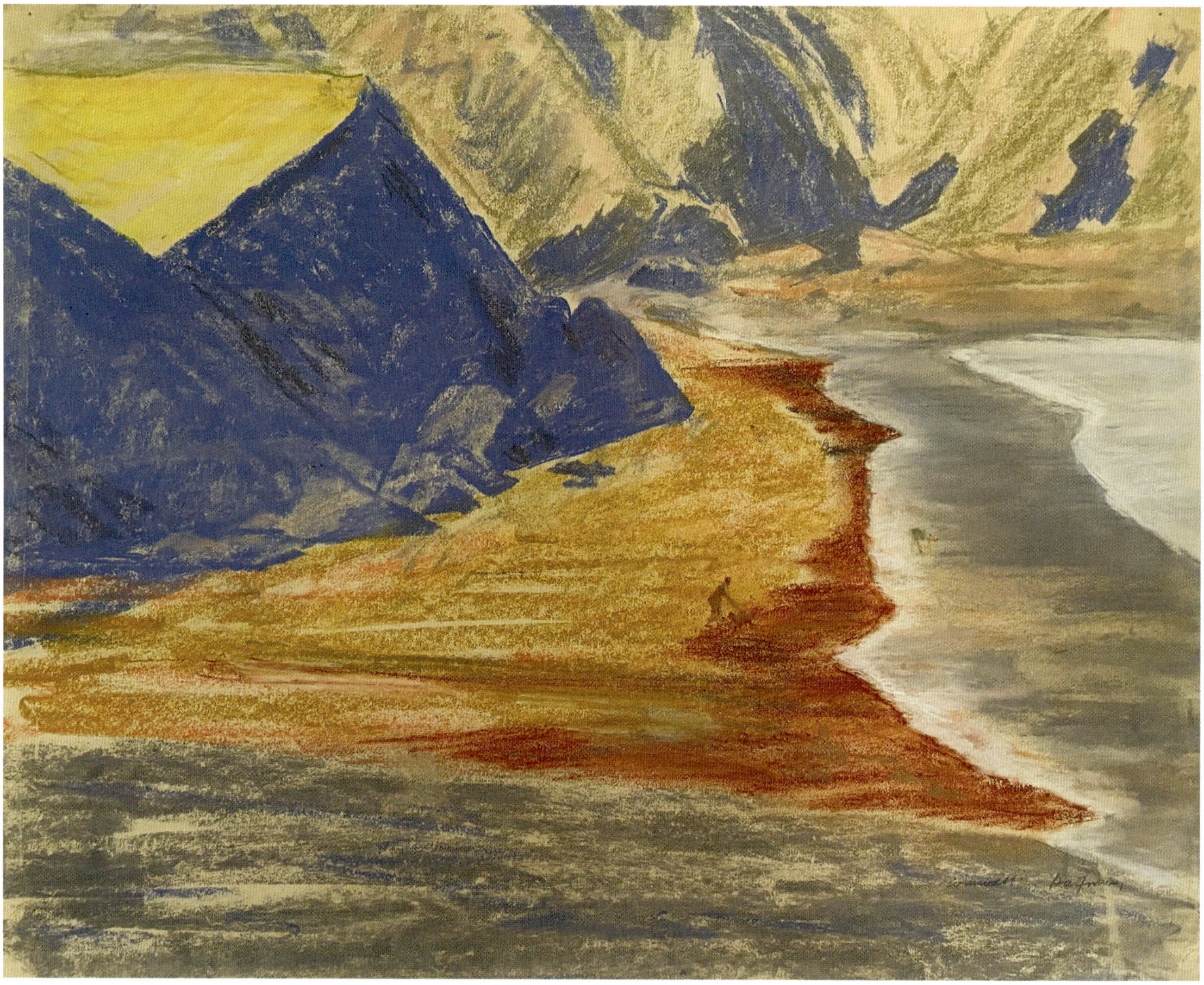

CAT. 38 – *Cornwall*, signed and inscribed 'Cornwall', pastel on paper, 15 x 18 in. (38 x 45.7 cm).

a CAT. 39 – *Dorset Jurassic Coast, Looking Towards St. Aldhelm's Head*, oil on board, 10 ½ x 13 ¾ in. (27 x 35 cm)

b CAT. 40 – *Cliffs near Dover with Couples Walking*, signed, oil on panel, 9 ¼ x 17 ¾ in. (23.5 x 45.5 cm)

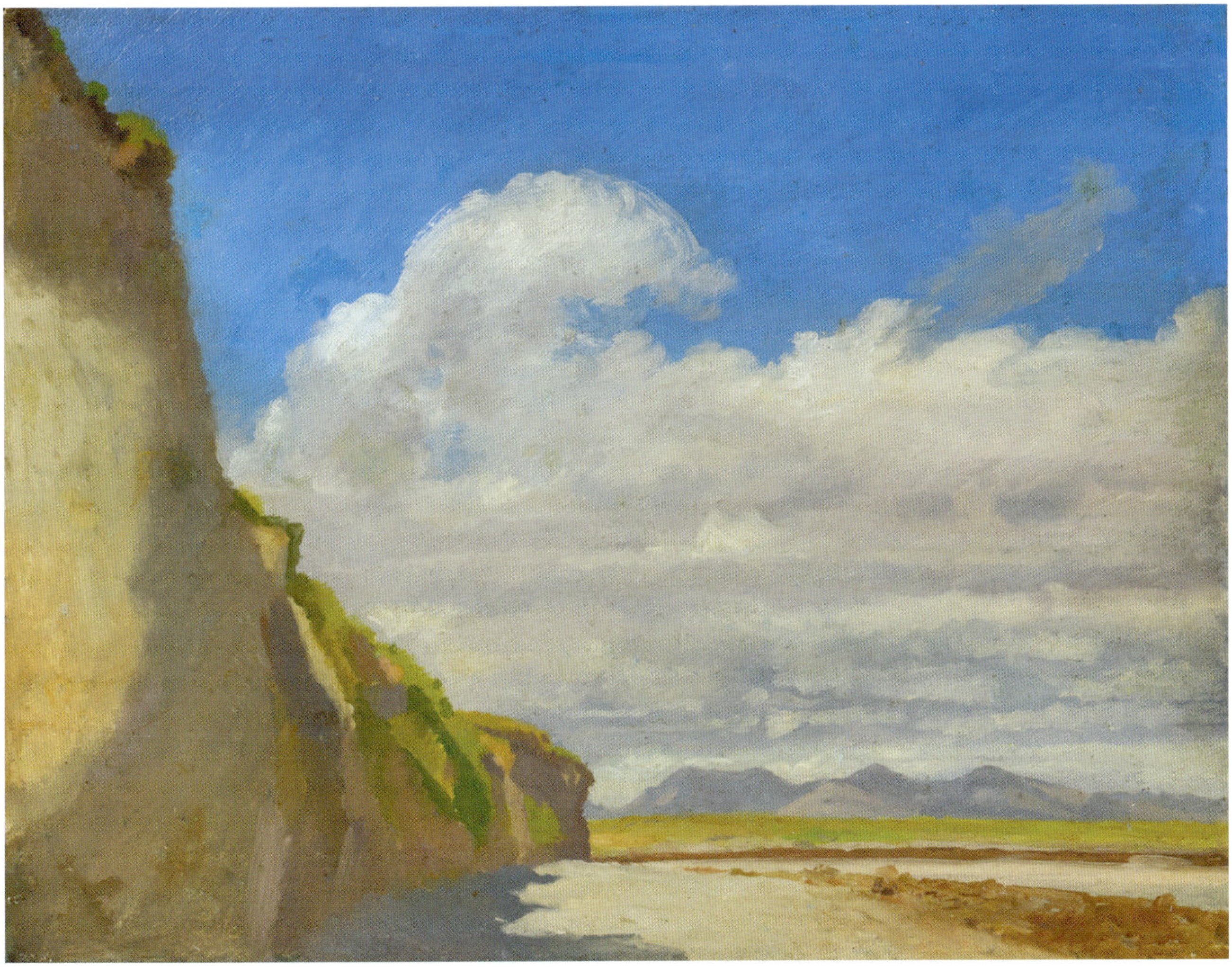

a

b

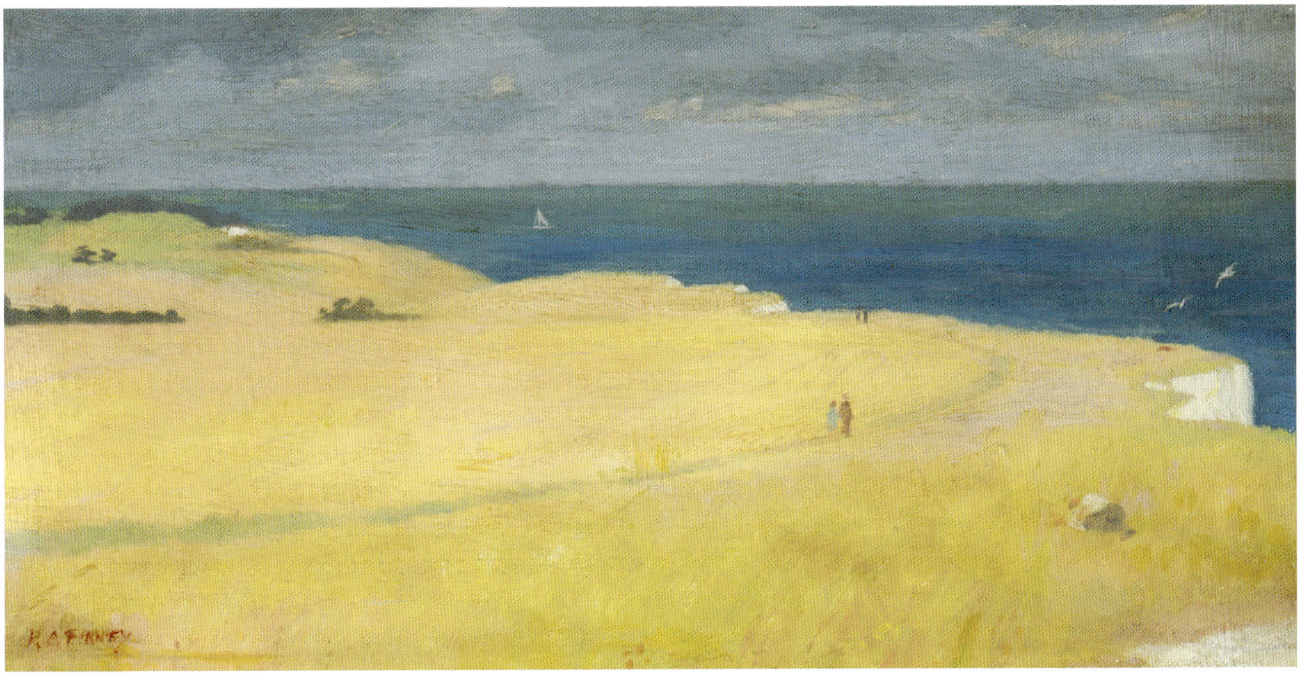

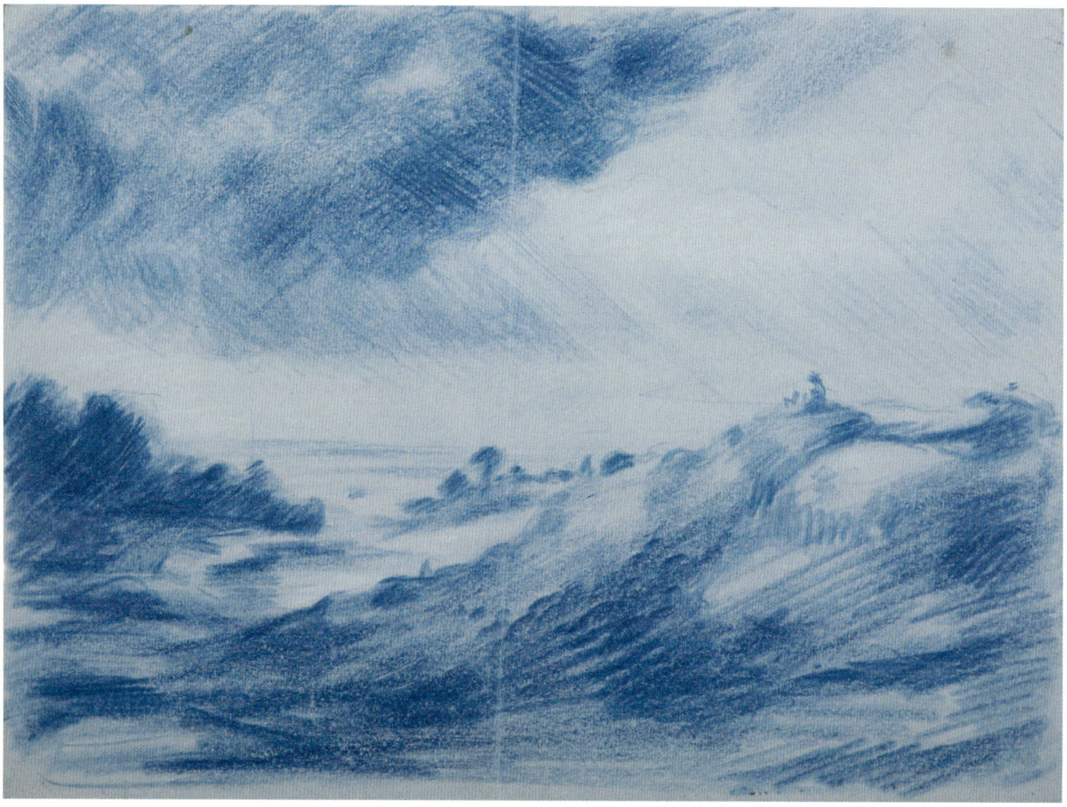

CAT. 41 – *Blue Landscape*, blue pencil on paper, 5 x 6 ½ in. (12.7 x 16.8 cm).

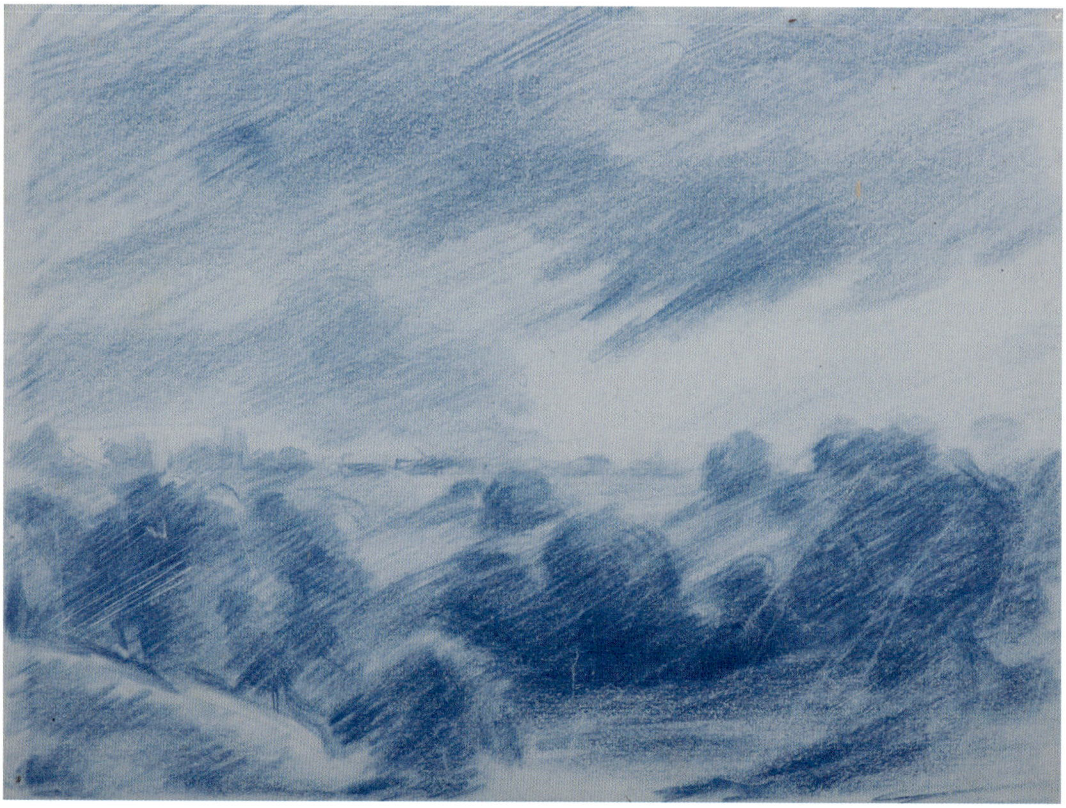

CAT. 42 – *Blue Landscape with Trees*, blue pencil on paper, 5 x 6 ½ in. (12.7 x 16.8 cm).

'However I do remember making a water colour of Siena Cathedral, large in scale with houses and gardens in front of it and which I thought I was seeing it, rather like a Cézanne. After soaking myself in Sienese art, and the work of Duccio, I took the train to Orvieto. The train follows the river Tiber as it approaches Orvieto, which is built on an extinct volcano, and from the train it is not visible, as one has to take a Funicular to reach the tower. It was here that fate took a hand in bringing to a termination my travels in Italy. I developed some form of dysentery through drinking some contaminated water. Waking up one night in a mental dazs, when the heat was suffocating I drank a few small sips of some water on the dressing table in my bedroom. The next day I felt ill and everything passed through me. I stayed in Orvieto two or three days, visited the cathedral, with its wonderful facade with the sculptured reliefs by Luca Signorelli of, "The Creation to the Last Judgement". And saw one of the most wonderful sunsets over the valley of the Tiber which one looks down upon from the heights of Orvieto.

I felt too ill to continue my stay at Orvieto, and I took the train to Rome hoping to find the British School of Rome, And then to be recommended a doctor. I never located it, as it is on the outskirts of Rome. By now I knew I was tired of travelling alone, and feeling very ill, I made up my mind that after seeing the Sistine chapel and the Velázquez portrait of Pope Innocent X. I would return home to England. I spent three days in Rome and then took the train to Paris, and England. I had intended visiting Naples, then travelling to Assisi, Ravenna, and finally Venice, but it was not to be. Because I had only been three and a half months in Italy, I had some scholarship money left which enabled me to live in a rented room near Hampstead until I was able to get a part-time teaching post. It was about this time that I found a friendship with a most gifted painter Edward Le Bas. He was the son of a wealthy industrialist, but Le Bas was a gentle person, sensitive and had high ideals. When his father died, he became a millionaire, but his passion, and love of drawing and painting dominated his life, and he was an indefatigable worker.

Now, I was back in England, I had nostalgia for Italy, and wished I had fought longer against my illness, but living and painting near Hampstead heath, and experiencing beautiful summer evenings on the heath helped to lessen my sadness that I was no longer in Italy. . . .'

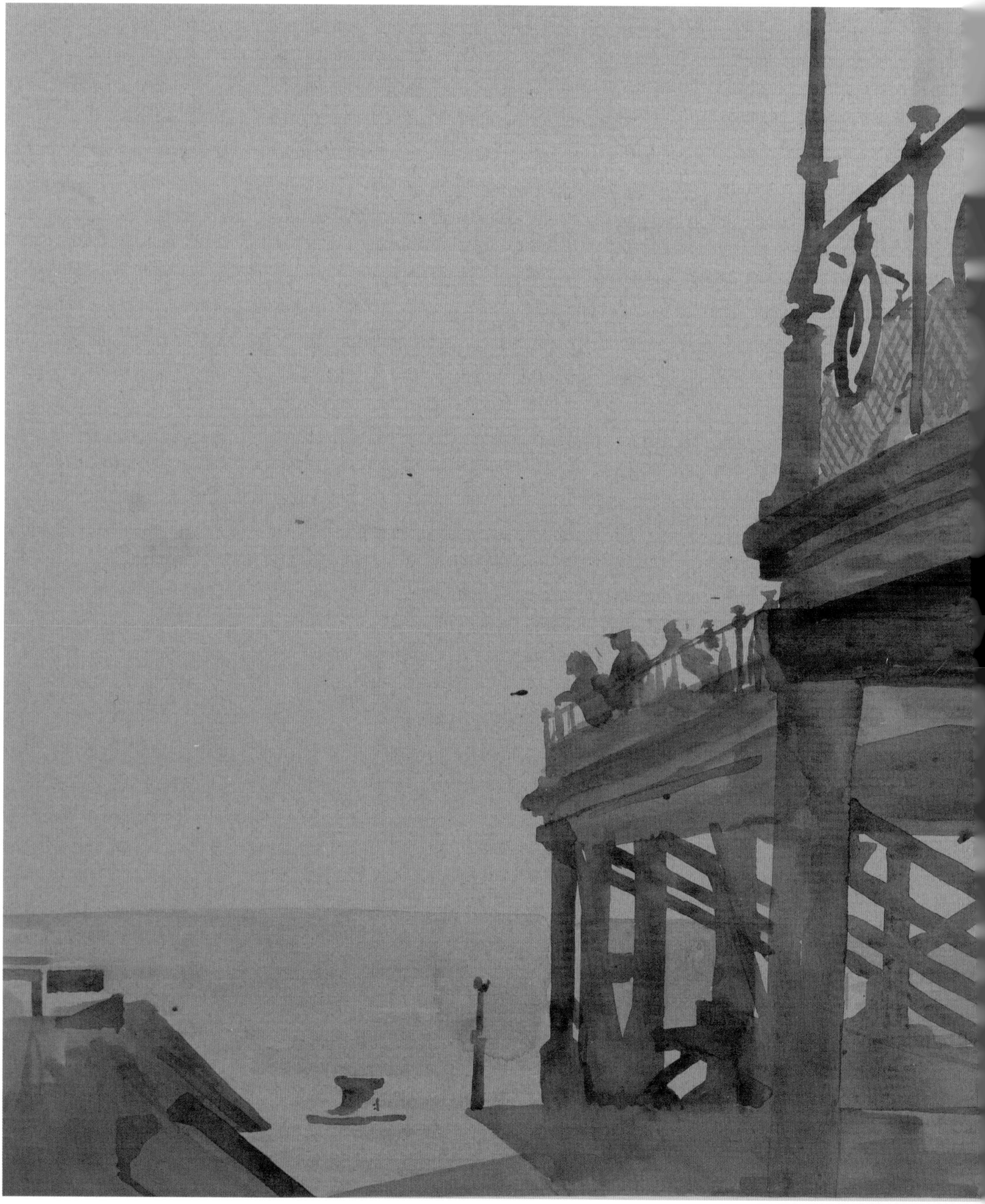

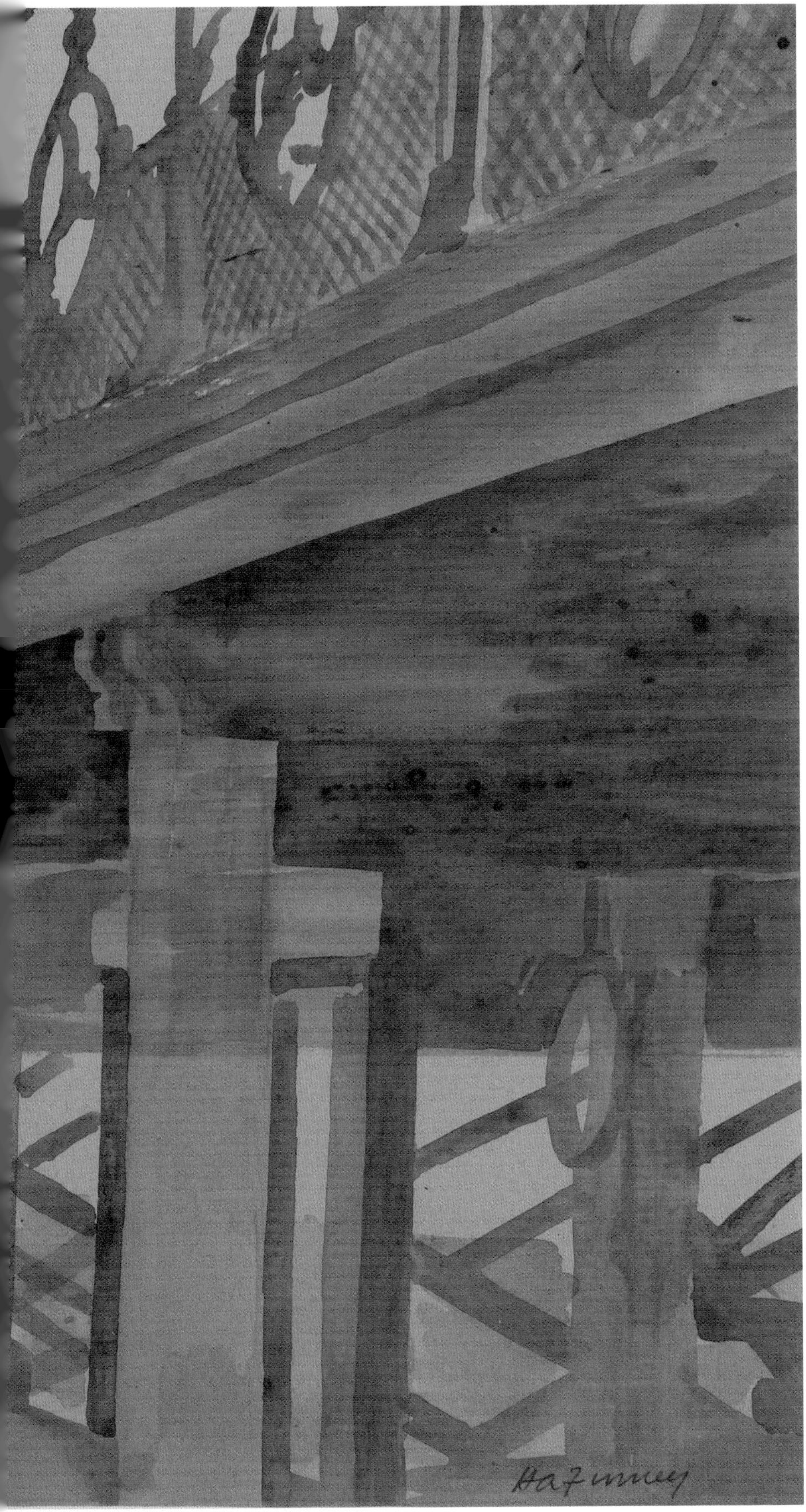

CAT. 43 – *Swanage Pier*, signed,
wash on blue paper mounted on card,
11 ¼ x 15 ¾ in. (28.5 x 40.2 cm).

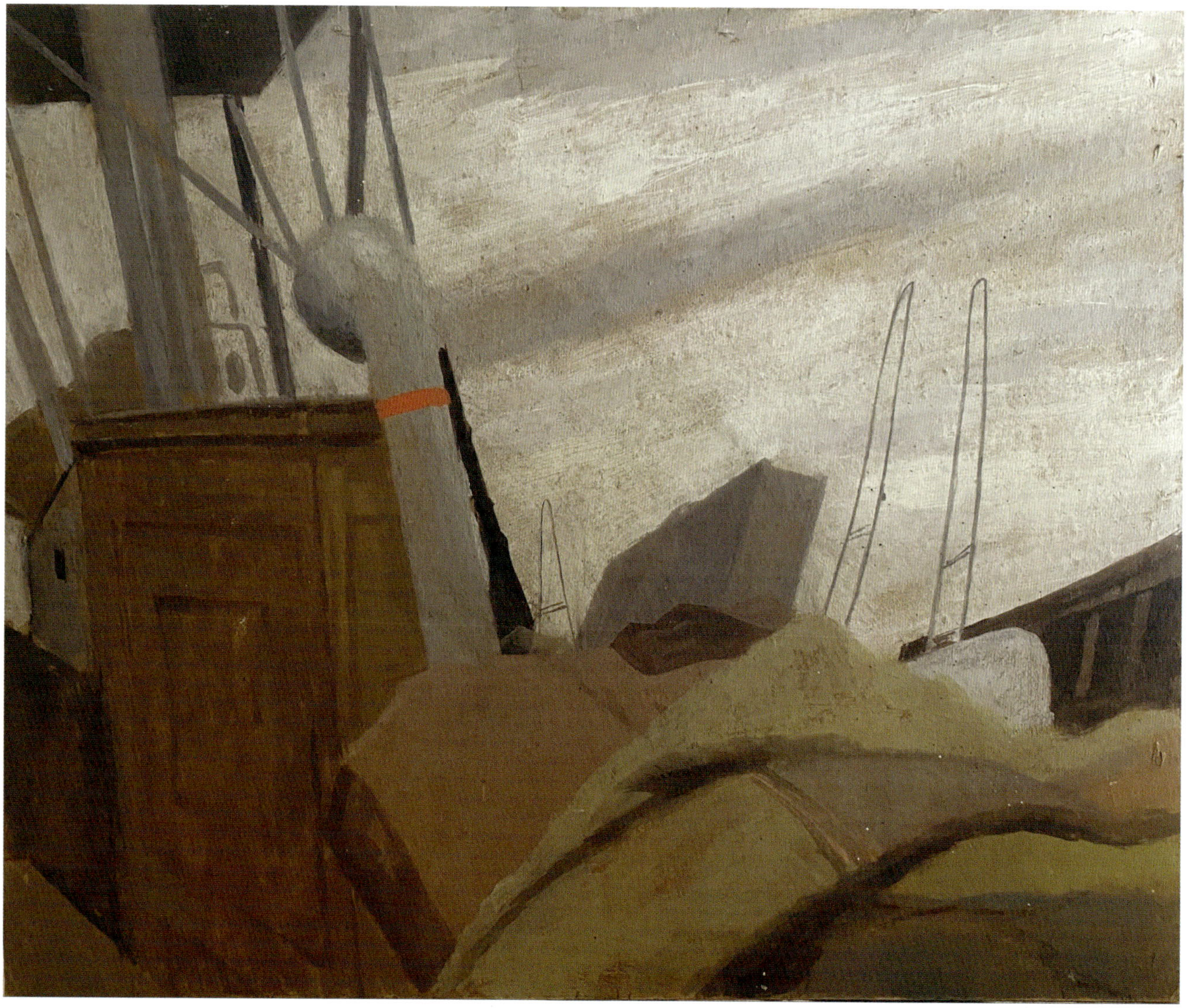

CAT. 44 – *On the deck*, oil on board 20 ¼ x 17 ¼ in. (51.5 x 44 cm).
Provenance: The Artist's studio.

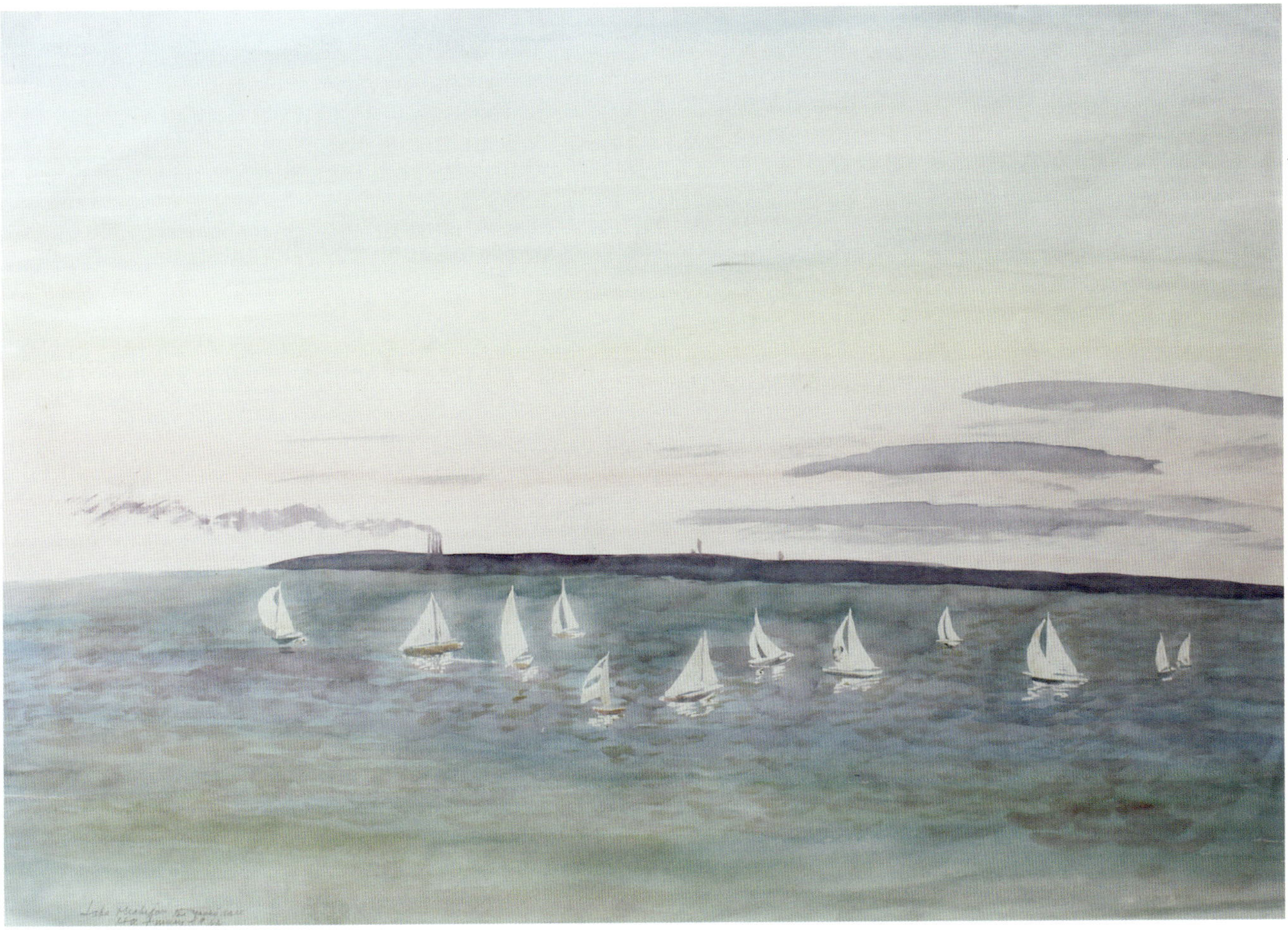

CAT. 45 – *Lake Michigan, The Yacht Race*, 1966, signed and titled, gouache on paper, 16 ½ x 23 in. (42.2 x 58.2 cm).

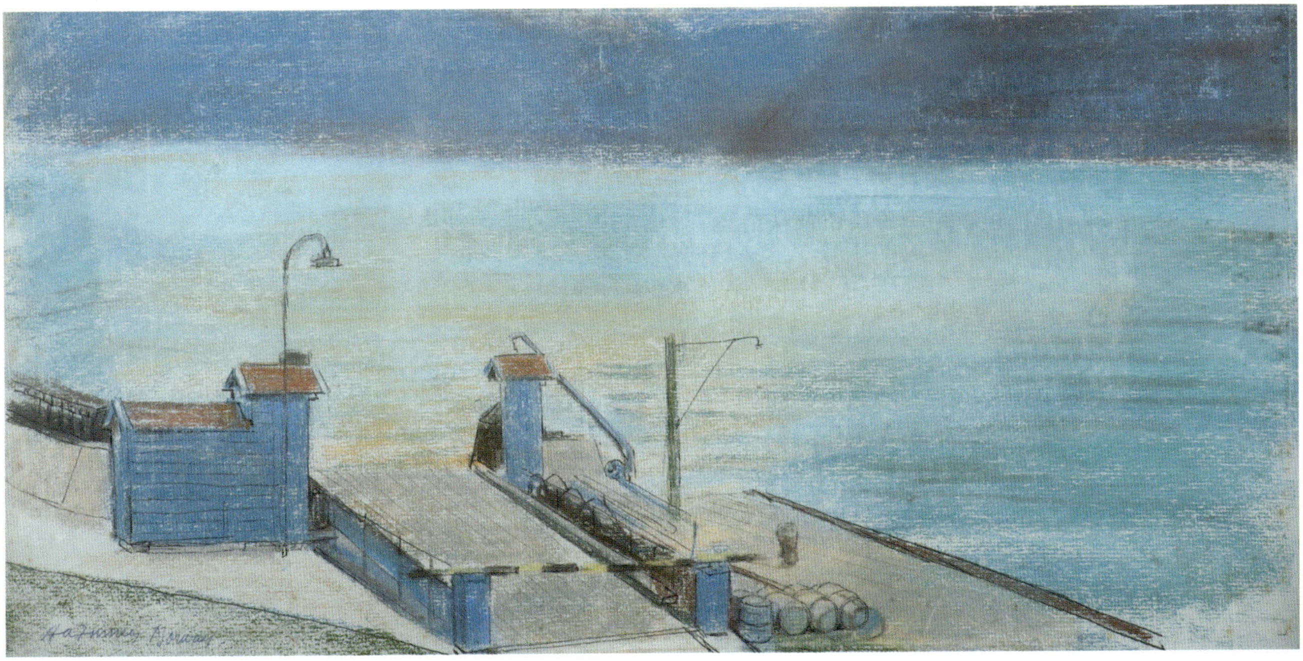

CAT. 46 – *Norway*, 1960, signed and titled, ink and pastel on paper, 8 ½ x 17 in. (21.8 x 43.3 cm).

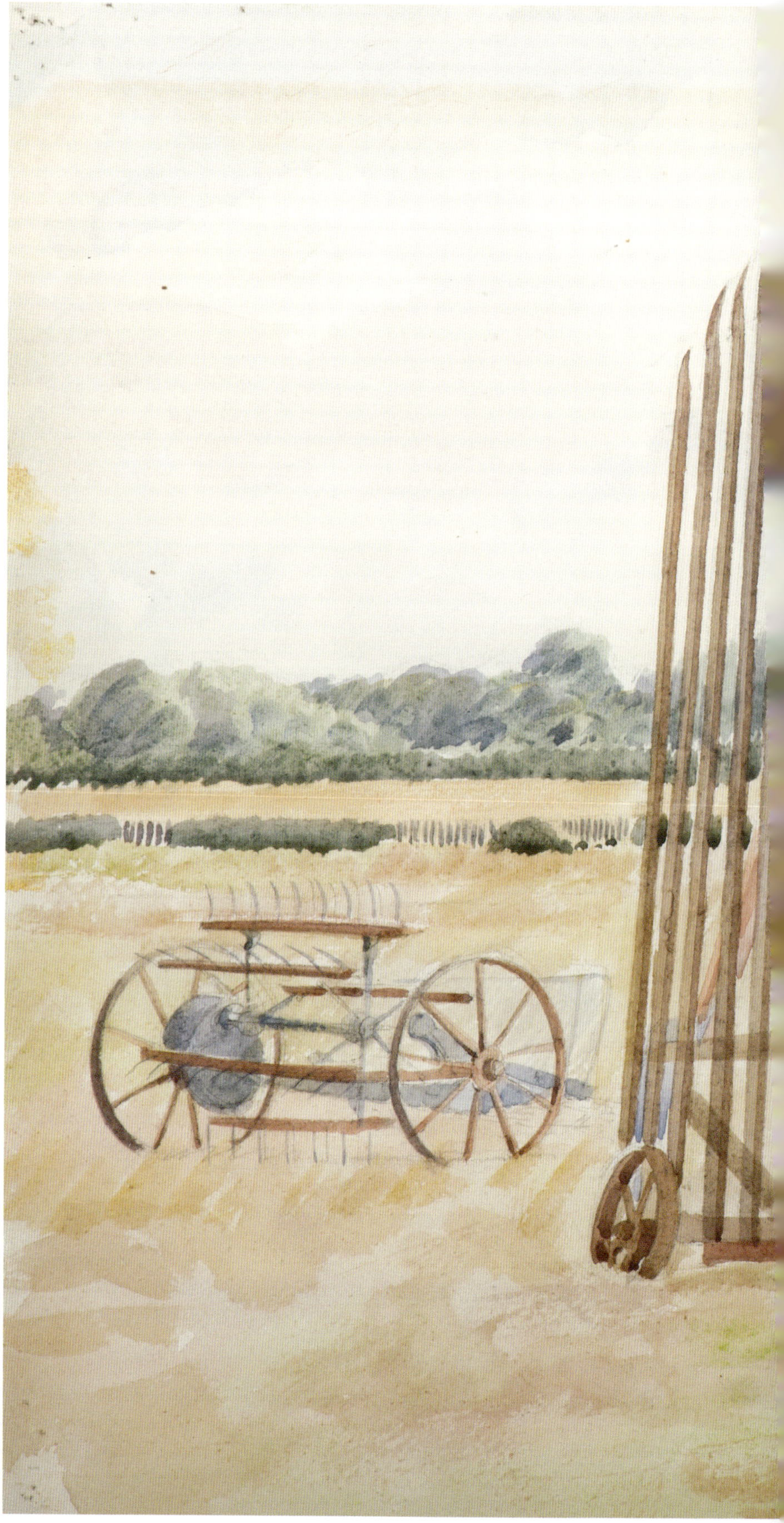

CAT. 47 – *Farm Equipment*, 1930s, pencil and watercolour on paper, 11 × 15 ½ in. (28 × 39.2 cm).

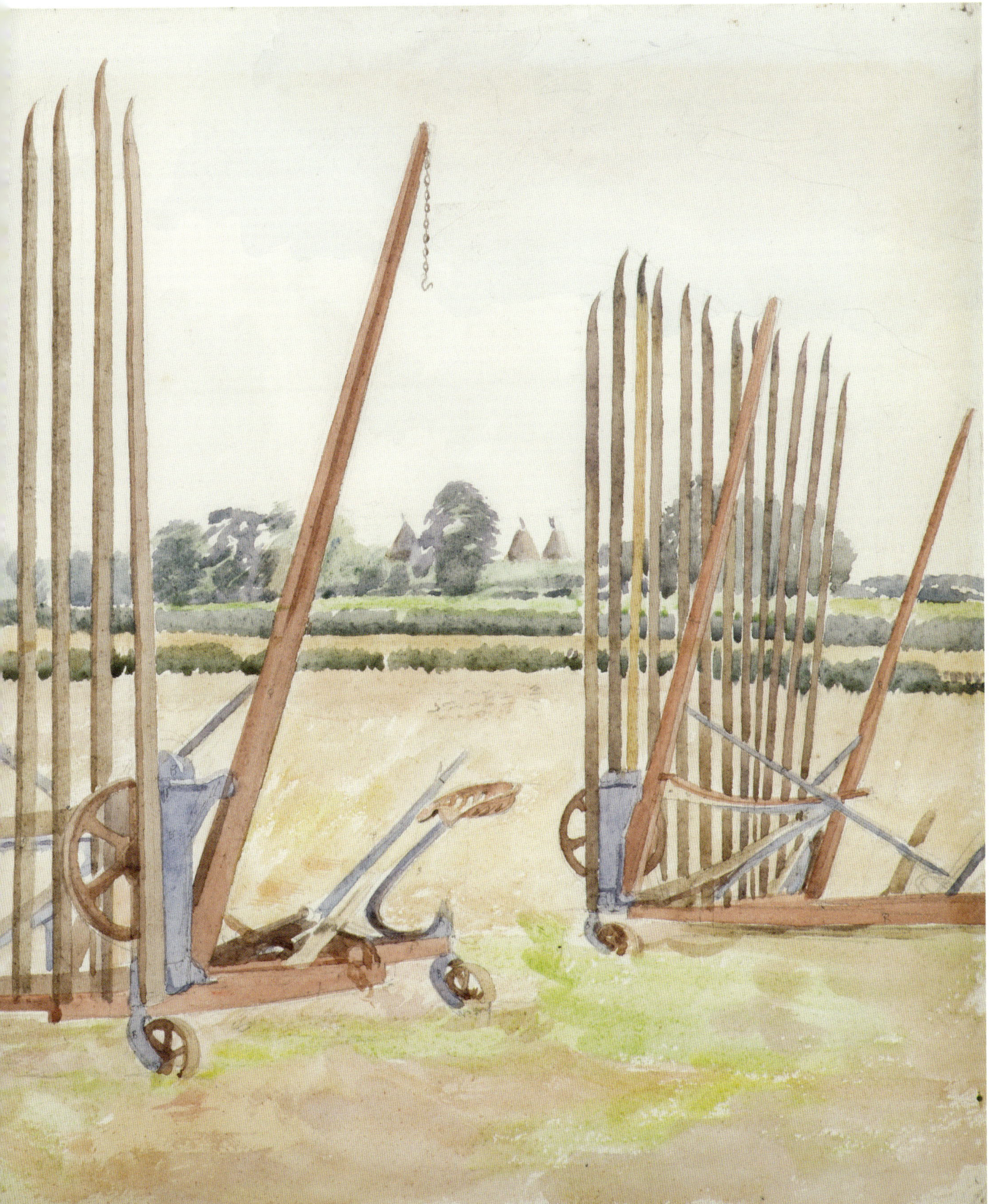

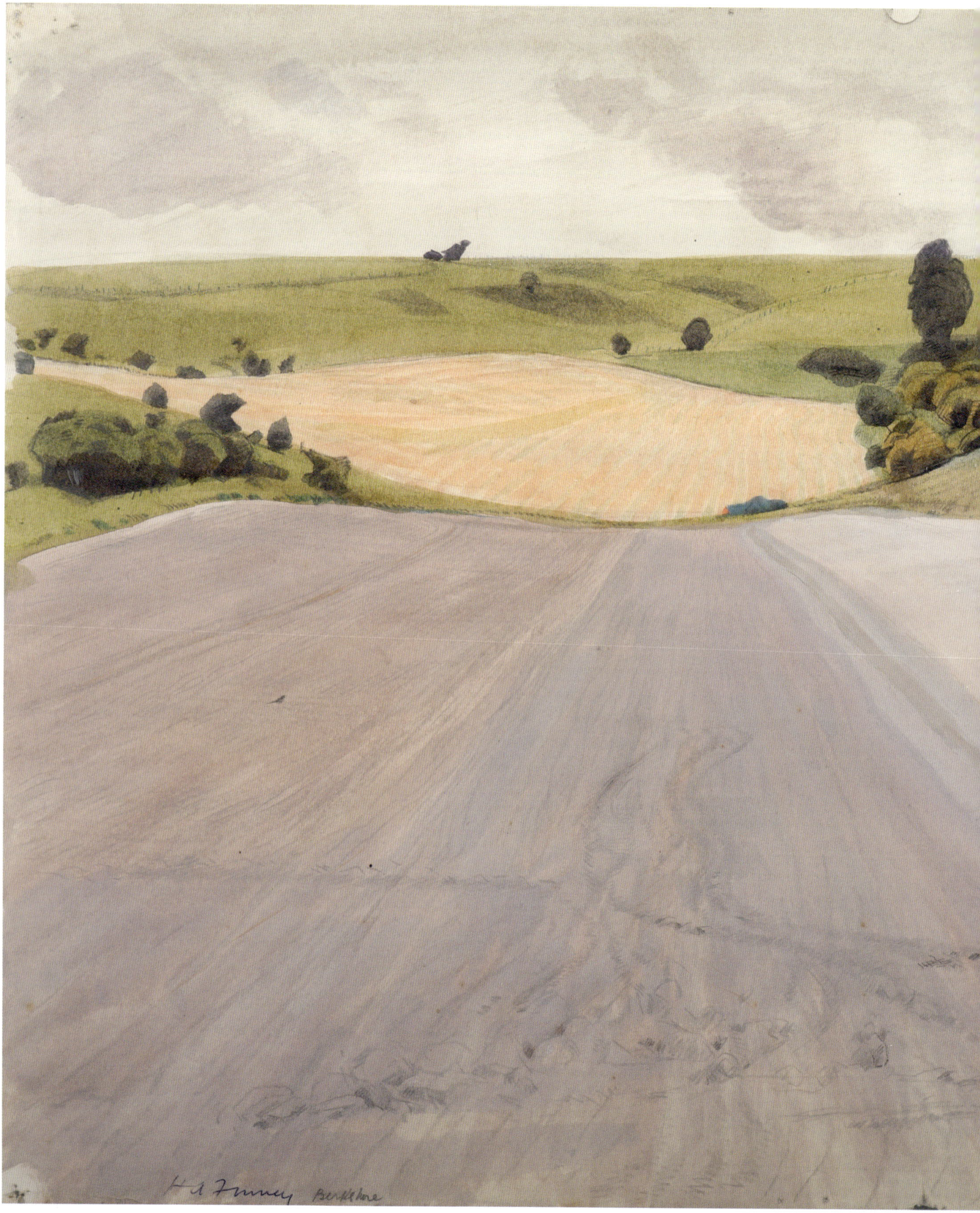
H A Finney Berkshire

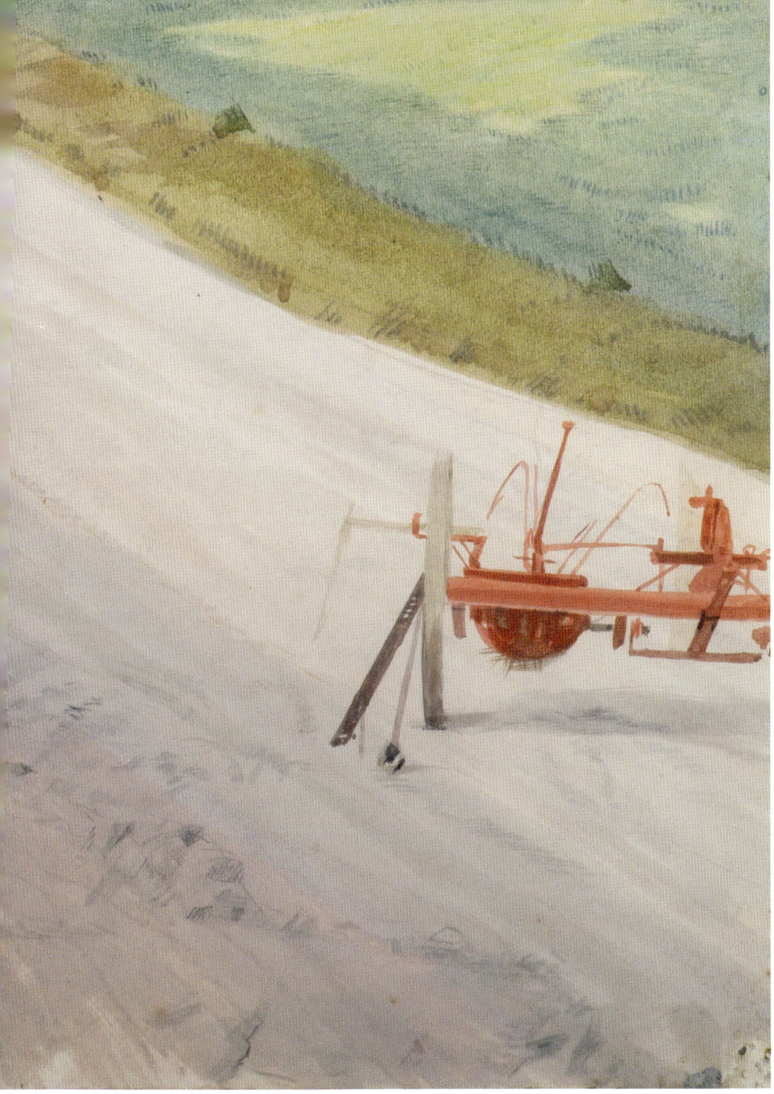

CAT. 48 – *Berkshire*, signed and inscribed 'Berkshire', 1960s, thinned oil on paper, 15 x 20 in. (38 x 50.7 cm).

'A most versatile personality took his place, H.S.Williamson a considerable musician, as well as an able and vital painter, a man with a great sense of humour, which often had a dart in it especially for me.

This teaching post. Which must have started four five months after I came home from Italy, enabled me to have contact with a few of the personalities, who were ultimately to make a name for themselves in the world of the visual arts. Henry Moore was in charge of the sculpture department and Graham Sutherland of the Department of design. I could have attended cocktail parties given by them, which would have led me into the arts circle. But being by nature antisocial, and having faced and inner happiness in communication with nature through the poetry of Shakespeare, Wordsworth, Shirley and others I cut myself off from social gatherings when it was possible. Looking back now over the years, I see I was wrong in my decisions. But we are what we are, and our life is the unfolding of our personalities as we pass through many different environments and contacts with other human beings. Most of the personalities I came into contact with at the Chelsea School of Art, were friendly, and found certain qualities in me likeable, but I think something told them that I was not to be encouraged into their fold, which consisted of personalities who felt that their destiny was moving on to make a reputation in the world of painting and sculpture. Two painters who showed genuine friendship and were always kind to me were Raymond Coxton and his wife and the memory of people's kindness helps one through life. . . .

After 40 years, looking back seeing life in a larger version, I know my painting would have benefited, if I had allowed myself to wait more often for the true creative spark to awaken, by an urgency to express some vision or emotion felt and experienced. But work had become a means of survival, in the battle for living.

Now began another struggle, for my love of nature, which has always been intense with not just a love of her beauty in all her extended forms, but an identity I felt between her and the revealing of the divine mind or creation of the Universe, was leading me to an awareness of the metaphysical. The retreating back to the world of the senses of matter of natural animals instincts, needed new adjustments to the art of living in this world. . . .'

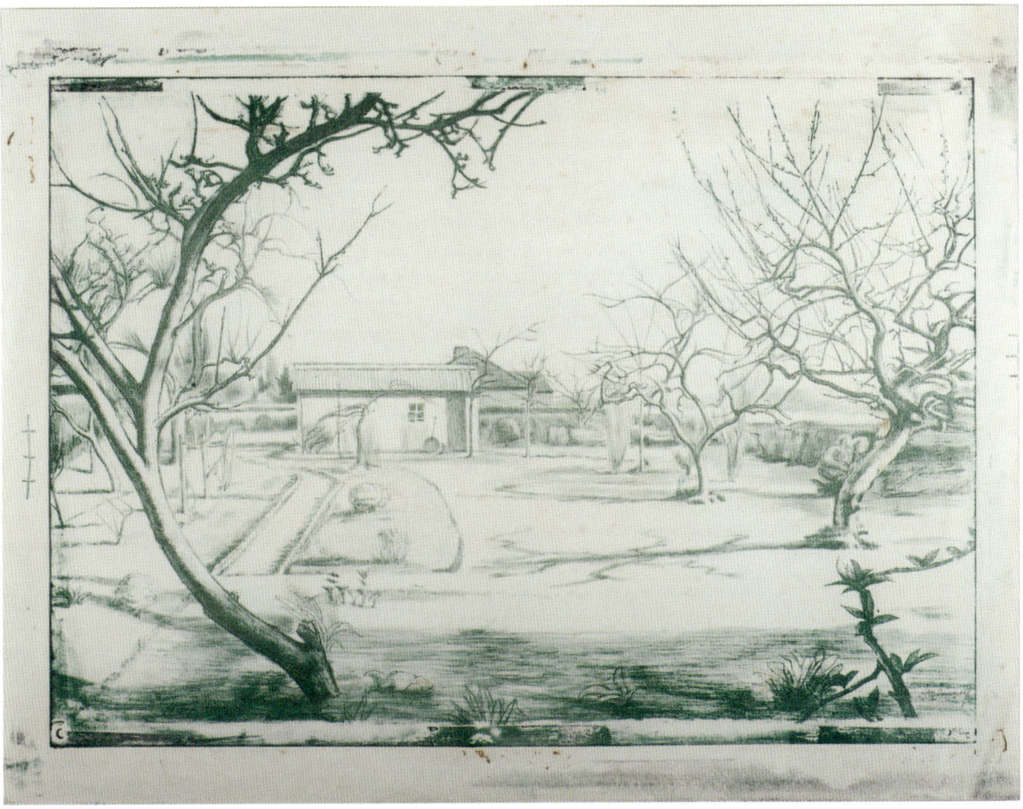

CAT. 49 – *White Cottage*, 1959, signed, lithograph, printed in green ink., 19 x 24 in. (48.5 x 61 cm).

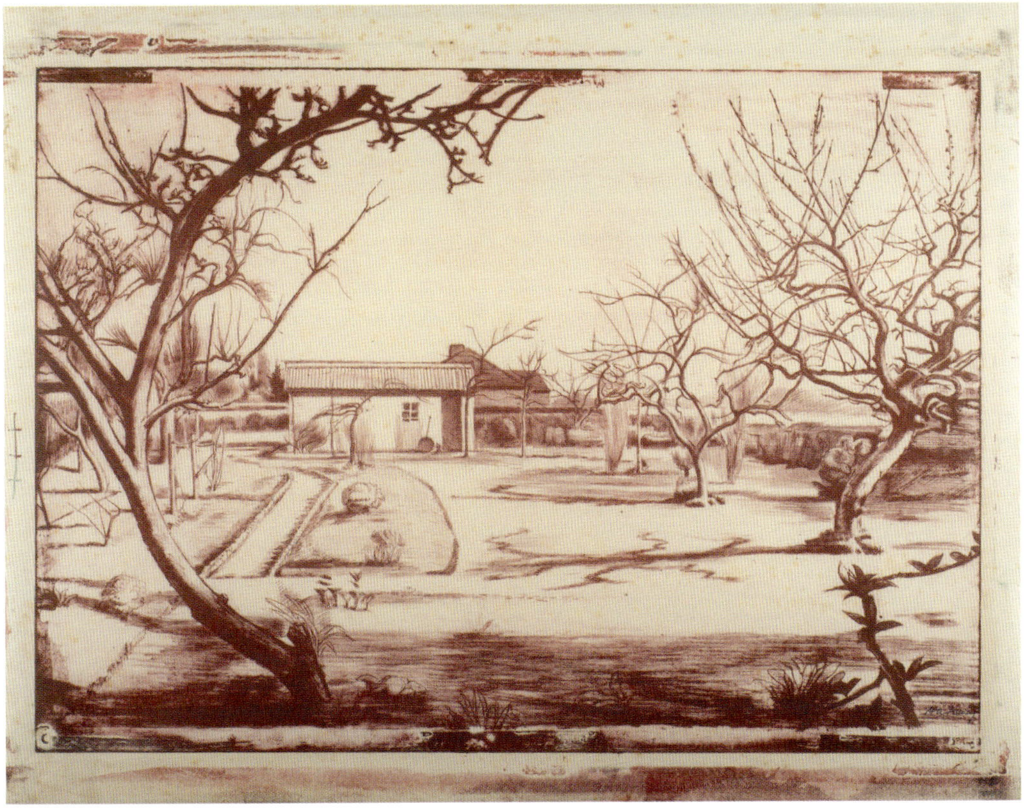

CAT. 50 – *White Cottage*, 1959, signed, lithograph, printed in red ink., 19 x 24 in. (48.5 x 61 cm).

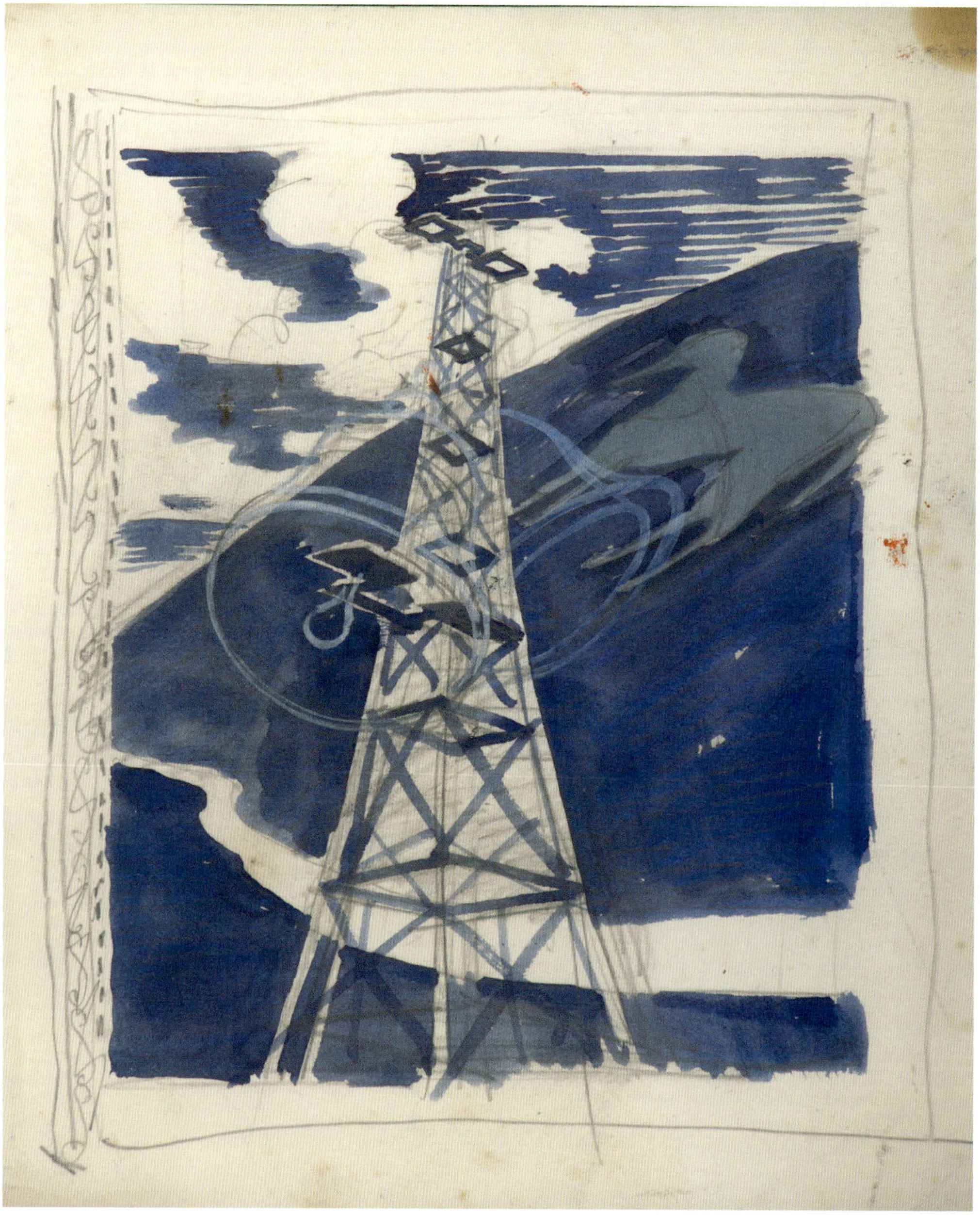

CAT. 51 – *A mast for a Radar Transmitting Station, part of the Chain Home System*, pencil and gouache on paper, 8 x 6 ½ in. (55.4 x 16.2 cm).

CAT. 52 – *Transmitting Station*, signed, inscribed, pencil and watercolour on paper, 17 ½ x 11 ¾ in. (55.3 x 36.8 cm).

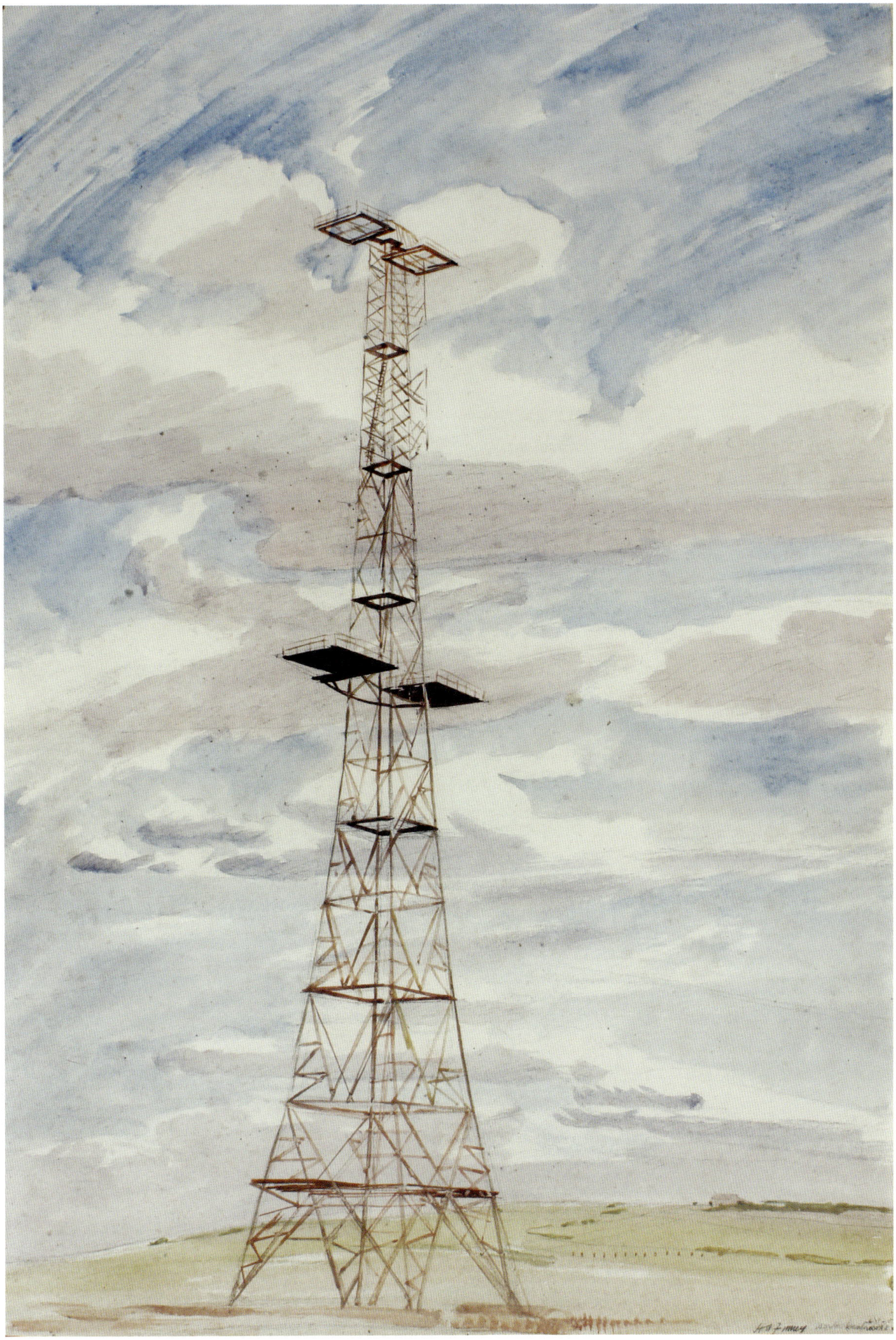

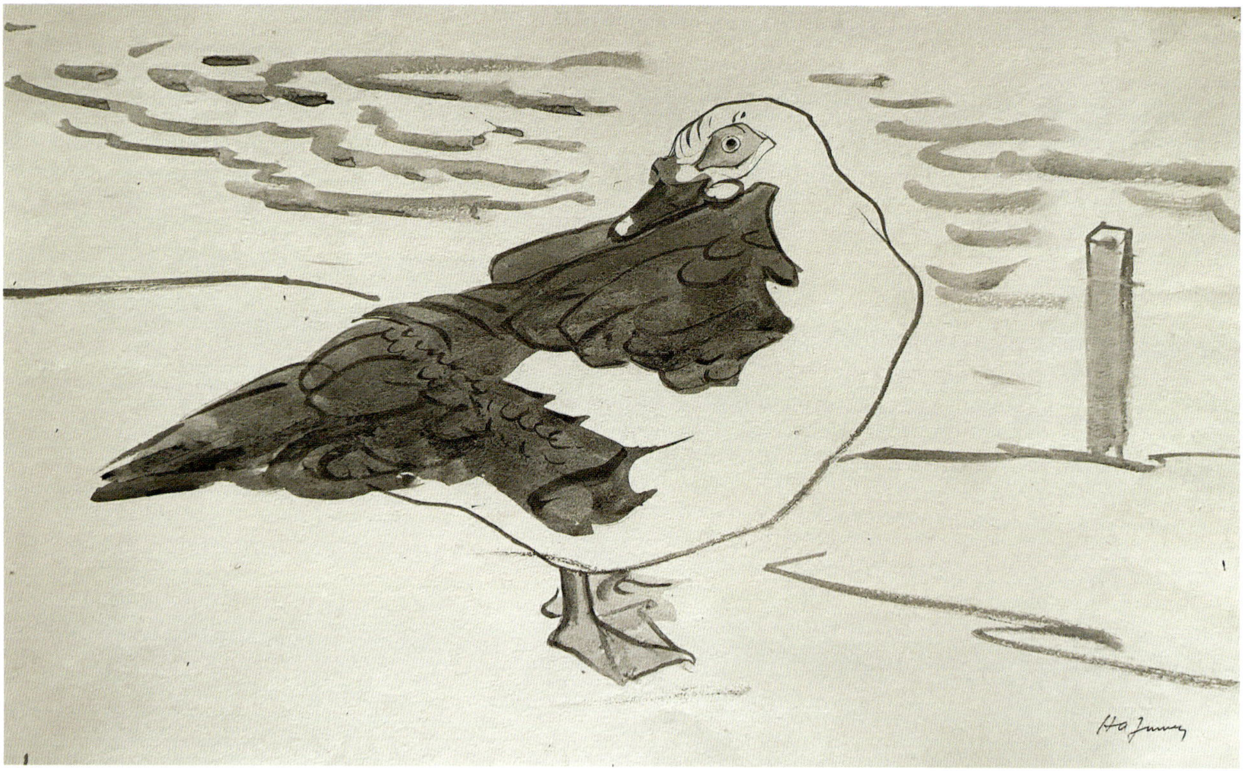

CAT. 53 – *Snow Goose*, signed,
wash on paper, 12 ½ x 20 in. (32 x 51 cm).

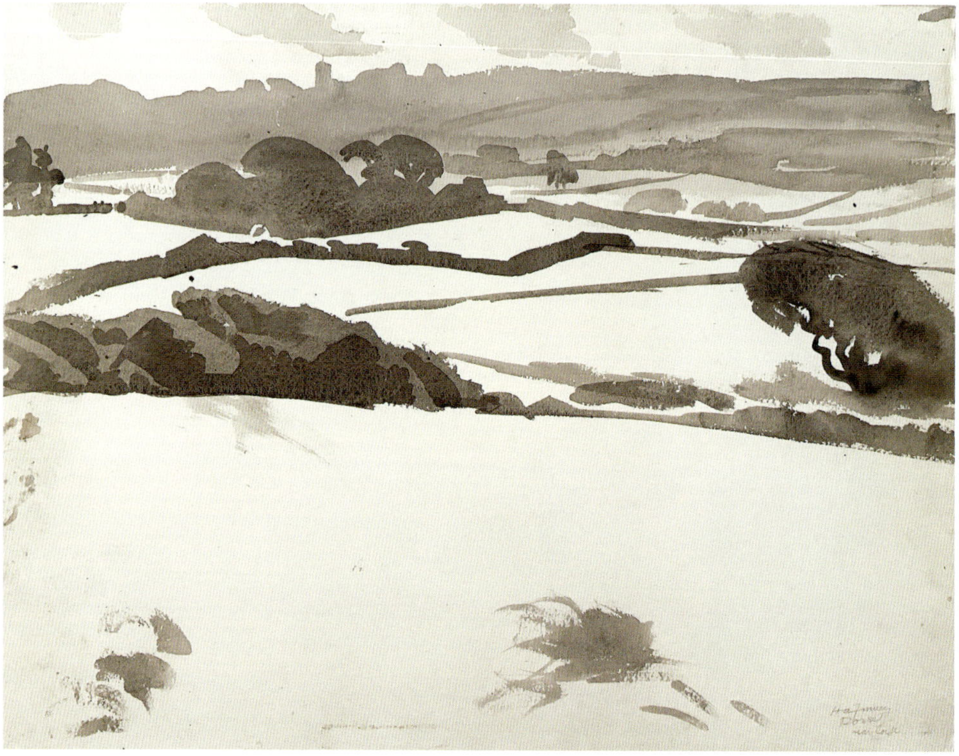

CAT. 54 – *Dorset near Corfe*, signed and inscribed with title,
inscribed on reverse 'View of Kingston near Corfe castle number 89',
wash on paper, 16 x 20 in. (40.7 x 50.5 cm).

'My thoughts turned inwards seeking consolation in exploring the different philosophies of east and west, but my passion for painting remained as urgent as ever. Seeking for some inner harmony, by falling in love with nature blinded me to the truth that art is not copying nature. I remember one day walking near Regents Park, and suddenly my mind seemed to be illuminated, I spoke the words "life is not chaos, there is an order behind this universe". That belief has never left me. It came like a flash and afterwards my thoughts seemed to form into verse and rhyme. Poetry began to speak to me with a new significance. The sonnets of Shakespeare seem to me a natural language and when reading them it was as though he was speaking to me. Wordsworth, Shelley, Milton, and other poets seem to my daily friends. Nature began to sing and I felt the greatest of all the arts was poetry, this was something unusual for a painter to feel, and I no longer feel this is true. My own efforts in this art never reached any satisfactory expression. Not because the content was lacking, but because my vocabulary was so restricted due to my lack of classical or advanced education. My formal general education stopped when I was 14, and I then became a self educated man. . . .

All that I had suffered left me suspicious of human nature. It is noticeable that in the recalling of my early life, no mention has been made of distinguished personages, painters, musicians, or writers. A withdrawal from life had taken place in me, fatal to a painter, unless one is a Fra Angelico. I attended an evening class at the working men's club at Camden town for drawing, as my friend Percy Horton taught there and I had contact with Edward Le Bas, but having been nearly extinguished by a blow from Life, which was none of my own seeking, I now lacked a flair for life, a courage and daring necessity for creative originality. I also had a platonic friendship for a woman, which was rich in its quality and friendship but eventually petered out because she hoped to marry me. During this time, I attended an evening ballet class held for business girls to get to practice at drawing the human figure in motion. The teacher was a pupil of Pavlova, I became friendly with her and perhaps would have formed a deeper attachment but she died suddenly, a tragic affair.

This was the time of the 1930s depression, but I was lucky in obtaining a part-time teaching post at Chelsea School of Art under P. H. Jowett. After I had been there a year, he resigned his post to become principal of the Royal College of Art, an ambition that had been consuming him since he left teaching at the Beckenham School of Art. . . .'

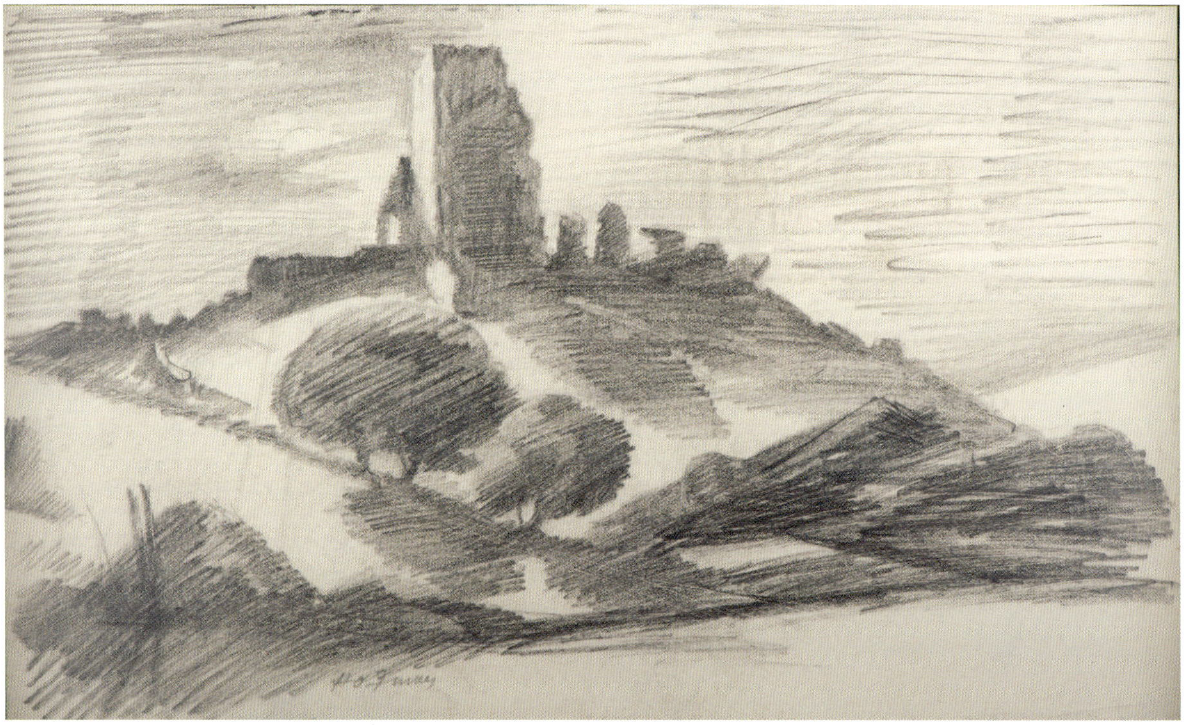

CAT. 55 – *Corfe Castle*, signed, pencil on paper, 8 x 13 in. (20.2 x 33 cm).

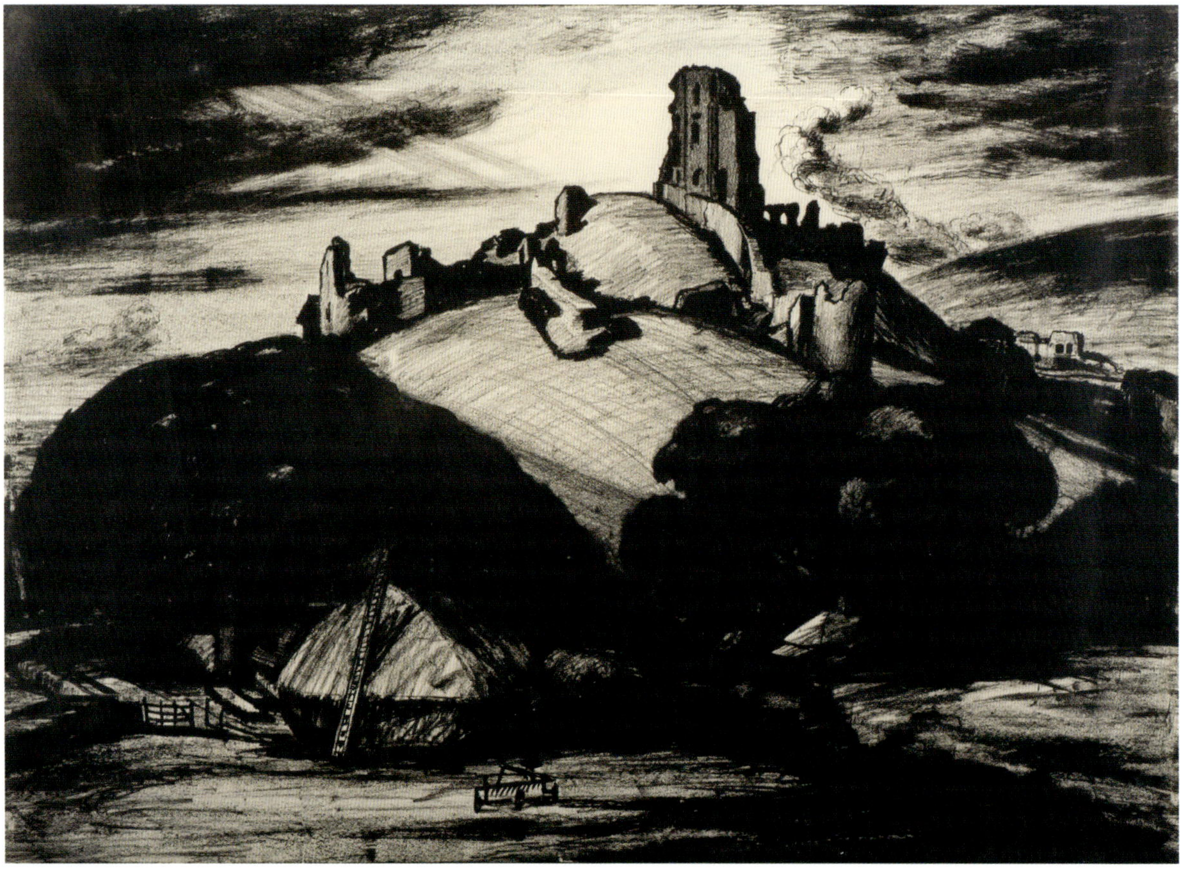

CAT. 56 – *Corfe Castle*, lithograph. 16 x 21 ¾ in. (40.6 x 55.1 cm).

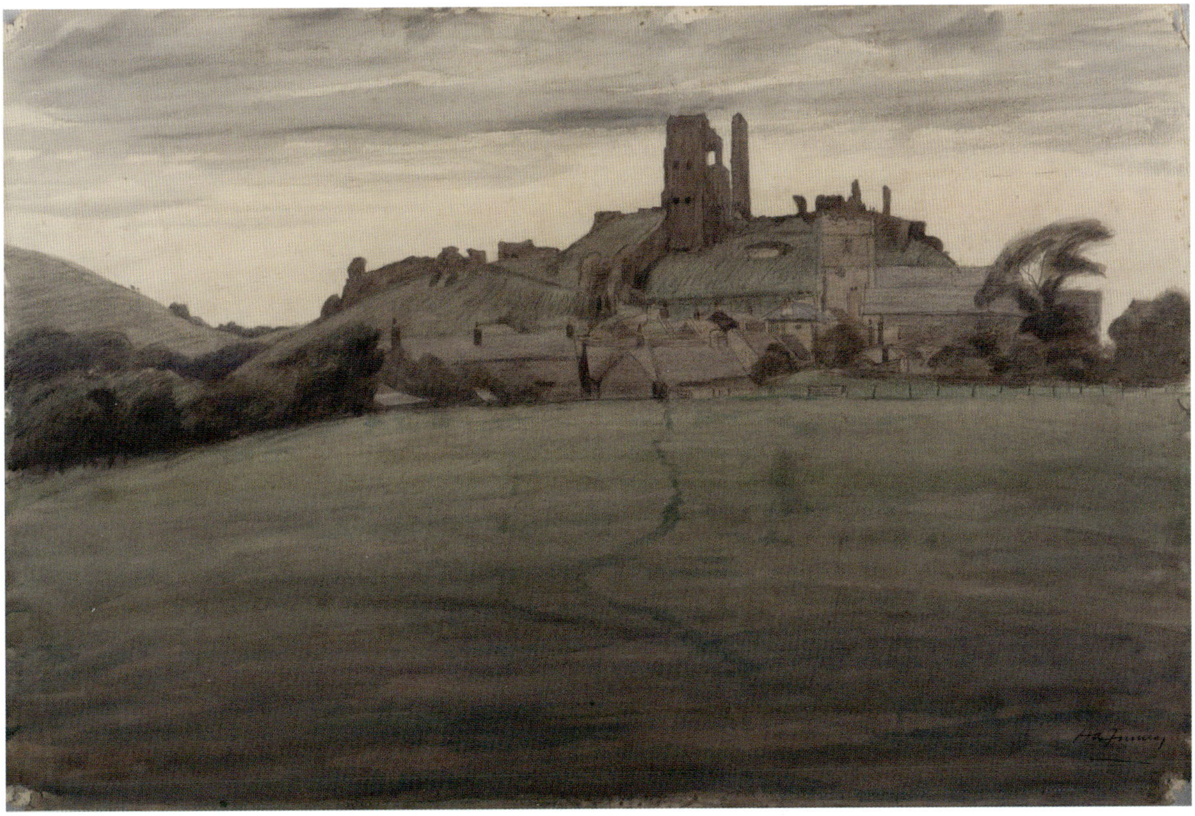

CAT. 57 – *Corfe Castle* signed, pencil and watercolour on paper, 15 x 22 in. (38 x 56 cm).

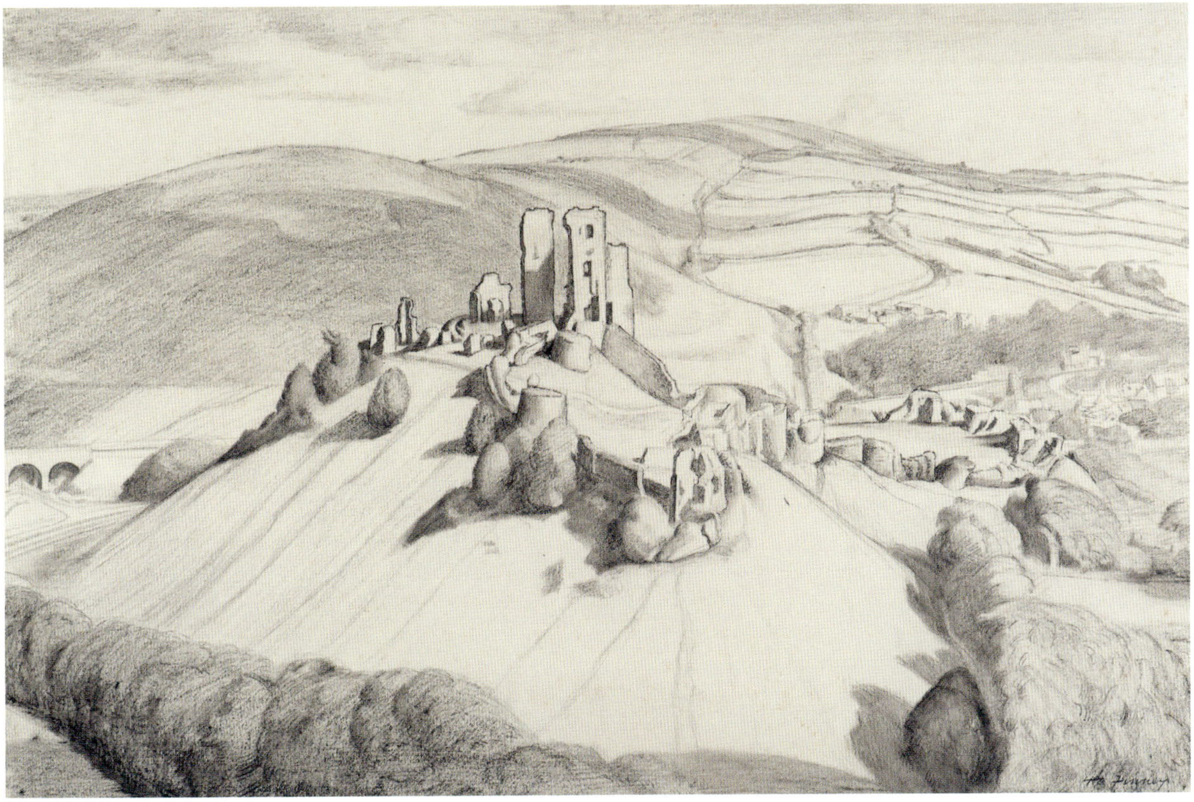

CAT. 58 – *Corfe Castle looking South*, signed, pencil and wash on paper mounted on card, 14.6 x 21.7 in. (37 x 55.1 cm).

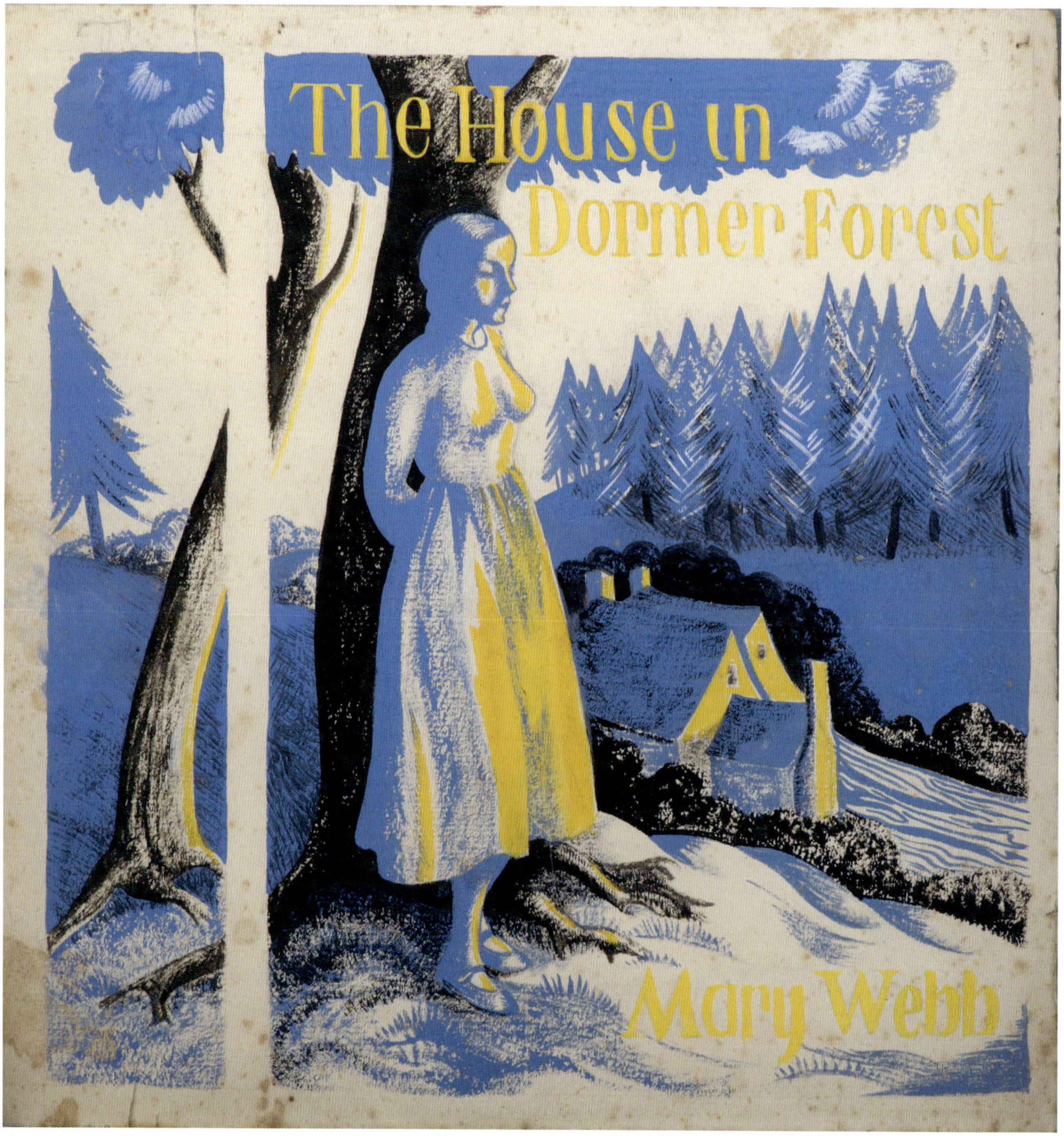

CAT. 59 – *The House in Dormer Forest*, design for book cover for novel by Mary Webb, pencil and gouache on paper, 9 ½ x 8 ¾ in. (24 x 22.3 cm).

'I find now, greater difficulty in proceeding with the unfolding of the memories of my past life and have doubts about whether they will prove tedious to the reader:

To analyse, to define all the various sensations and experiences of the next year or two is impossible when so many years have passed and to penetrate to the mind of women's unspoken thoughts is impossible, and perhaps for the best. Nita went into a nursing home to give birth to her child, and I distinctly remember that when I visited her in her room in the nursing home, I mentally saw a cord stretching from her to her child who was in a cot in the room.

When she came home with a child named Brian, I had a feverish activity to draw and paint the mother and child theme and in this small house I painted a large painting which was sold to Carlisle Art Gallery (through the influence of Sir William Rothenstein) I consider it was a distinguished painting of a figurative subject, but I wonder now if it has been sent to the basement and a more fashionable, abstract painting exhibited in its place.

We were living on the edge of property, two days a week part-time teaching at Chelsea School of Art, and finding the small house and restricted environment of the Hampstead Garden suburb so restricting made us find a bungalow at Otford in Kent. This was the beginning of our estrangement. Nita after some months decided to find a secretarial job in Croydon, where some past friends of hers were living. But I must record an incident of significance which happened before we left the house in the garden suburb and before Brian was born. Nita's mother who never gave her any of a mother's love, left a note for her with the name and address of a woman who performed abortions because she did not want Nita to have the child. Here is where fate came in, I found the note and persuaded Nita not to have anything to do with the suggestion in the notes. . . .'

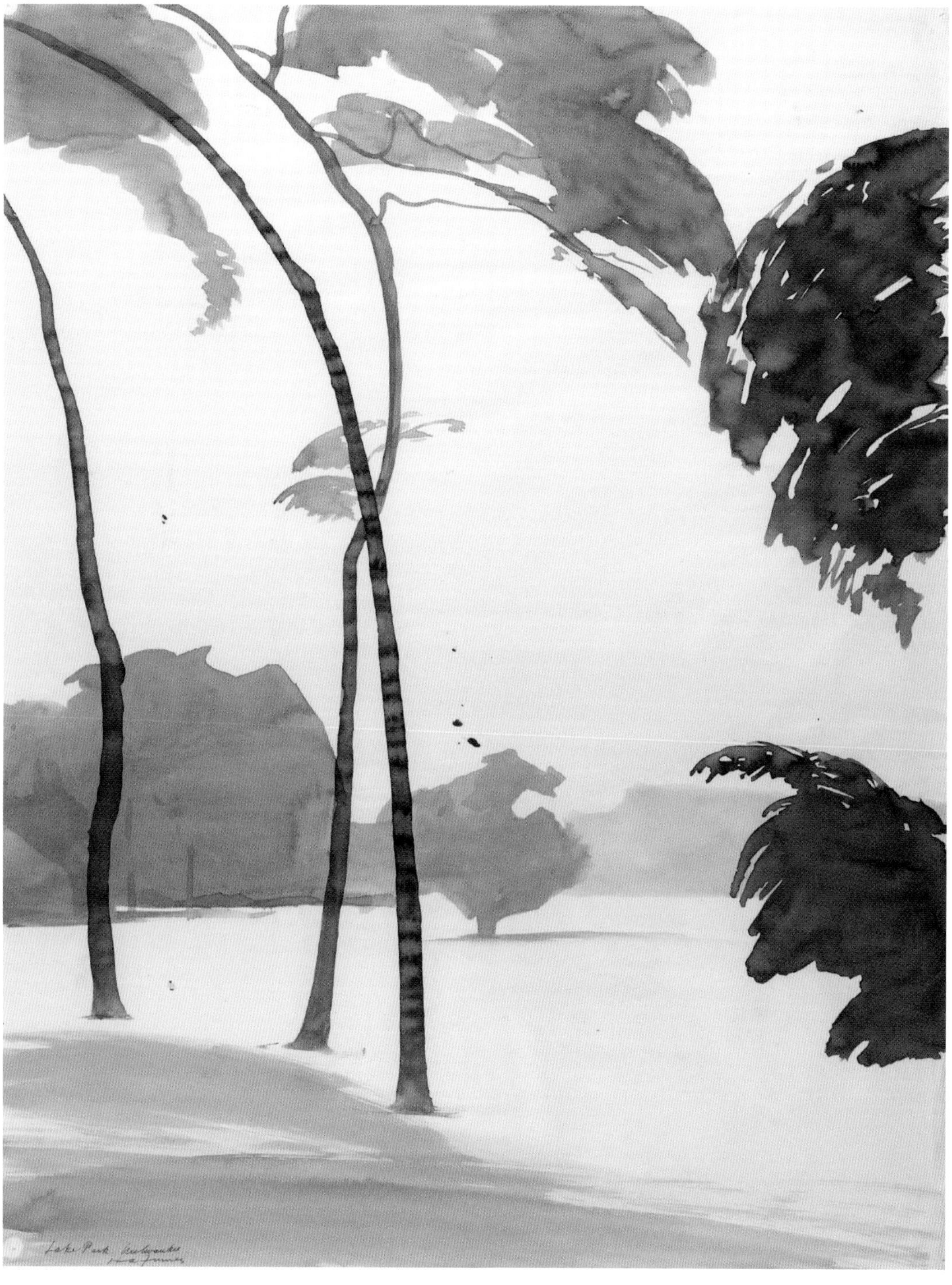

CAT. 60 – *Lake Park, Milwaukee*, 1966, signed and inscribed with title, wash on paper; 24 × 18 in. (61 × 45.8 cm).

CAT. 61 – *White Cottage, Winnersh*, blue pencil and gouache on paper; 22 × 15 in. (55.8 × 38.3 cm).

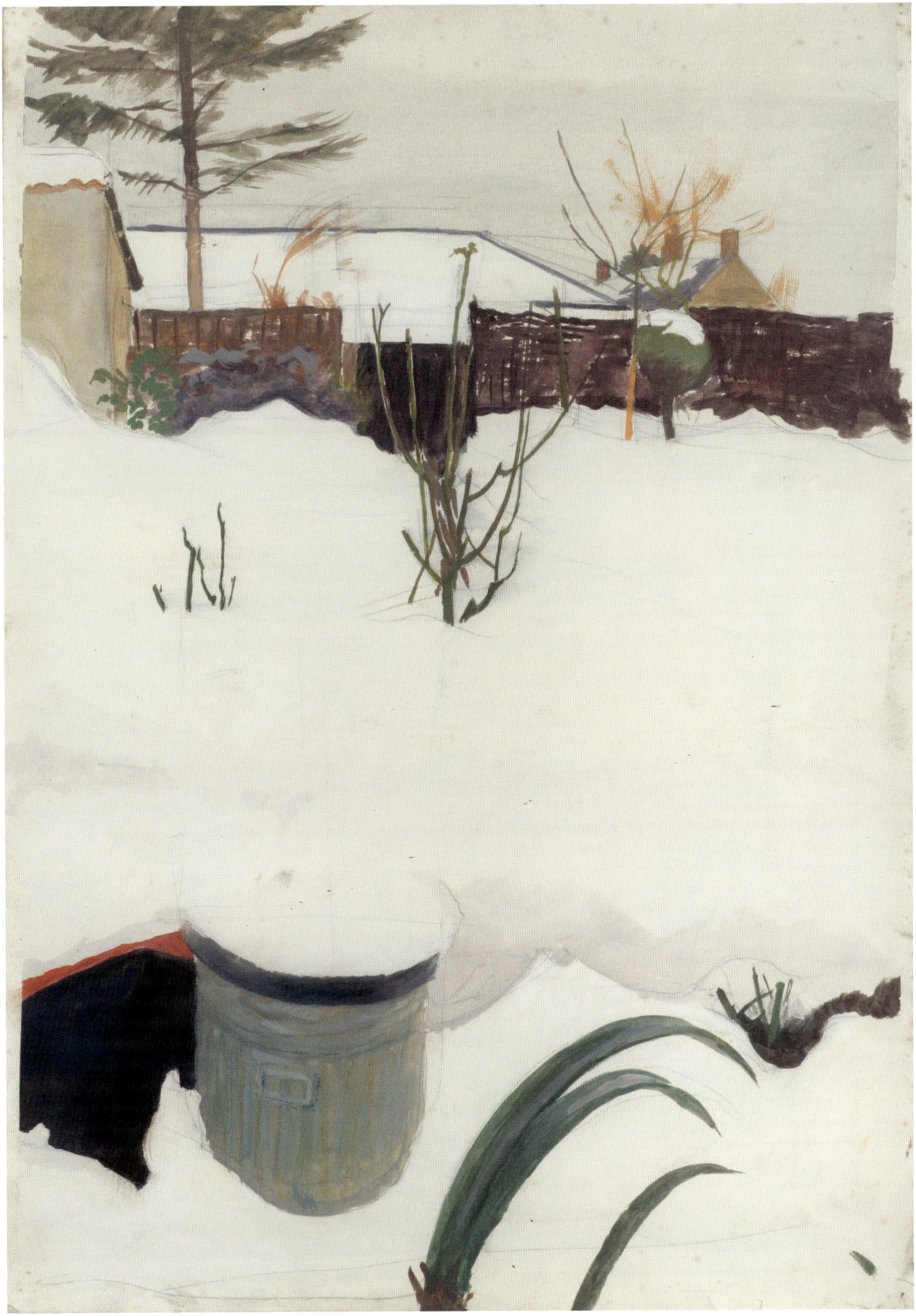

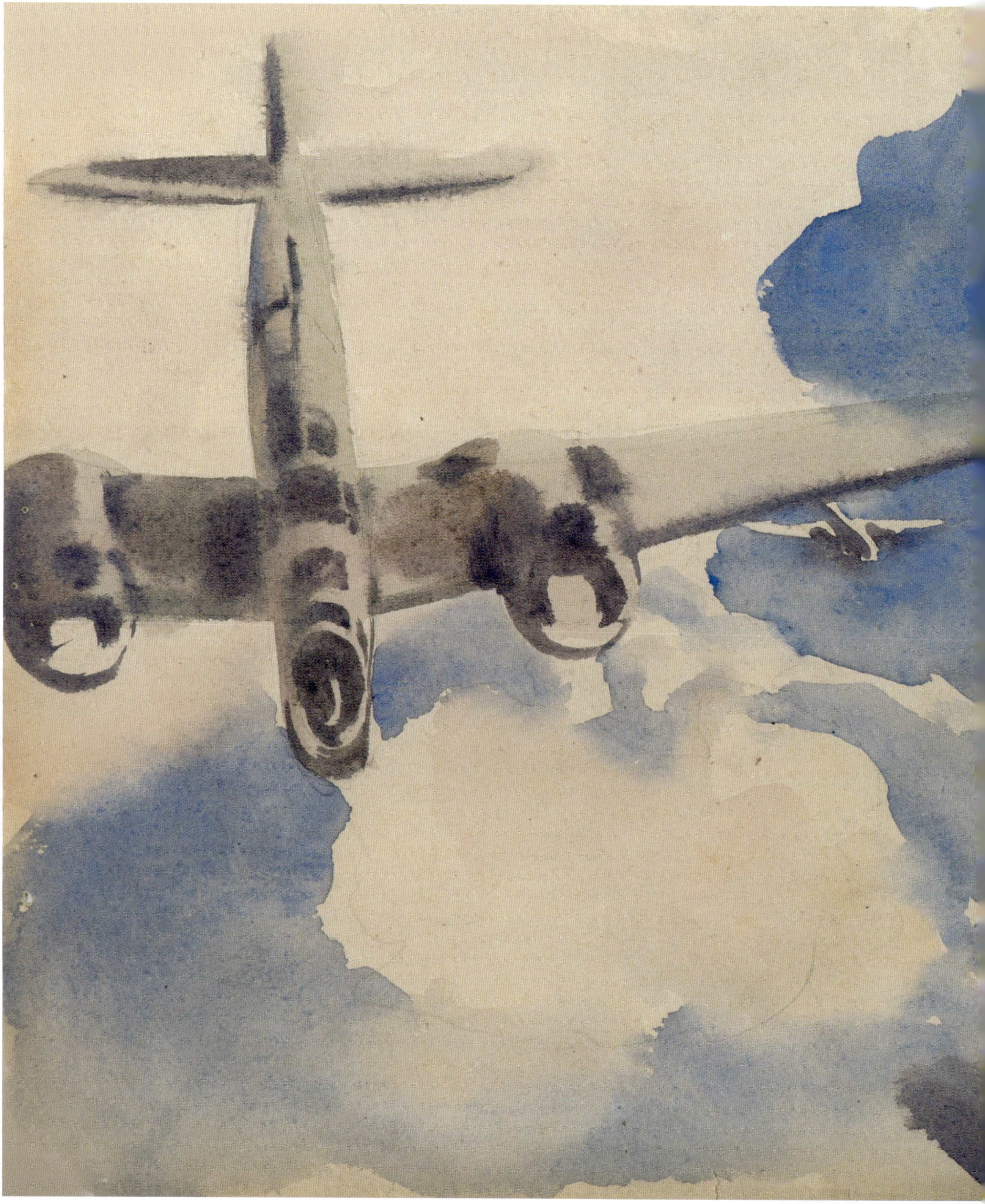

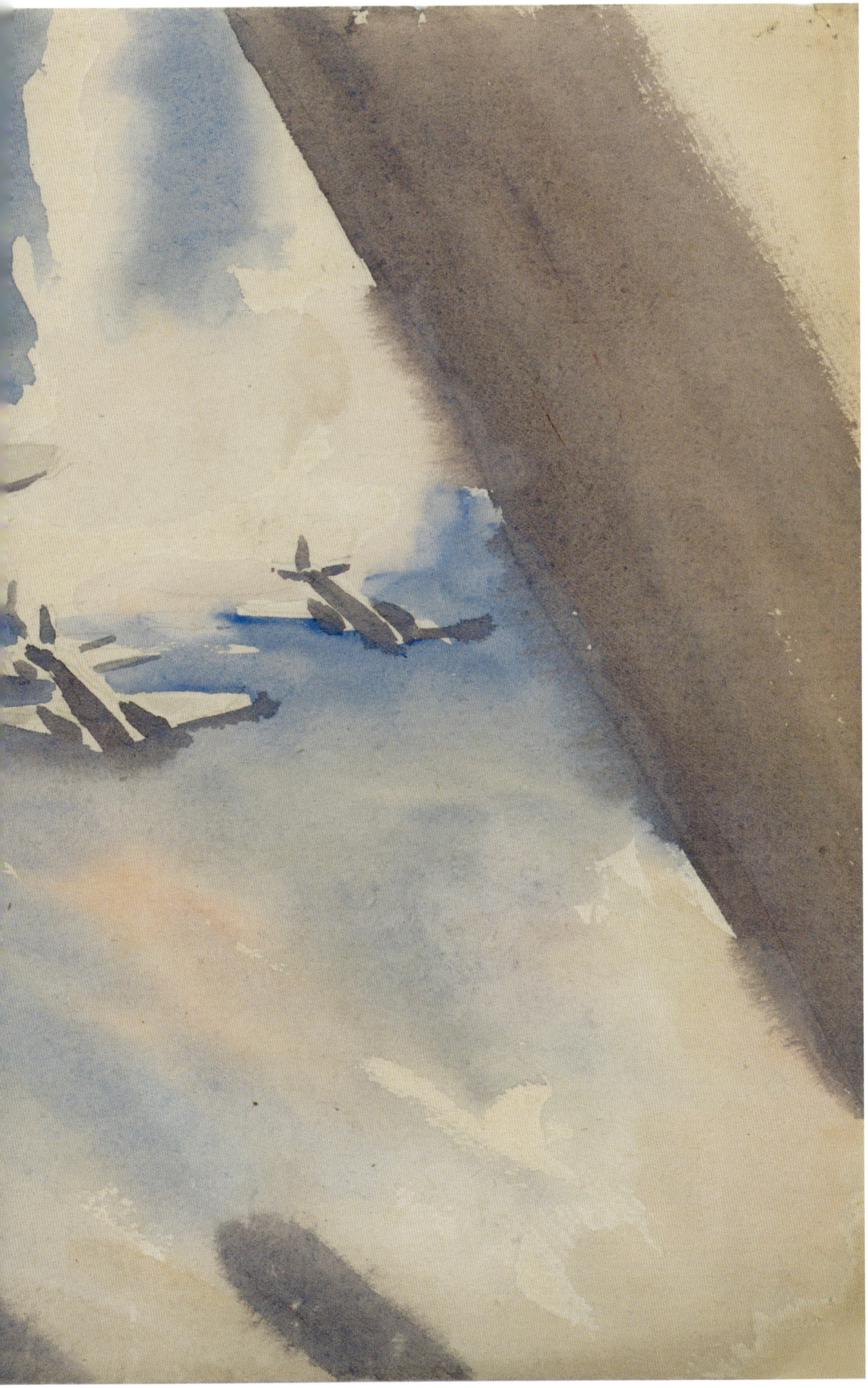

CAT. 62 – *A formation of Douglas A-20 Havocs*, early 1940s, watercolour on paper, 10 ½ x 15 ¾ in. (27 x 40 cm).

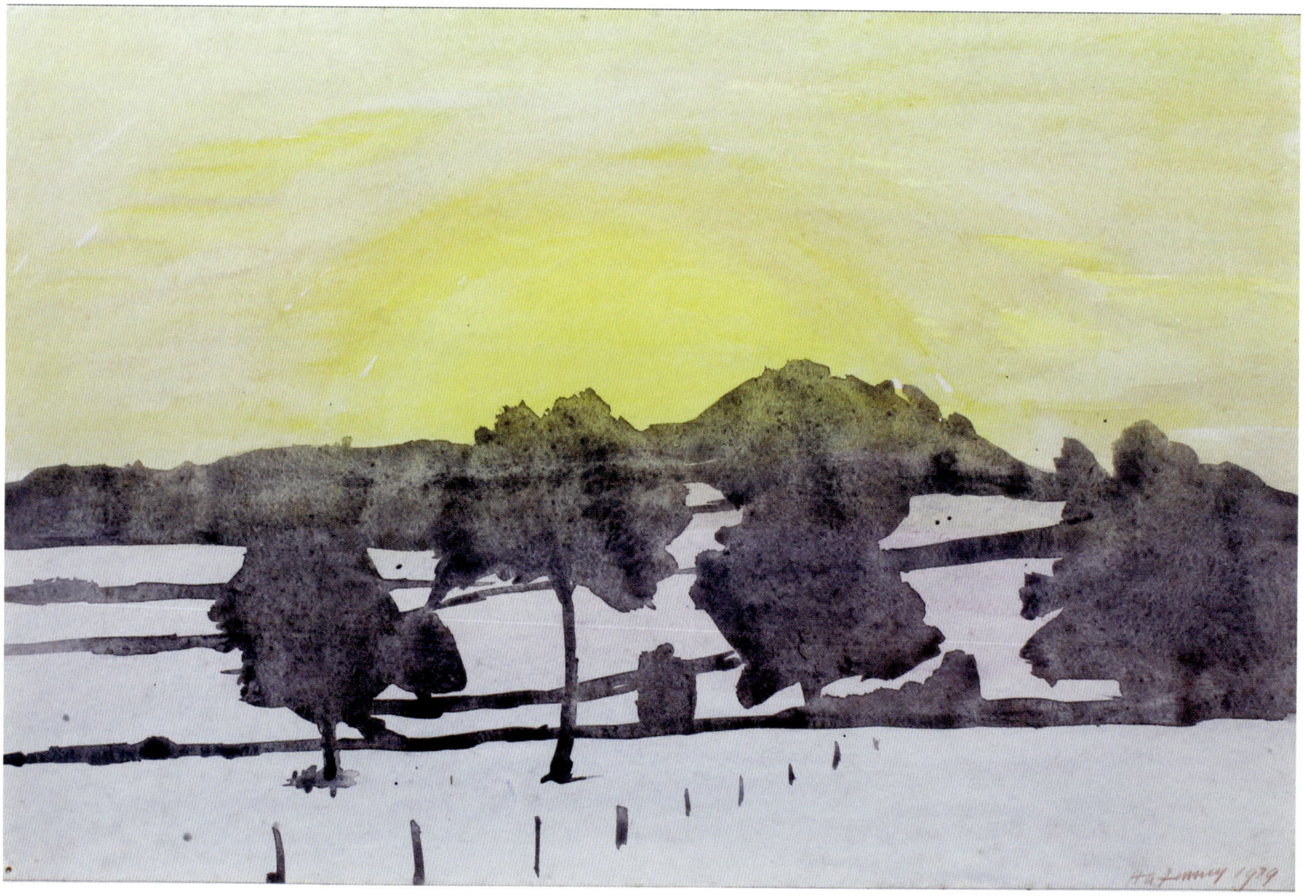

CAT. 63 – *Winter Barrington, Sunset*, 1939, signed and dated, watercolour on paper, 11 x 16 ¼ in. (28.3 x 41.2 cm).

a CAT. 64 – *Raising a barrage balloon in Hyde Park*, 1940, signed and dated, wash on paper, 14 x 22 ½ in. (35.4 x 57 cm).

b CAT. 65 – *Barrage balloon in Hyde Park*, 1940, signed and dated, wash on paper, 18 ½ x 12 in. (47 x 30.5 cm).

a

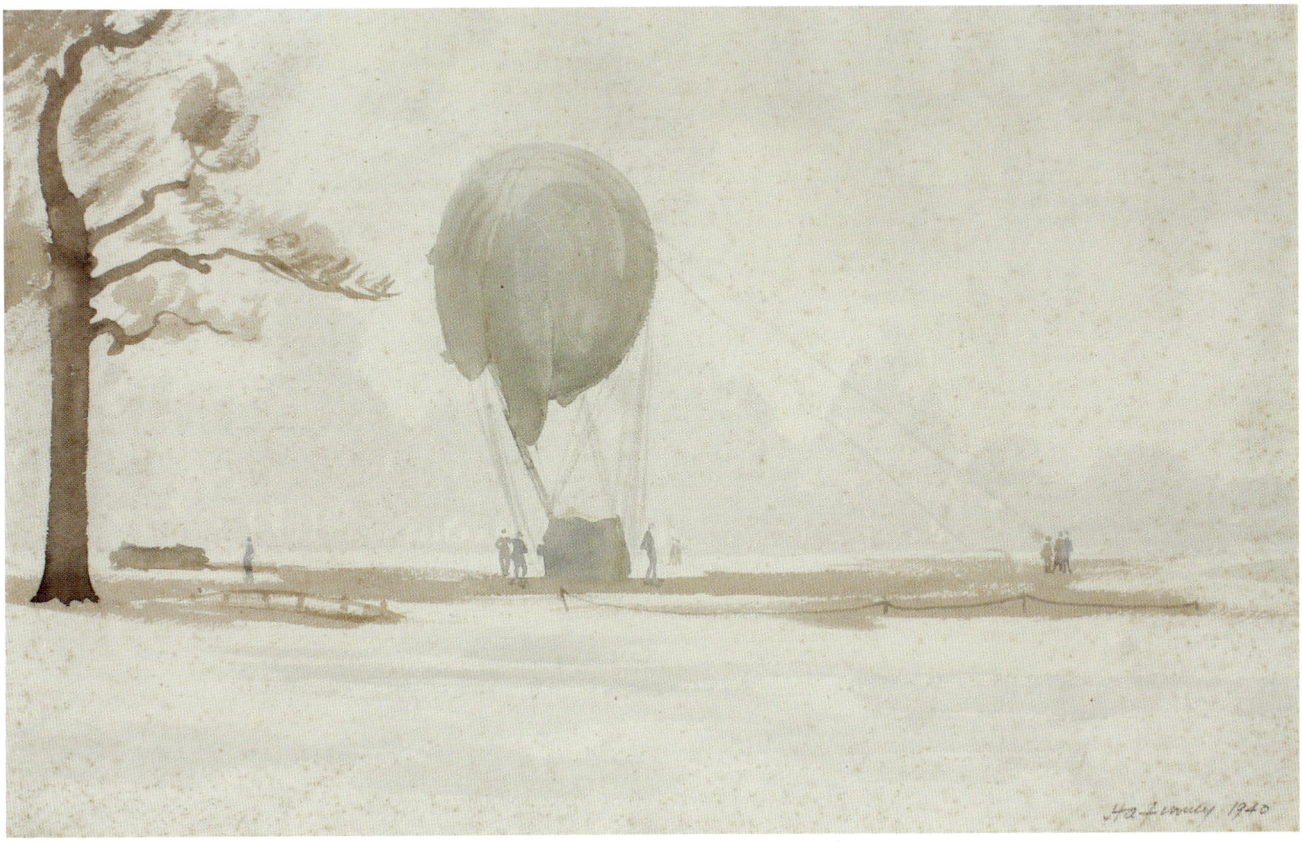

b

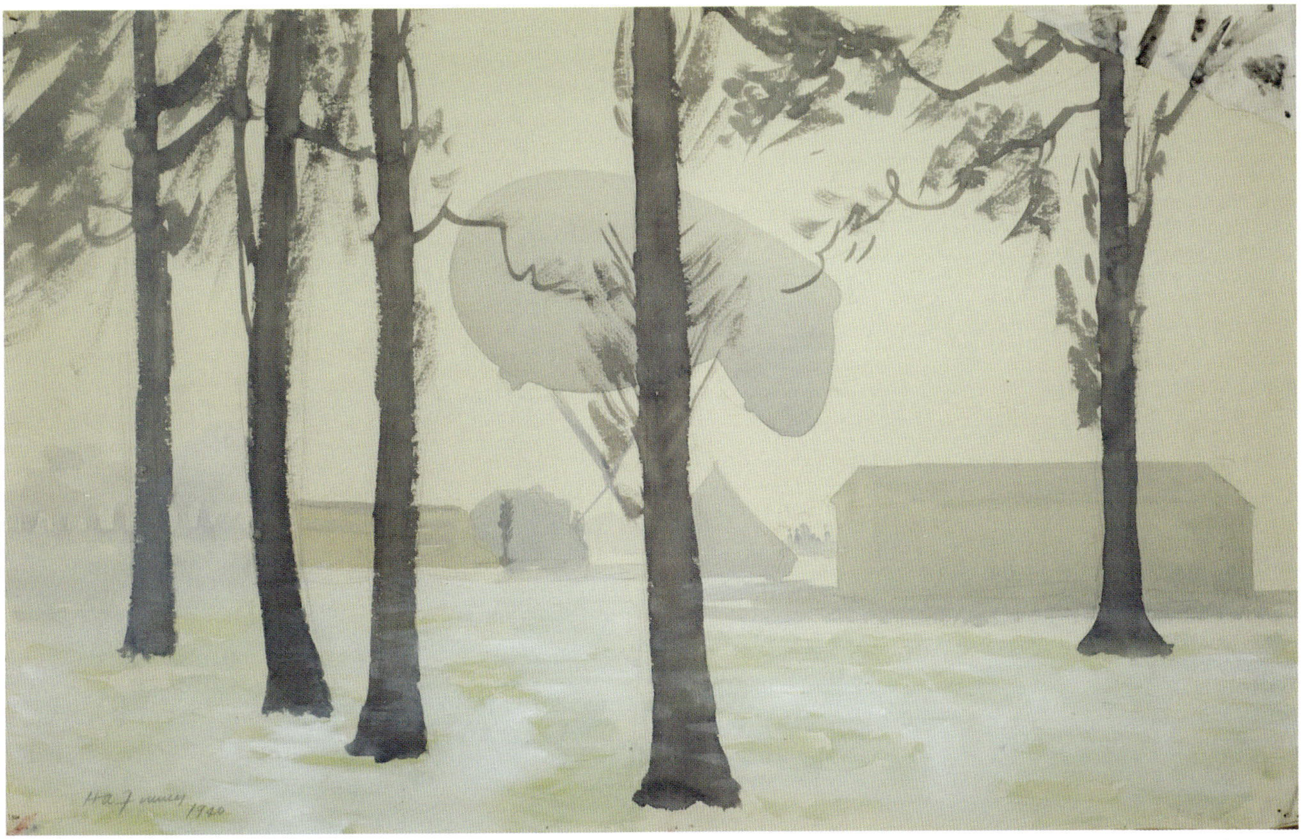

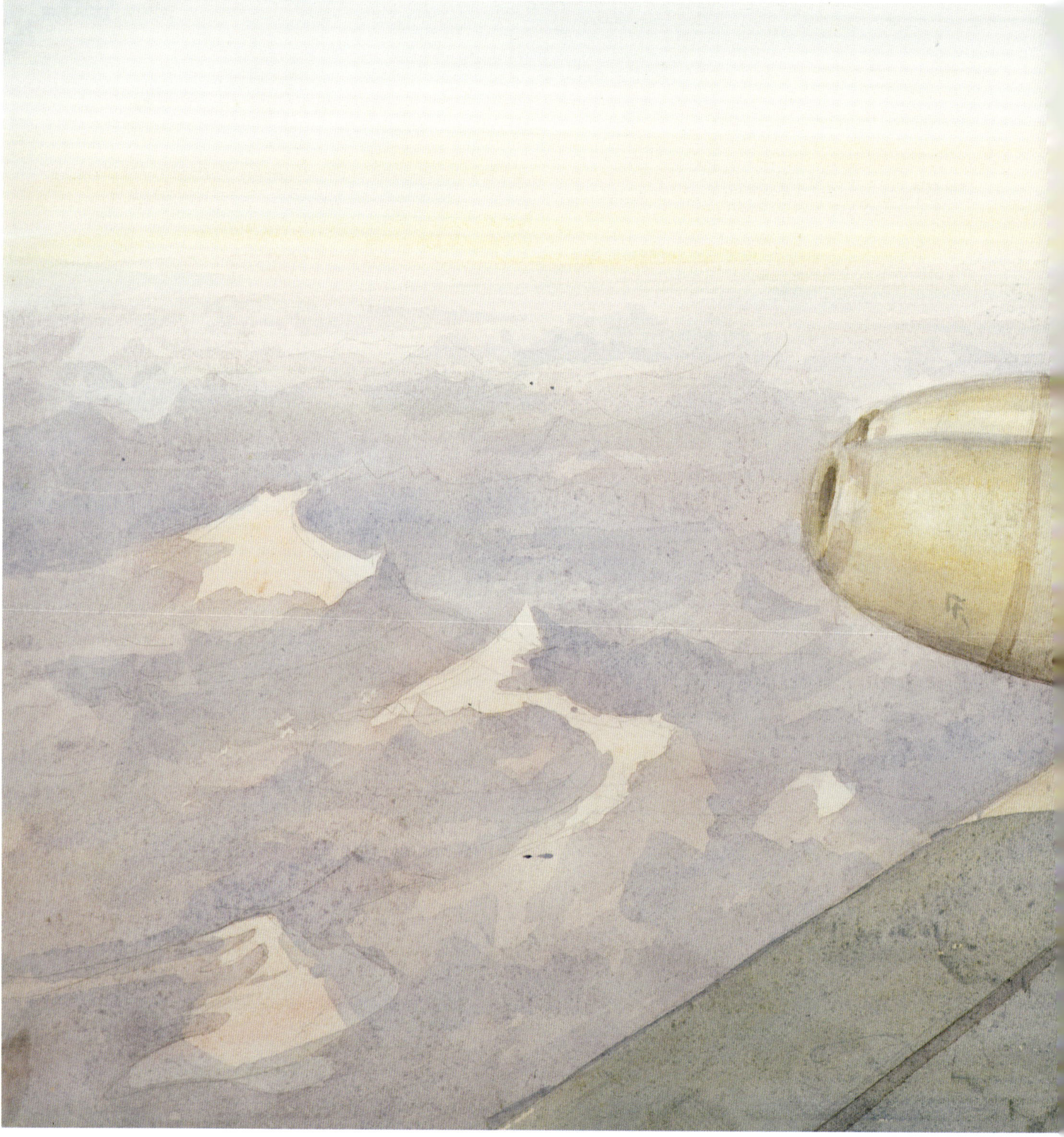

CAT. 66 – *View of aircraft's wing over mountains*, signed, pencil and watercolour on paper, 8 ½ x 16 ¼ in. (21.3 x 41.5 cm).

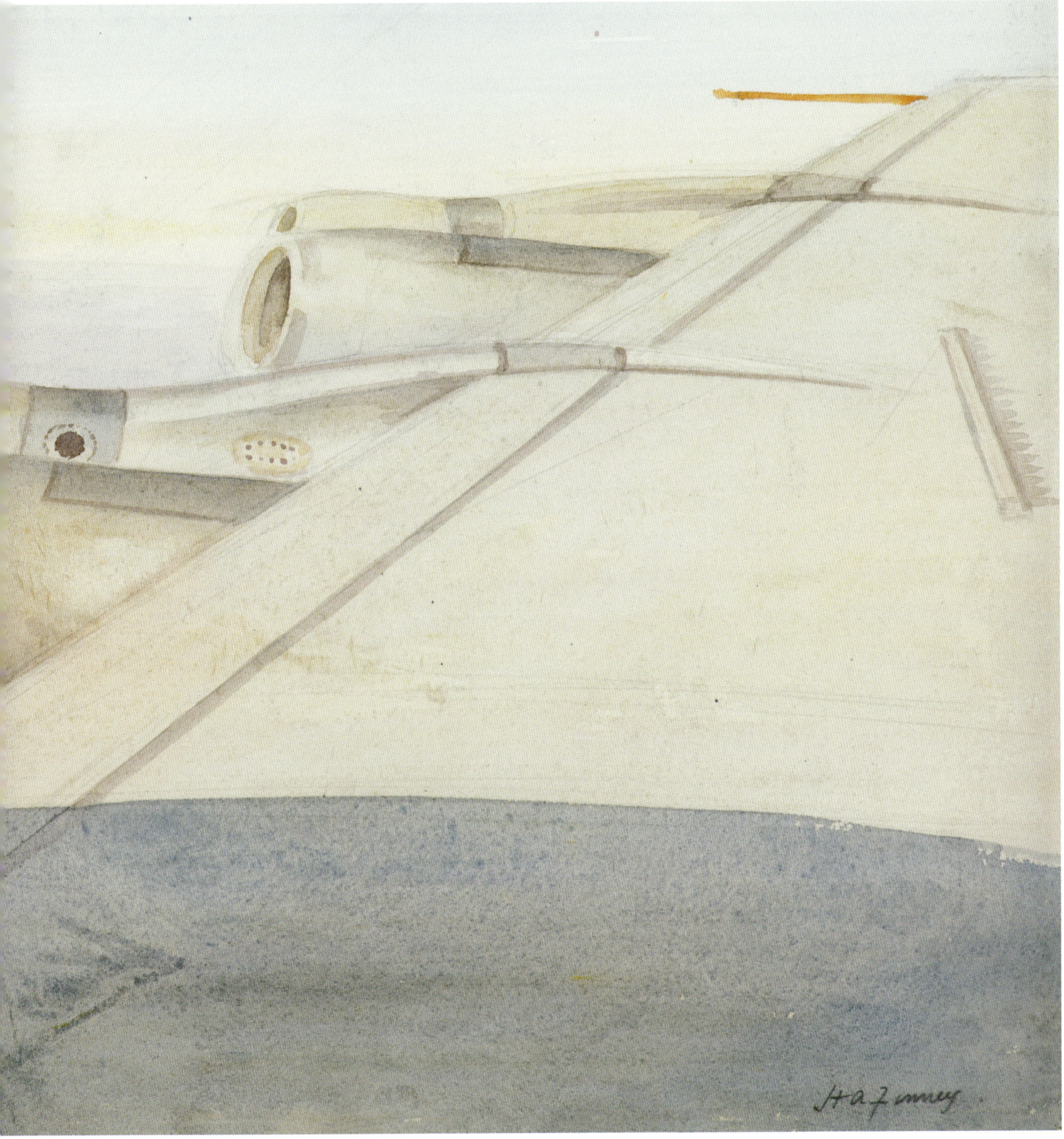
H A Finney

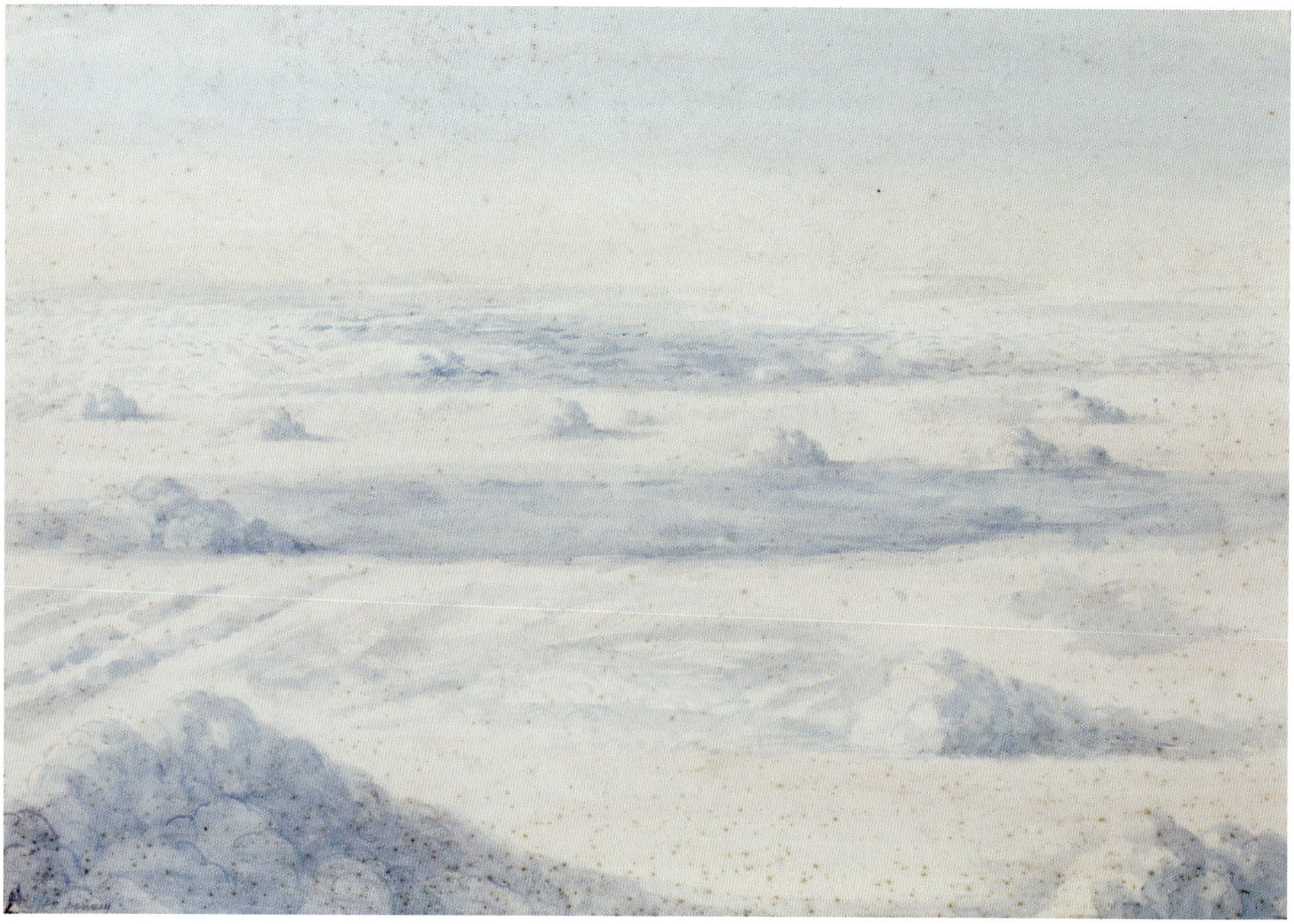

CAT. 67 – *Over the Atlantic on the way to New York, Sunrise*, signed, watercolour on paper, 13 ¾ x 19 ½ in. (35 x 49.2 cm).

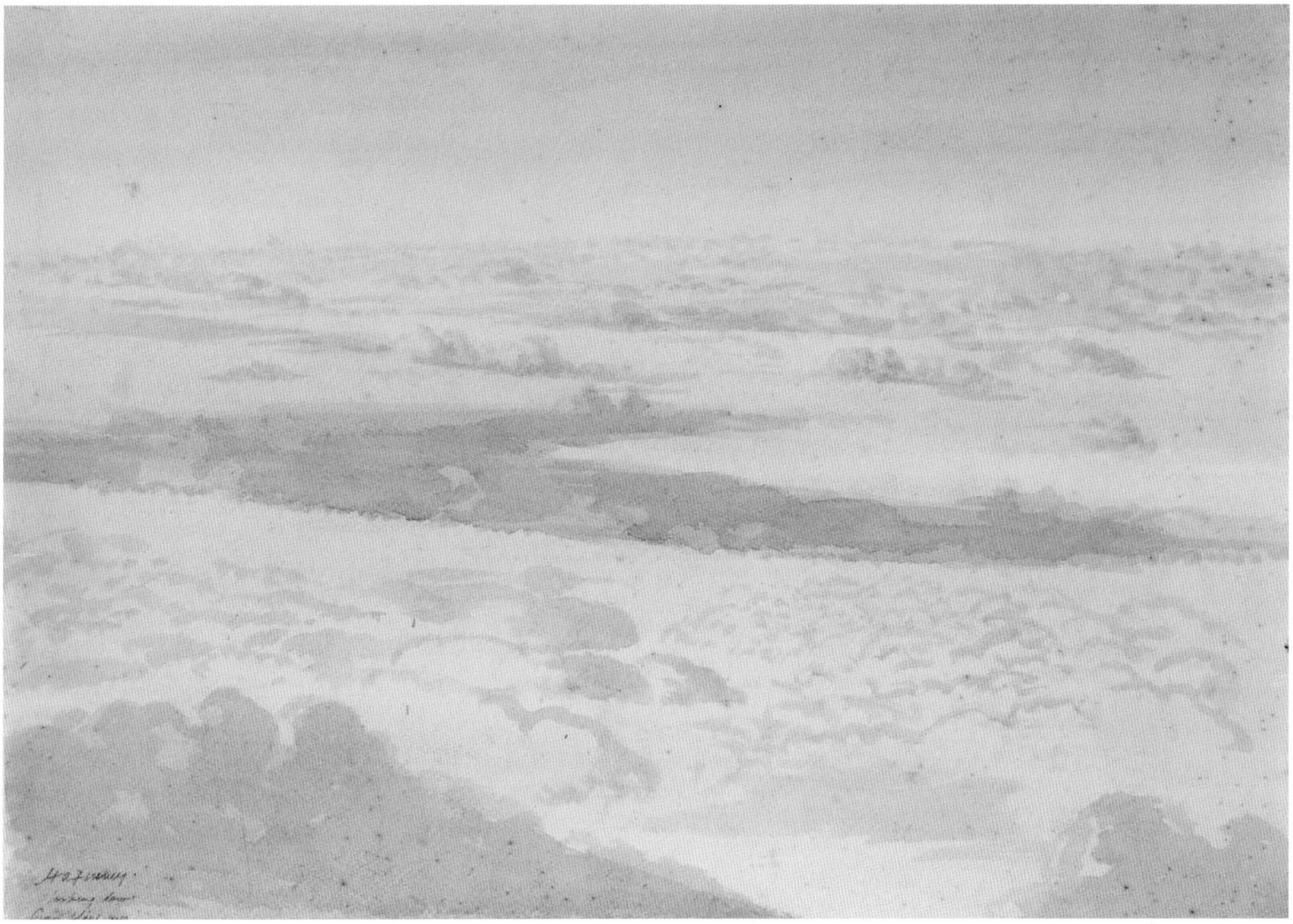

CAT. 68 – *Looking down from plane over Atlantic, Dawn*, signed, and inscribed 'Looking down from plane over Atlantic' watercolor on paper, 16 x 21 ¼ in. (40.4 x 54.2 cm).

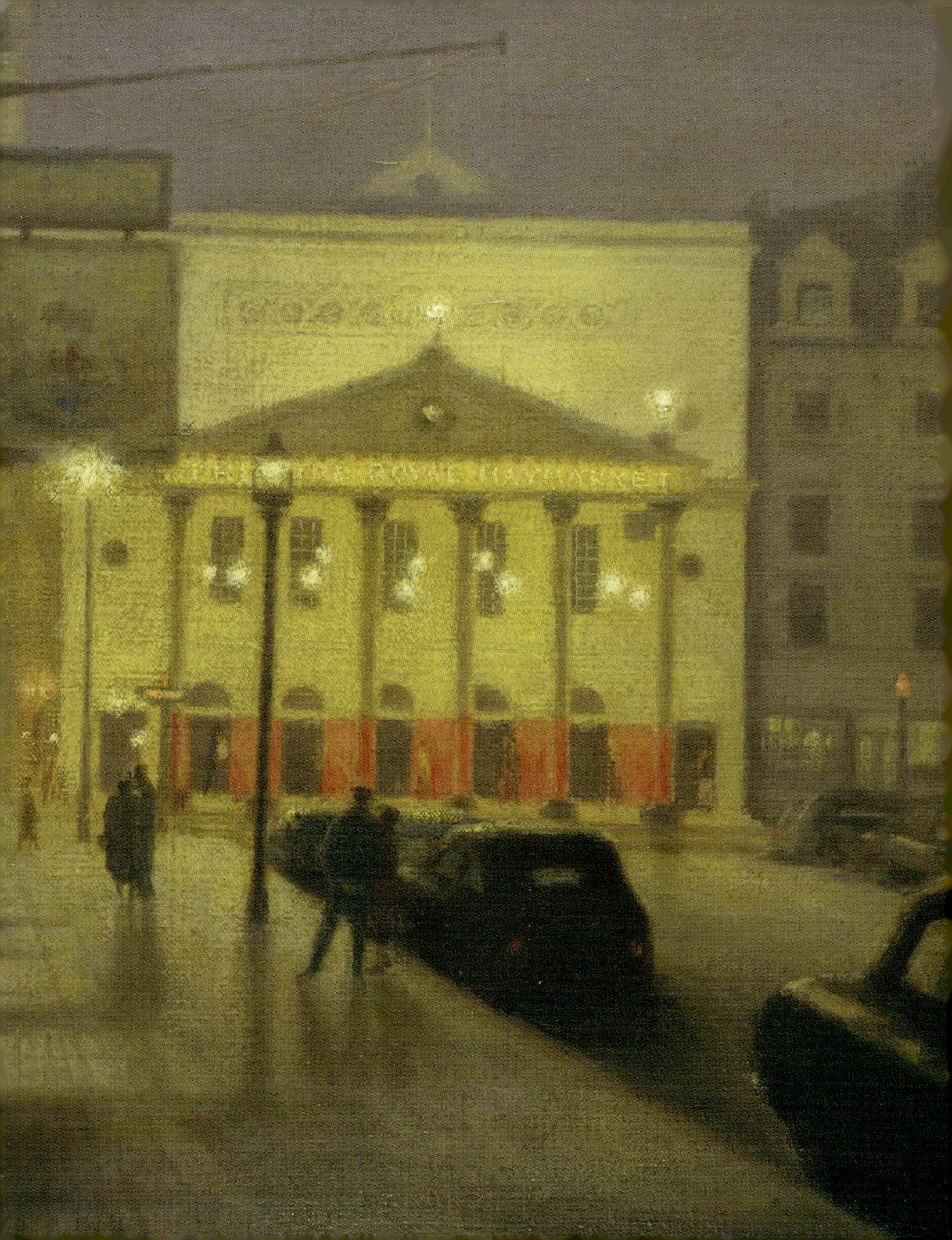
ROYAL HAYMARKET

Night

'I travelled to London by what was then called a Workman's train from Otford to save money as I saw living on my two days teaching at Chelsea School of Art. I would arrive in London by 8 o'clock in the morning although I did not start teaching until 9am. The deep suffering appeared once more in my life. When I was left alone in the Otford bungalow, the feeling of poverty and the hope of a sympathetic human spiritual and material companionship seem to have faded, and a forlorn mood descended upon me. Once again nature in the form of the Kent landscape seemed a vehicle for a distorted mental suffering, so I decided to move from Otford, as Nita was working at secretarial work in Croydon, and visited me at weekends. Yet in spite of this unhappy period I was beginning to become an inspired teacher at the Chelsea School of Art. In an effort to try and earn more money, I completed three or four large posters of the Kent landscape hoping to sell one of them to the southern Railway, but there was no luck in this distinction and in a mood of despair I applied for a steward job on board a ship at Liverpool. Here is where fate stepped in for if I had been successful in getting this work my life would have been changed. I eventually persuaded Nita to move to a flat in Shepherd's Bush in London, and the clouds of war were drawing nearer.

Foreseeing that war was inevitable I went to evening classes in first aid during the months before war was declared. I was not a conscientious objector in principle but felt I would avoid taking human life if it was possible. I was sympathetic to the true Christian belief which the conscientious objectors held but I don't think I could have stood firm against the pressure brought to bear on them. . . .'

Theatre Royal Haymarket by Night, DETAIL. See CAT. 84, pages 112-113.

'Before war was declared, I was staying with a painter friend Percy Horton and his cottage near a village named Lamarsh in Suffolk about 10 minutes from Cambridge. He was always a good friend to me, and I enjoyed his company and his deep interest and passion for drawing and painting, he was also a fine scholar. When he heard on the radio that war had been declared, we both felt the necessity to return to London, when I arrived at my flat in Shepherd's Bush, there was a letter awaiting me, calling on me to join the light rescue party of the Civil Defence. As Percy Horton was a member of this teaching faculty of the Royal College of art and they were evacuated to the Lake District at Ambleside, I did not meet him again until after the war, and this applied to all my other friends except Le Bas.

During the first year of the so-called phoney war, I moved from the flat at Shepherd's Bush to a room in Hammersmith. As Nita was away on a secretarial job but she came to see me at at weekends. Brian was away at nursery school on the edge of Croydon Airport when the first German air raid began. It was a bad raid and many planes were destroyed while on the ground. Now the war began in earnest so in the early hours of the next morning I went to Croydon and brought Brian back to my room at Hammersmith. Nita was there at the time. She then sent him to a nursery school on the outskirts of London somewhere in Hertfordshire and as he was unhappy there, he was again moved.. . . .

. . . my life in London was a lonely one and I was only allowed about four or five days vacation from my civil defence duties are year. My work consisted of 24 hours on duty and 24 hours off and we were eventually organised into squads of five men including a driver to each rescue car. There was a lot of training first aid and stretcher bearing and for the first year during the so-called phoney war, conditions were primitive. This life was a new world to me, because I came in contact with every type of human being, from a young lad who had been to Wellington College, Berkshire, to thieves and near criminal types, and men from every walk of life. This new environment made me realise that if there were not millions of people who worked at humble occupations, what we call civilisation would not function. Among all these different types of human beings, I never saw any violence between them and strangely enough after a year or two I felt they had an unspoken regard for someone who possessed my gift because I made many portrait drawings of them on condition that they sat for me twice, I sold the first one (which usually was the best) for five shillings. . . .'

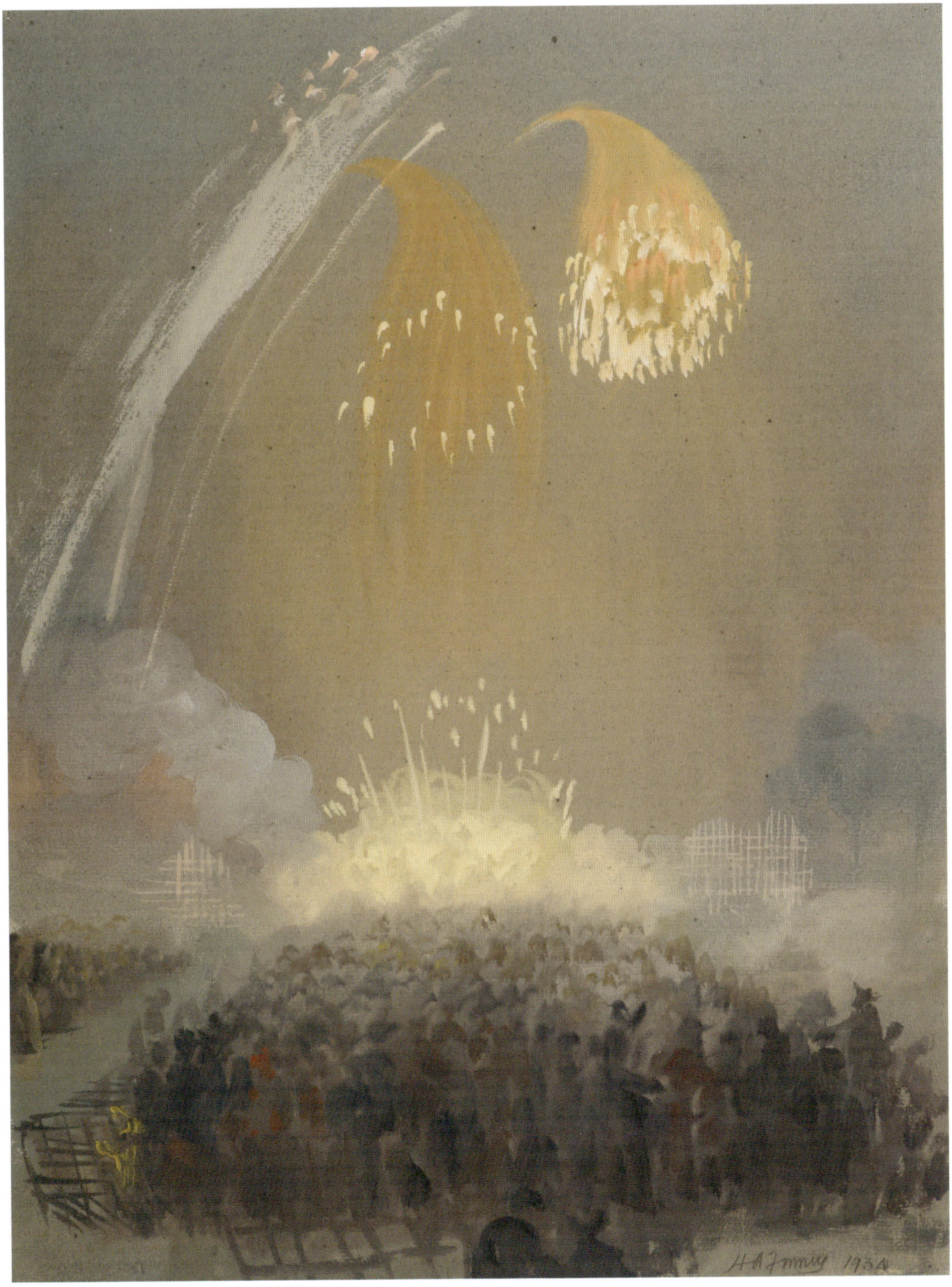

CAT. 69 – *Firework Display on Hampstead Heath*, 1934, signed and dated, titled on label to reverse, gouache on grey paper, 16 ¼ x 11 ½ in. (41.3 x 29.2 cm).

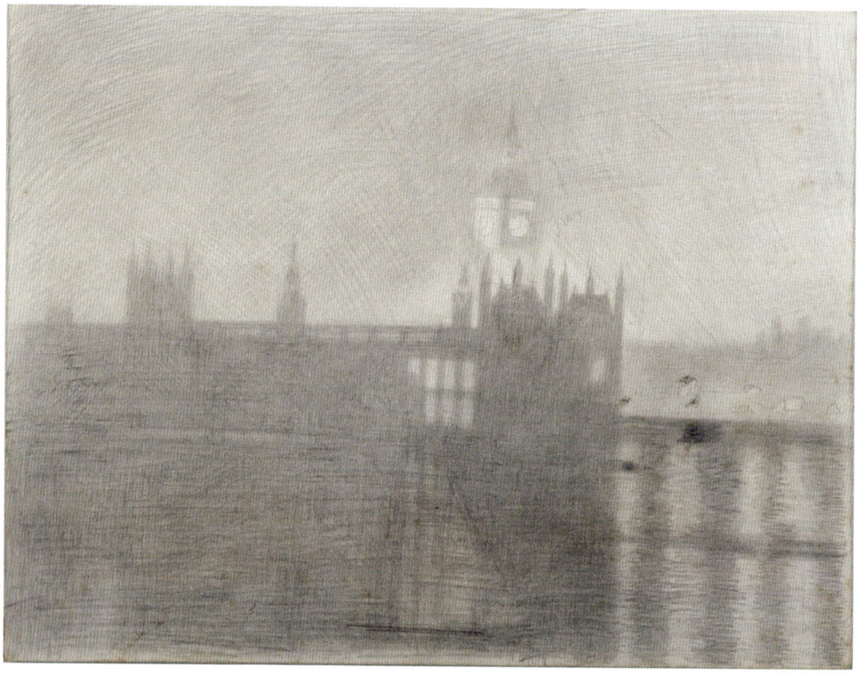

CAT. 70 – Study for
Houses of Parliament
from St Thomas Hospital at Night,
inscribed with notes, pencil on paper,
9 x 11 ½ in. (22.7 x 29 cm).

CAT. 71 – *Houses of Parliament at Night from St Thomas*, signed and inscribed with notes, pencil on card, 10 x 12 ¼ in. (25.4 x 31.2 cm).

'Hard work combined with the healing power of worship for nature and the Sun, and much metaphysical thinking and searching for the meaning of life enabled me to gradually find a harmony, and so became a reasonable human being in society.'

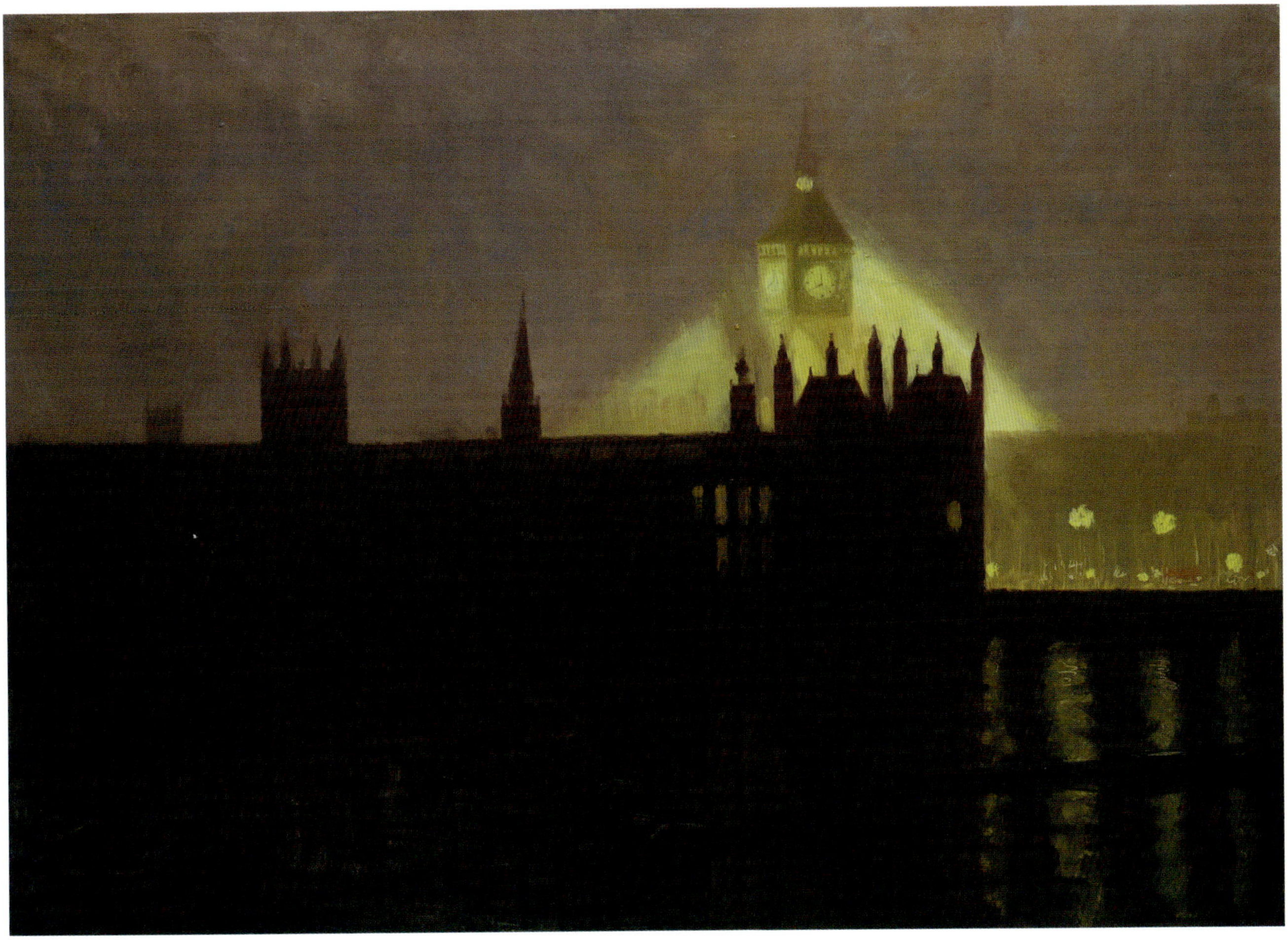

CAT. 72 – *Houses of Parliament from St Thomas Hospital at Night,* signed and inscribed with title to reverse, oil on board, 15 ¾ x 21 ½ in. (40 x 54.5 cm).

'My health was beginning to show signs of breaking. I was sent to a Civil Defence Convalescent home after serious bronchial cold. I never ceased to draw and paint and presented one painting to the Convalescent house before I left. I also painted the ceiling in an improvised theatre, and the backstage in the Depot of Kingston House, and held a drawing class one evening a week for the ambulance and rescue service personnel. Nita during most of this time was secretary at Bunce Court School. She also had a sexual affair with one of the staff at the school and on my last visit to her at Wembley on my annual leave we had separate rooms, and the new relationship was beginning to develop between us. One day in my Chiswick studio when I was recovering from influenza a friend of mine in ambulance service brought along a woman friend of his wife's who wanted to look through my portfolio drawings as she was a lovely intelligent woman with gifts in the visual arts as a designer.

I believe about this time my moral fiber was weakening and women were occupying too many of my thoughts. As much of my work in the rescue service was composed of occasionally taking people out of rubble but chiefly, cleaning houses filled with debris dust, my lungs were beginning to coat with this dust and therefore my health deteriorated. I was evidently destined to survive the war, because when the night bombing started and Victoria station was one of the targets for German planes, we received a call from squad of rescue men and ambulance to go to the station as a bomb had fallen directly on the station. My squad was chosen to go but the last moment but as we did not have a driver available, another car with five men went. And another bomb fell on the station when they were there so I was saved because they were all killed. In my spare time throughout all my rescue services during the war I drew and painted men and women around me asleep and awake, the depot Itself, memory sketches of the bombed sites I had worked on, my creative urge never left me. . . .'

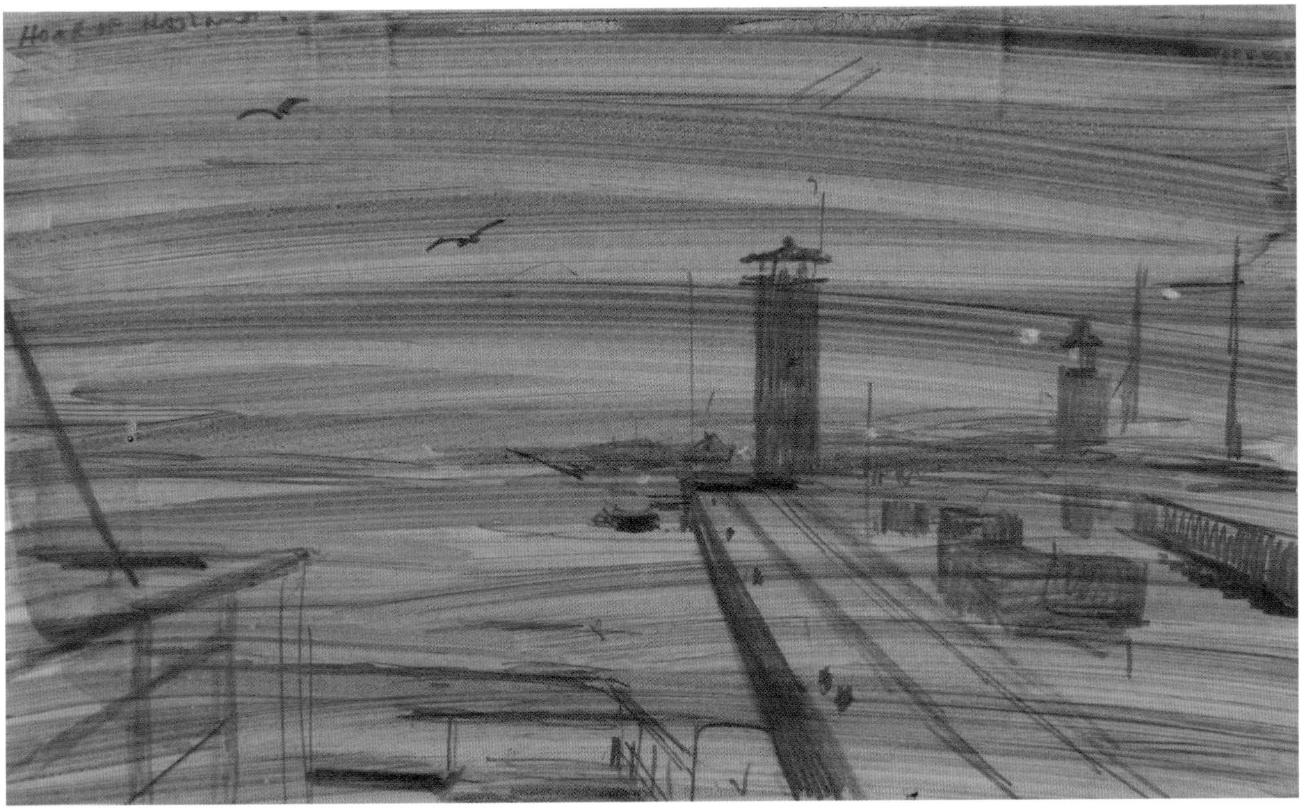

CAT. 73 – *Harbour Scene*, pencil, wash and white highlights on paper, 5 × 8 ¼ in. (13 × 20.8 cm).

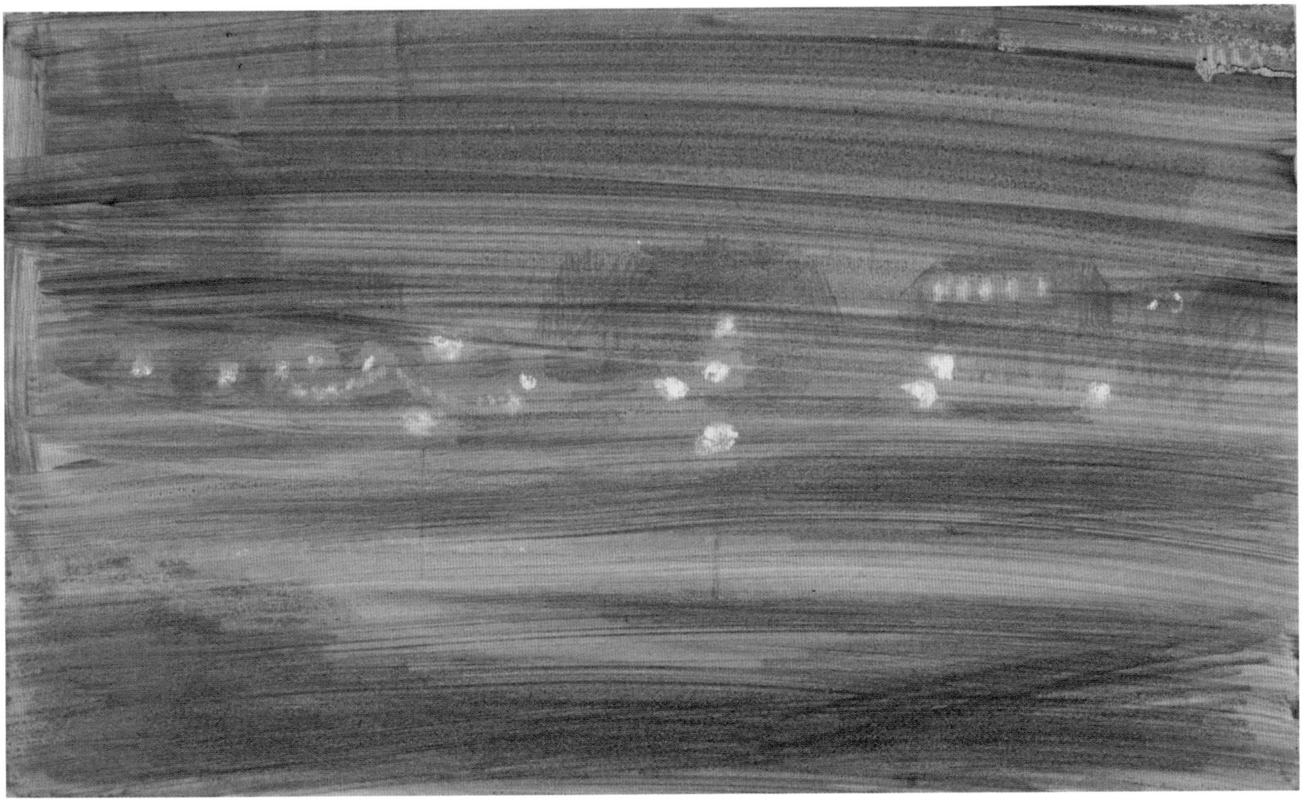

CAT. 74 – *Night Scene*, pencil, wash and white highlights on paper, 5 × 8 ½ in. (13 × 21.4 cm).

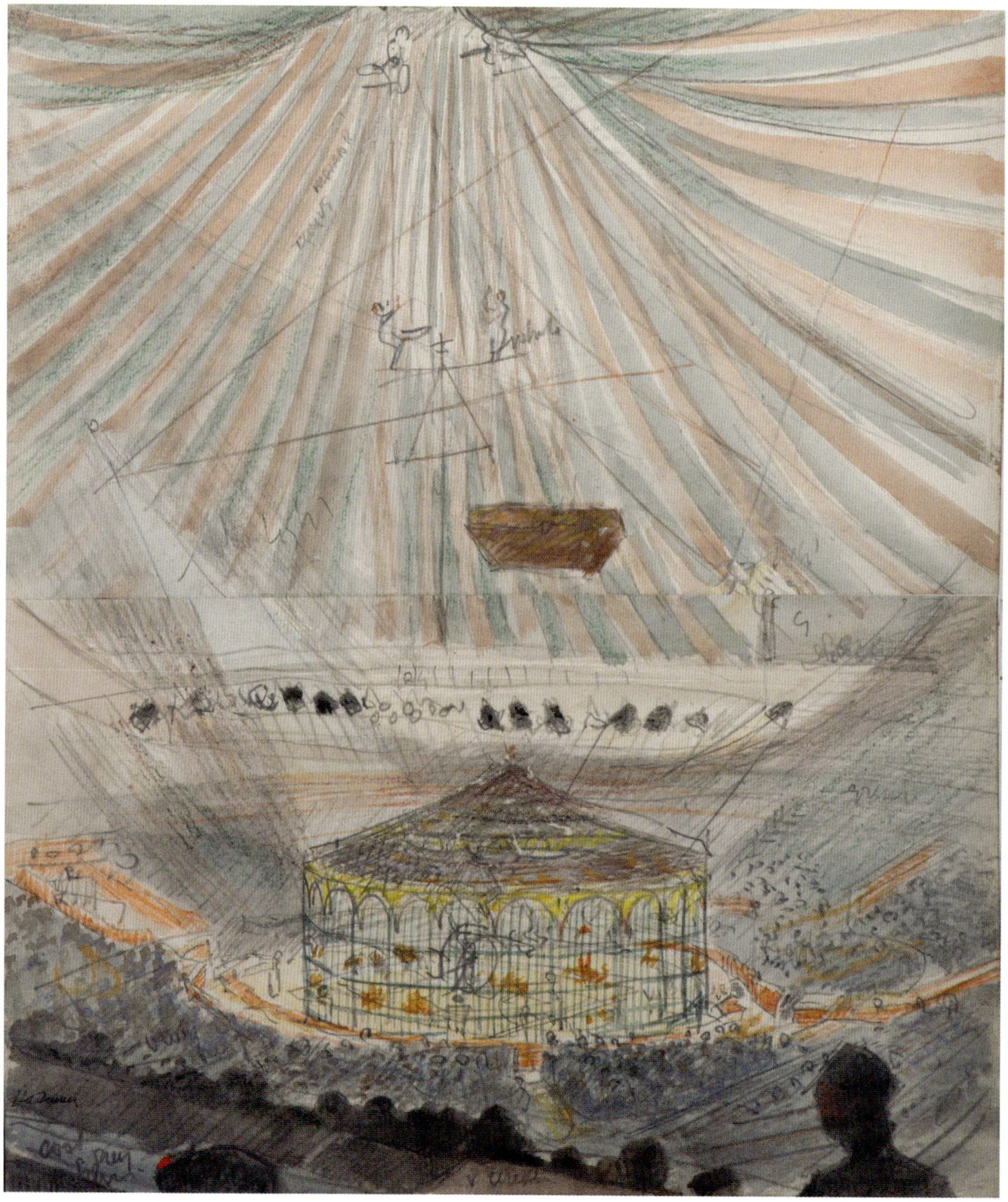

CAT. 75 – *At the Circus*, signed and inscribed with notes,
pencil and watercolour on paper, 10 x 8 ½ in. (25.7 x 21.5 cm).

CAT. 76 – *Self Portrait,* signed, titled to reverse, oil on board, 26 ½ x 21 in. (67.3 x 53.4 cm).

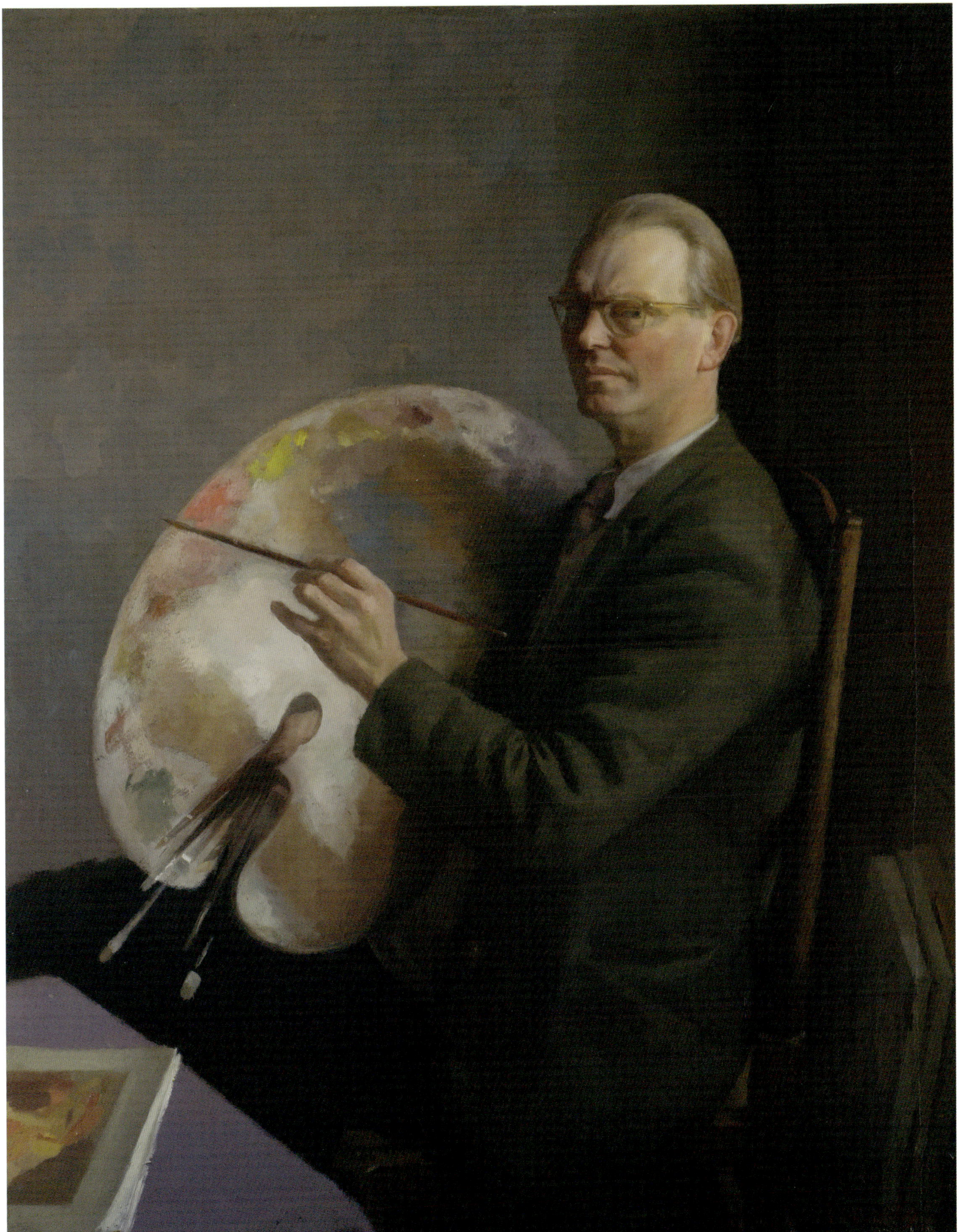

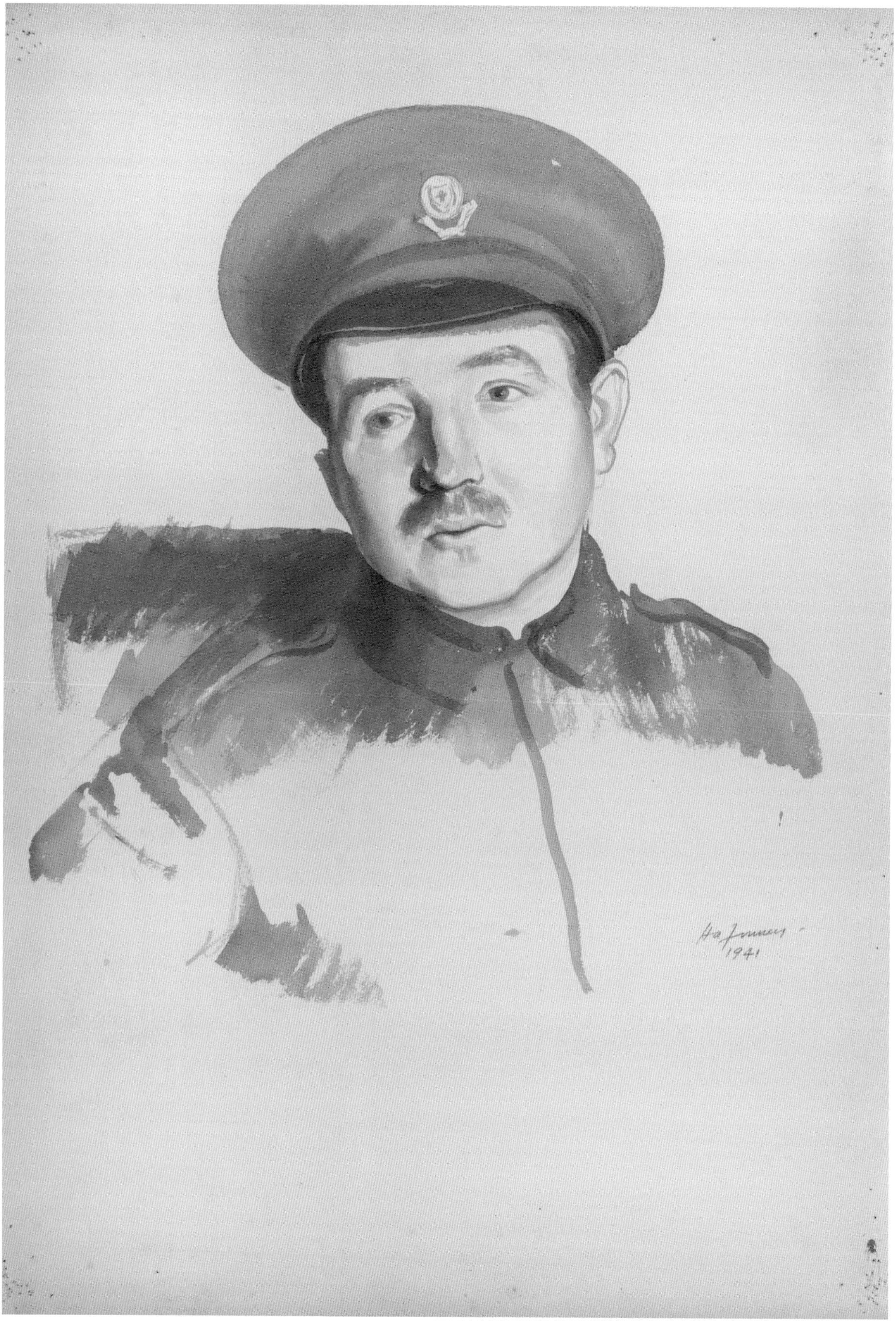
1941

'In my thirst for beauty I practised hard on learning the concert flute and had a few lessons on my days off duty with a charming flautist Mr. Claudius who lived on the outskirts of London. His patience with a raw and not naturally gifted musician, was rewarded because my flute has enabled me to get through many anxious and dangerous hours and after nearly 40 years I am still playing it and getting pleasure from my instrument.

To return to my Chiswick studio, while I was occupying the studio, a flying bomb fell in the street nearby and it shattered all my windows. This happened on the night when I was invited to spend a day with this new friend Amy Dyer at her house in Berkshire in a country town called Wokingham. I was therefore saved from being injured as my studio except for the wall against the railway embankment was glass, and when I returned next day it was all shattered. I can remember nights in the studio when the aircraft raids were active. The flying bombs were falling. On my nights off duty from the rescue service, playing my flute alone in the studio helped to combat my fears. To comment about the whole of my life and activities during these war years in London would be tedious to the reader and much of the memory of it is fading, so I will continue to remember and write down those feelings events and adventures which I consider significant to the development of the next phase of my life. After my weekend with Amy at Wokingham our relationship grew more intimate, and as I had been granted leave, because of ill-health, I transferred all of my belongings at Chiswick studio after it had been bombed, to a garage belonging to Amy's sister in Wokingham. . . .'

CAT. 77 – *Portrait of a British Red Cross Society Volunteer*, 1941,
signed and dated, wash on paper, 22 ½ x 15 ¼ in. (57.5 x 38.6 cm).

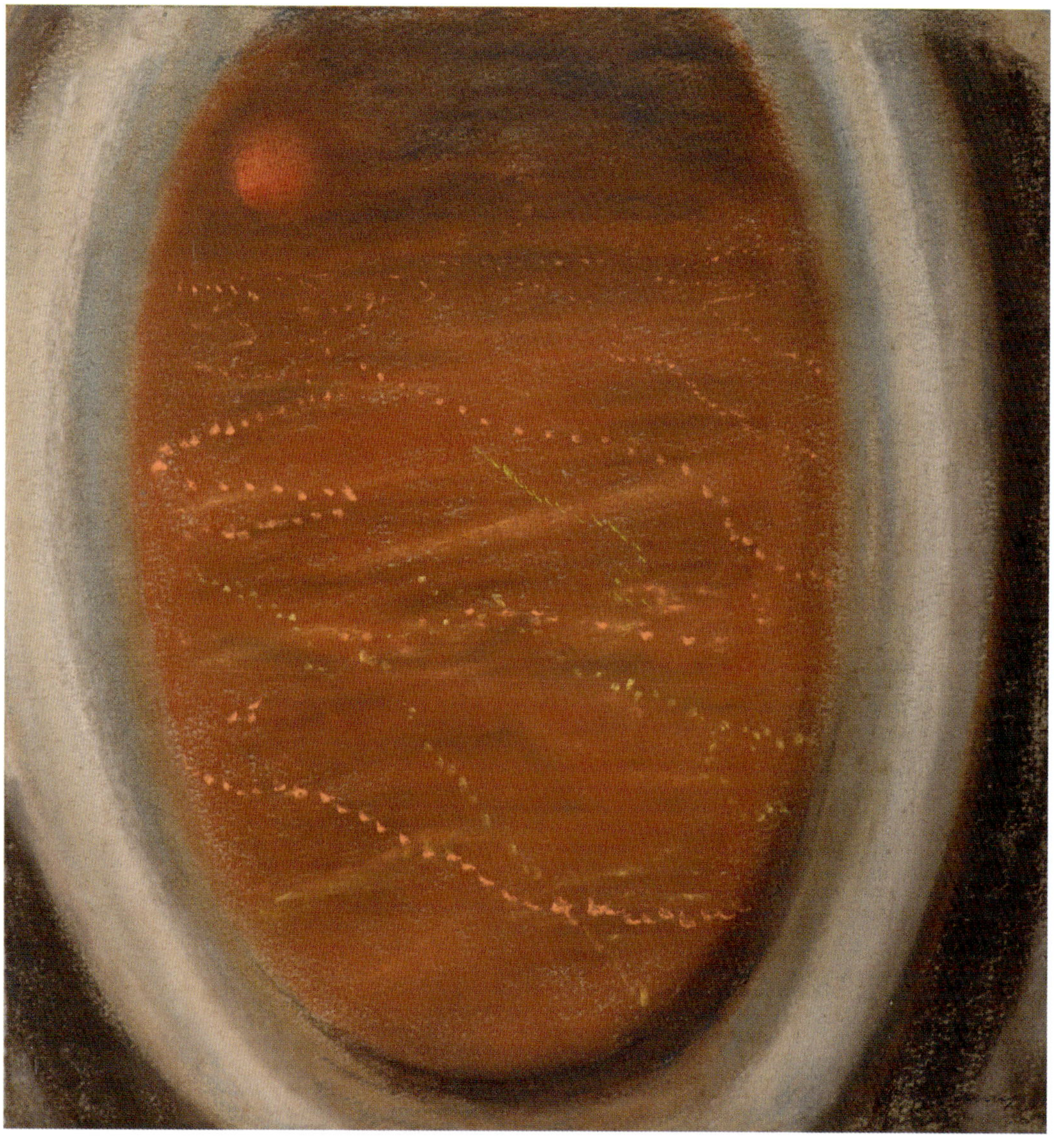

CAT. 78 – *View from an aeroplane by night*, pastel on paper, 11 ¼ x 10 ½ in. (28.8 x 26.5 cm).

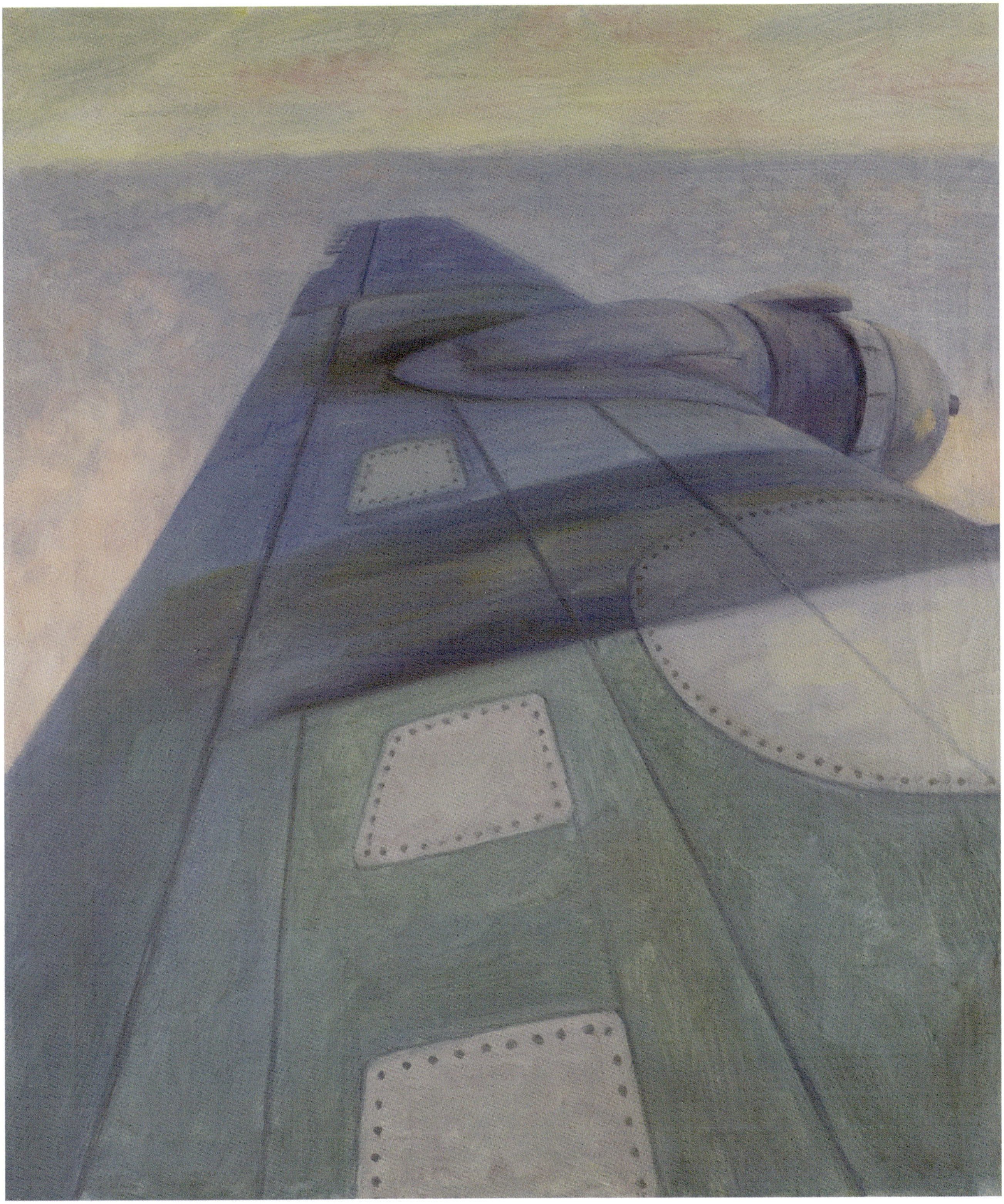

CAT. 79 – *Wing of an aeroplane over the horizon line*, oil on canvas, 23 ¾ x 19 ¾ in. (60.4 x 50.2 cm).

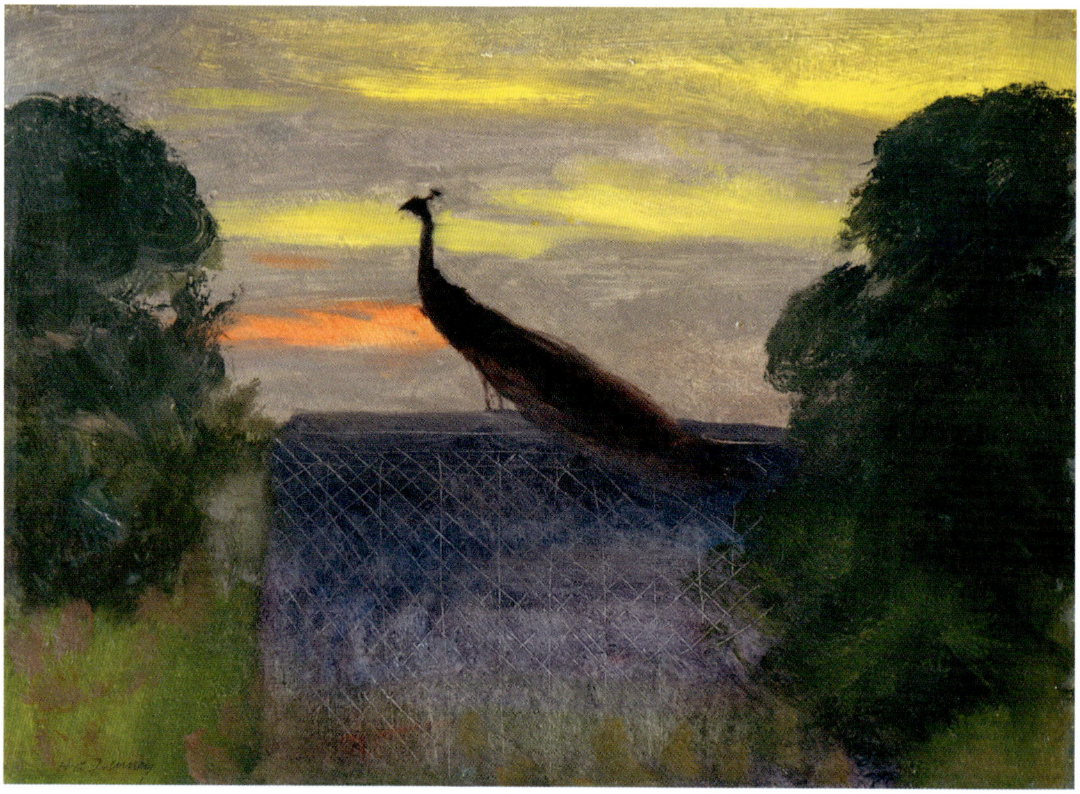

CAT. 80 – *Sunset with Peacock*, signed, oil on canvas, 12 x 16 in. (30.5 x 41 cm).

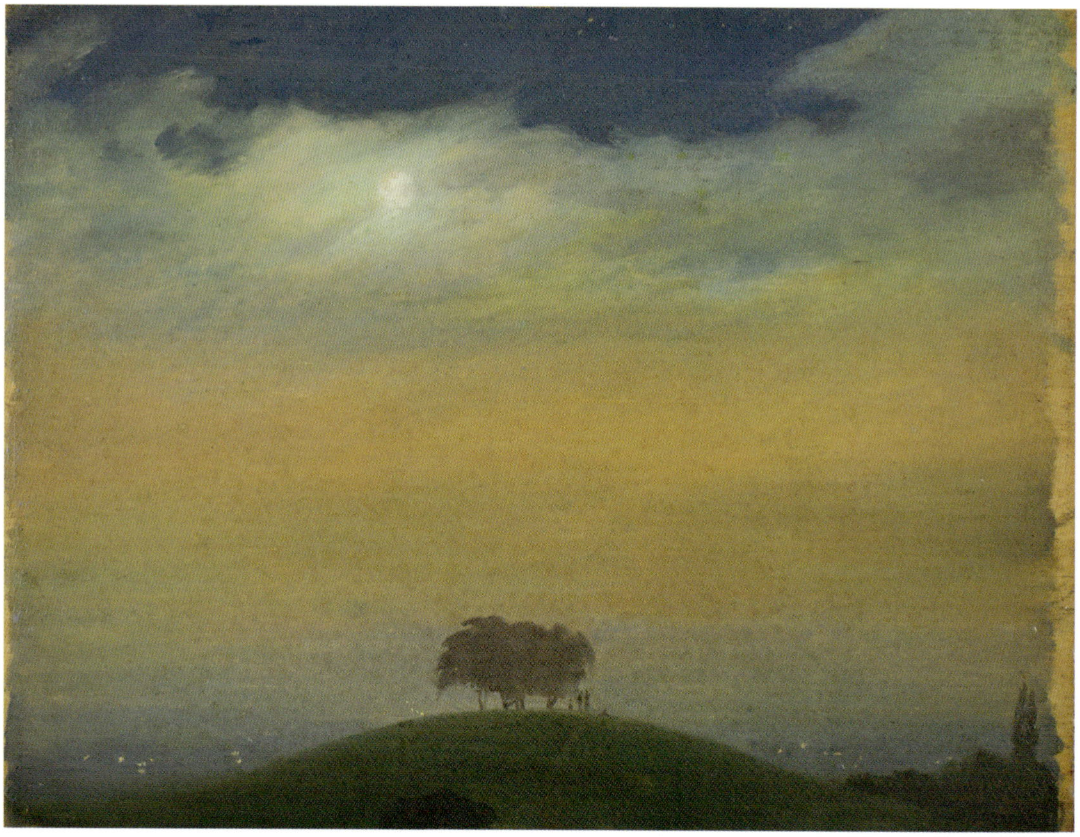

CAT. 81 – *Parliament Hill by moonlight with view of London beyond*, thinned oil on panel, 10 ¾ x 13 ¾ in. (27.4 x 35 cm).

'As we were in contact with the ambulance service, I also made many drawings of the nurses, I had admiration for many of the ambulance personnel who were young girls of good breeding and social standing, for their courage during their work when the night bombing of London began. I dreaded my nights of duty in my room alone when the night bombings started and we had no defences. During the early part of the Battle of Britain, I would go down to an Anderson shelter in the garden of the house, in which I rented a room and the tenant above me a woman with two young children also shared the shelter through the long night while the German planes did what they liked in the sky above because except for barrage balloons and our little aircraft fire we had no defences in the beginning of the second year of the war.

On the night of the great fire of London when I would see the red glow increasing over central London, It was my day off from duty, and when I was in my room at Hammersmith I could hear the German planes approaching at about 6:30 pm and I watched the fire gradually increasing around the city centre and this went on until almost midnight. To pass the time away, being on my own I put a records on, the record of Casals playing Bach's "Come Sweet Death" was my favourite one.

My passion for painting and drawing was always with me and because the building we were housed in at the beginning of the war was dreary and my associates were unawakened to the sense of beauty, my own yearnings to create increased not diminished. Perhaps this was why I decided to try to learn to play the concert flute after hearing a beautiful recording of a flautist in a children's hour broadcast given by Walter Davies. I made a painting of a crater made by a time bomb in the garden of Kingston house where we were housed, and the management bought it. . . .'

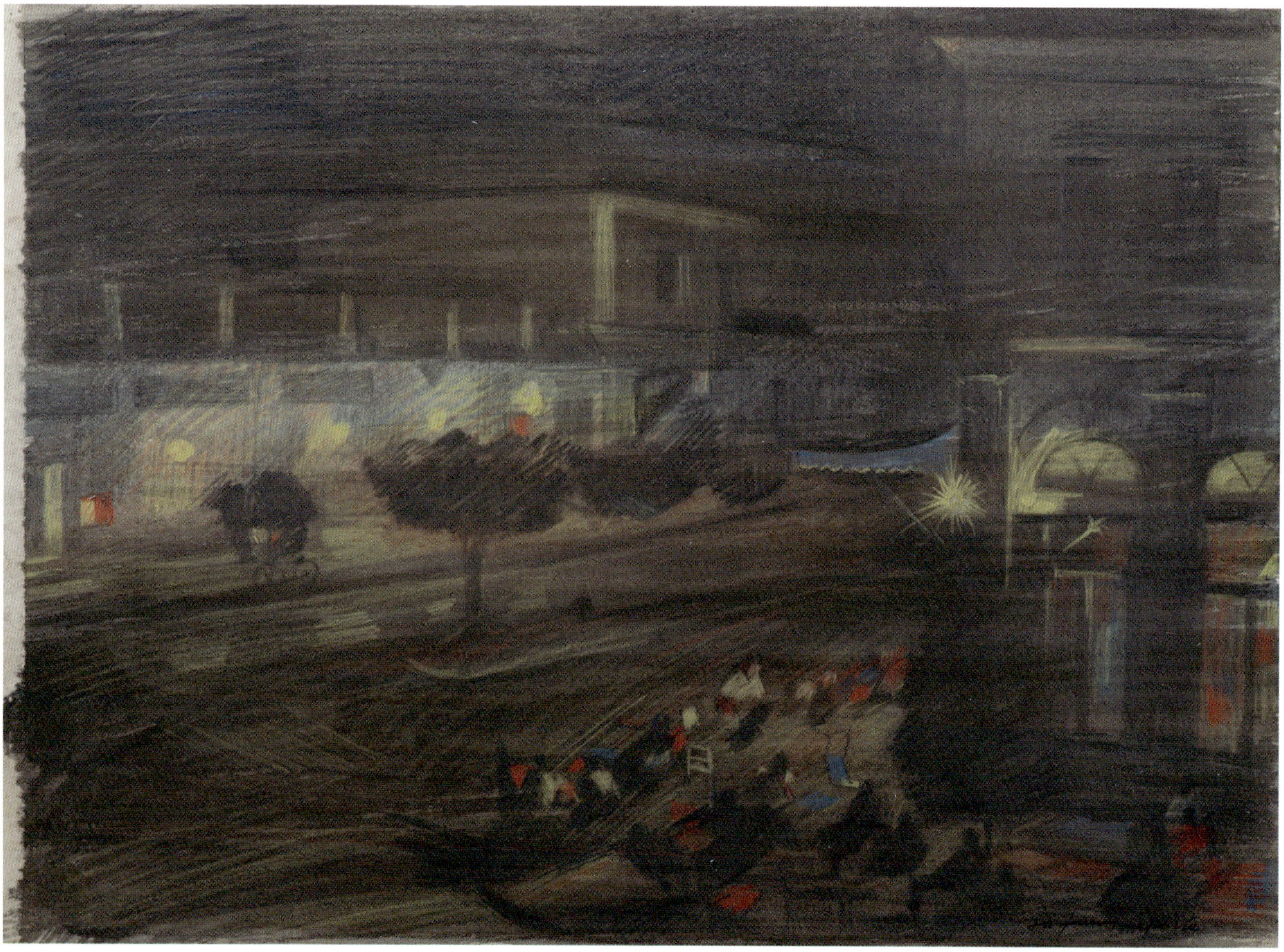

CAT. 82 – Study for *Night Café, Sparta*, signed, inscribed 'Sparta', pencil and thinned oil on paper, 11 x 14 ¾ in. (28 x 37.5 cm).

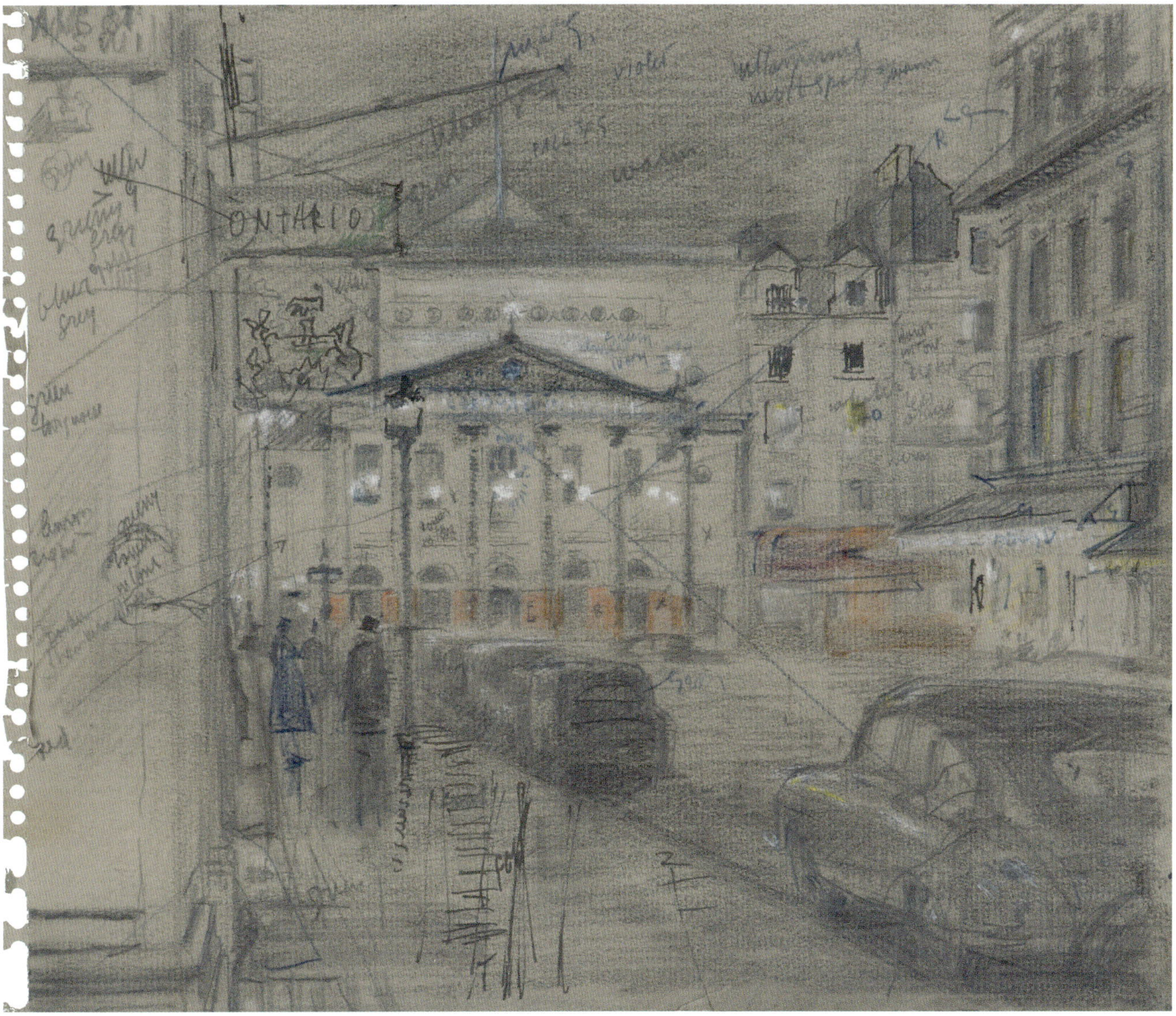

CAT. 83 – Study for *Theatre Royal Haymarket by Night*, inscribed with notes, pencil and pastel on grey paper, 7 ¾ x 9 in. (19.8 x 22.8 cm).

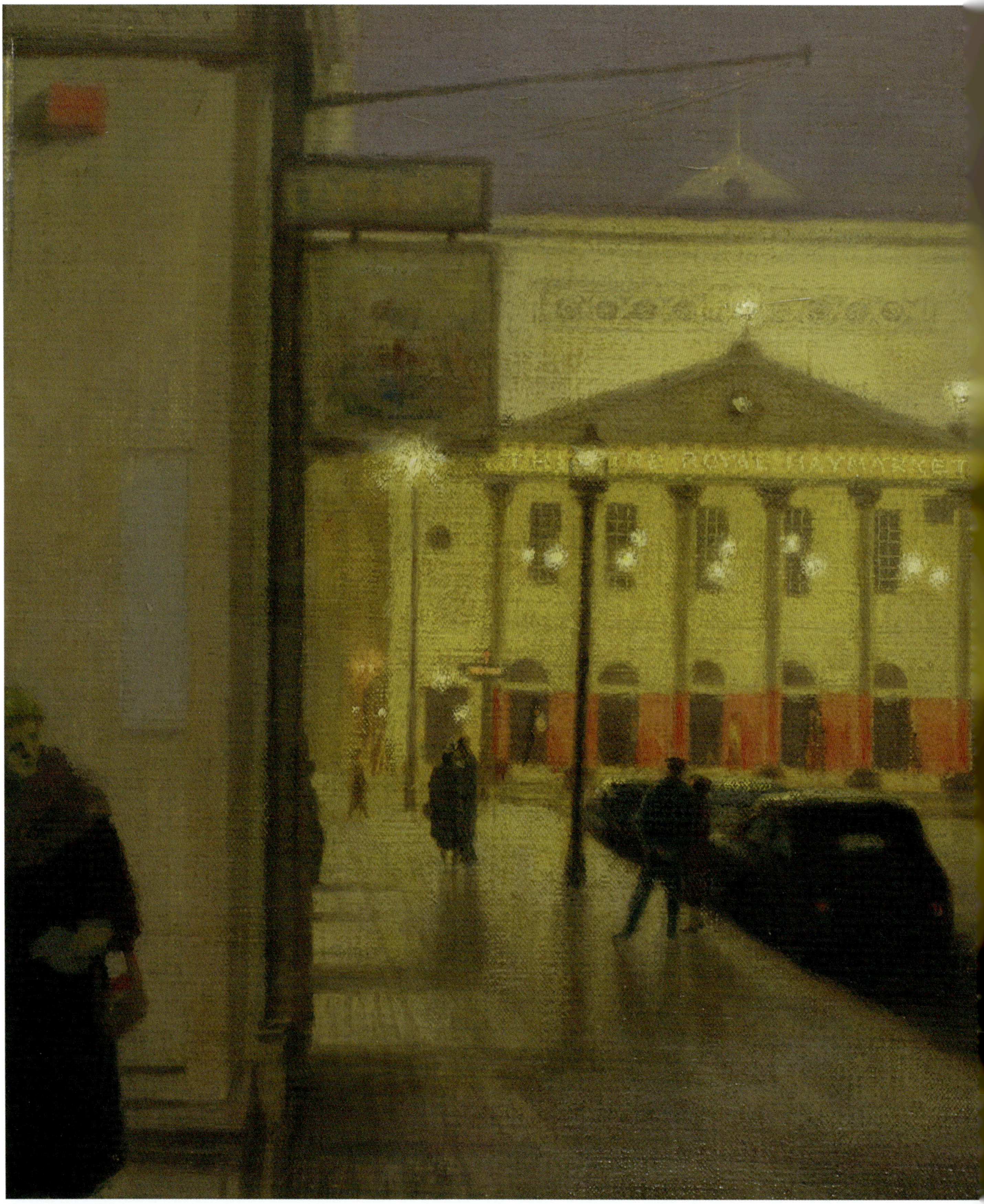
ROYAL HAYMARKET

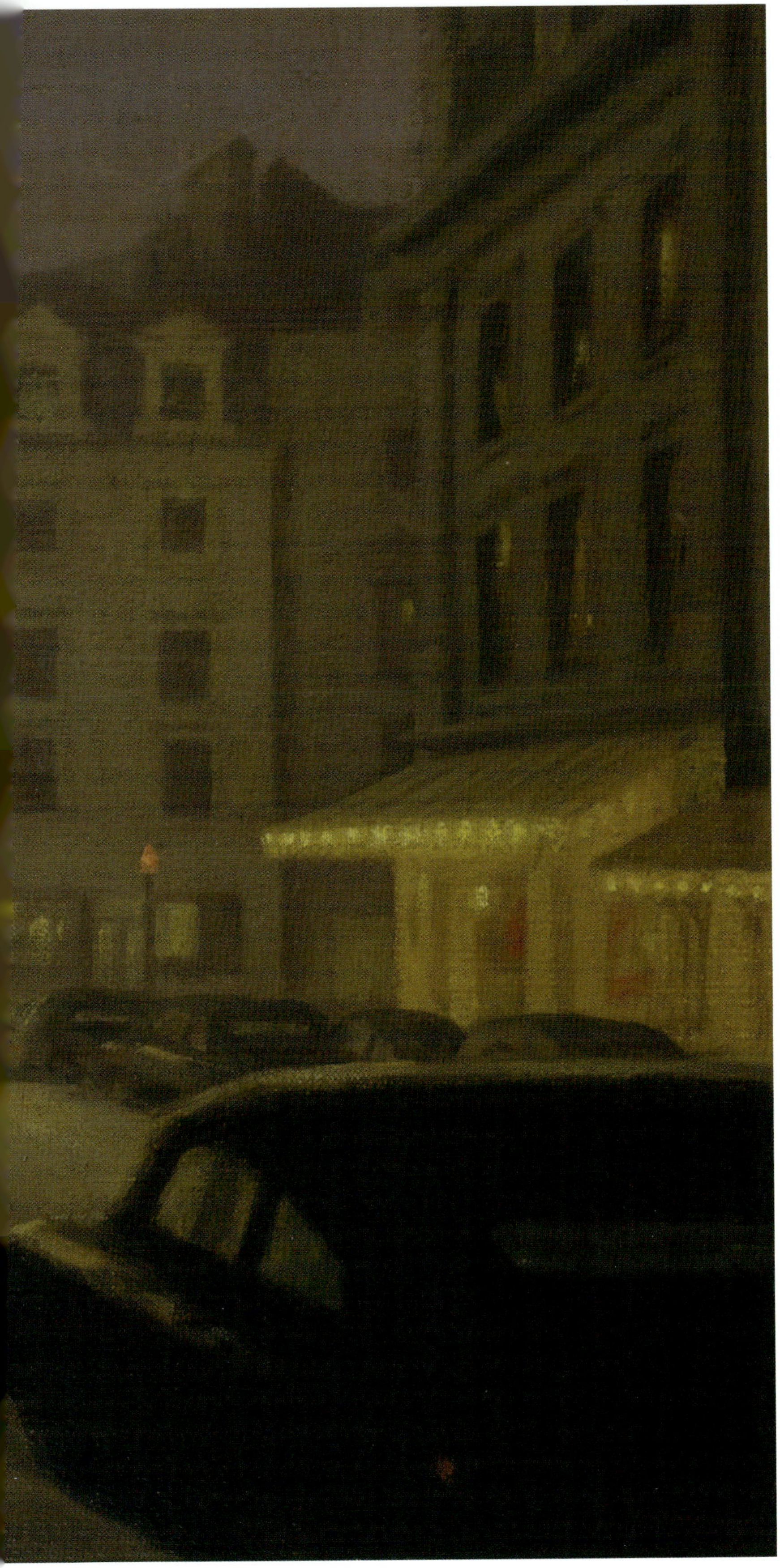

CAT. 84 – *Theatre Royal Haymarket by Night,*
signed, titled to reverse,
oil on canvas, 16 x 12 in. (40.5 x 30.5 cm).

'Nita came to London one weekend before I left this Chiswick studio, but she stayed with a friend, and visited me with Brian at home. Even if we had been able to start a home again, I believe she would have left me as the pull (perhaps hereditary) to live in Europe and then to the US was so strong I believe wishing to give Brian some permanent home influenced my decision to eventually live with Amy in Wokingham as she had a house to share. Her husband was in the forces and she had been separated for three years and there was hatred between them. I felt like a cockatoo in another's nest, but her mother and father and a paying guest were in the house as well as the two children. Brian was still at boarding school in Bruce Court School at Wem, when the significant events in my life occurred. My fascination for the opposite sex was beginning to weaken my direction in life and Amy also wanted an anchor for her sexual cravings and desire for a permanent object of love. She, like many women during the war, had much toying with so-called love, or affection, or attraction for men of the American forces in England but felt the need for something more permanent. I was the object of that desire. I remember just before I met her I joined the Communist party, because after the Battle of Stalingrad, there was much sympathy for the Russians. There was even a Mrs Churchill fund held in the depot for which I was asked to make a poster. The Communist party at the time, said they only wanted members and that one had no need to be an active one. One of The subtle ways of getting people to join. After two years I responded. Through Amy's influence I found her intellectual vitality and extroverted personality, combined with her interest in the visual arts and attractive and mesmeric influence in my life, and this is how the new direction in my life took place. The landscapes and strain on my constitution of these war years was showing in the deterioration of my health as something had to give way. I would be ill with influenza and have to nurse myself in a room at the top of a tall Victorian house with no heat for a week. The constant working when on duty of moving furniture and people amongst the debris dust and hours of sleepless nights. The strain of being alone when off duty in my own room with nights of bombing undermined my health. I had such bad sore throats that Amy persuaded me to have my tonsils out. The most painful and unpleasant operation at my age. I finally asked the release from the light rescue party as the war showed signs of victory for the Allies, and it was eventually granted to me. . . .'

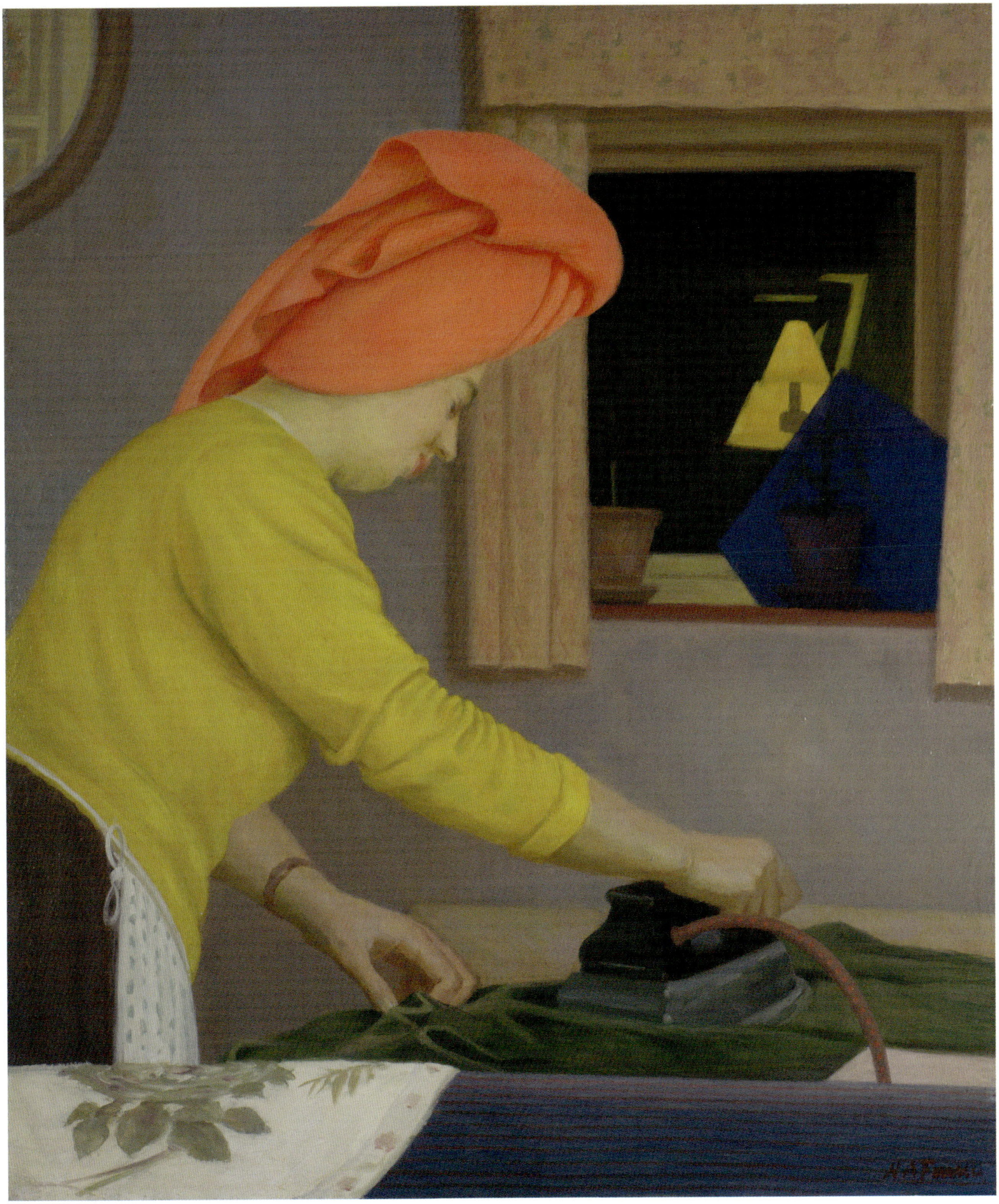

CAT. 85 – *Amy Ironing*, c.1953, signed, inscribed on stretcher 'Women Ironing after washing her hair, no 33', oil on canvas, 30 x 25 in. (76 x 63.5 cm).

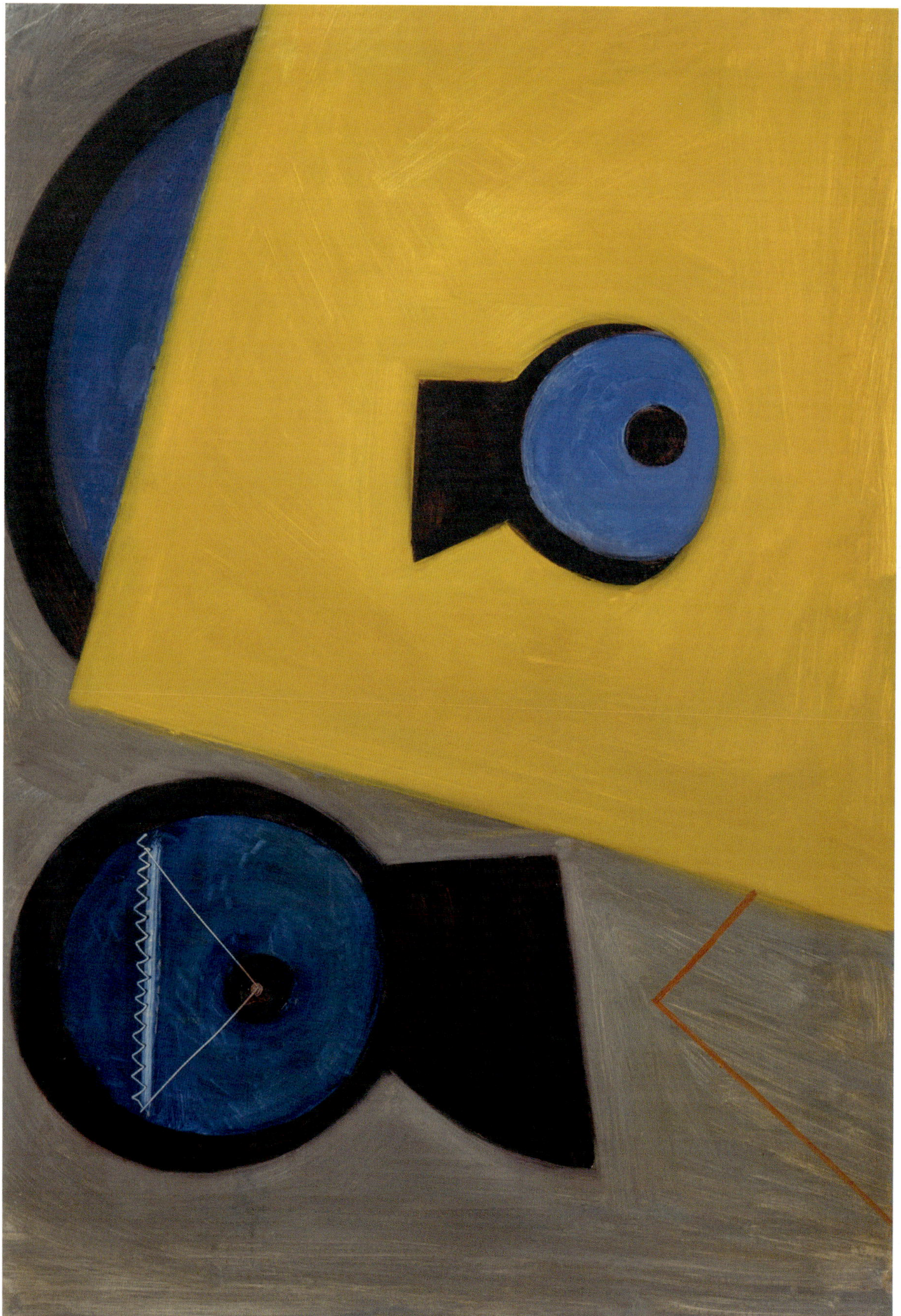

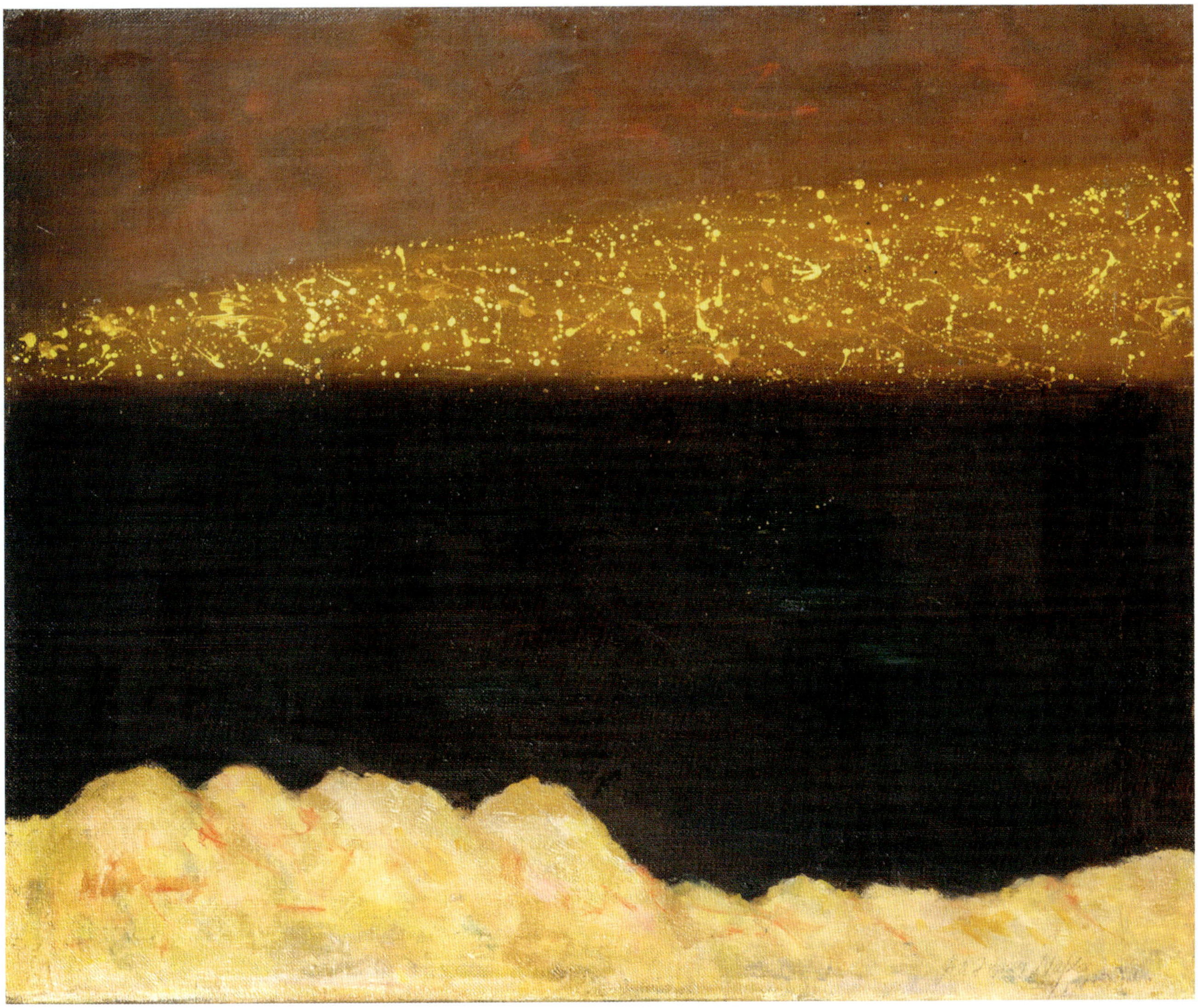

CAT. 87 – *Bay of Naples at Night, en route to Athens*, signed, oil on canvas, 20 x 23 ¾ in. (51 x 60.5 cm).

CAT. 86 – *Bay of Naples*, titled to the reverse, oil on card, 30 ¾ x 21 in. (78 x 53.5 cm).

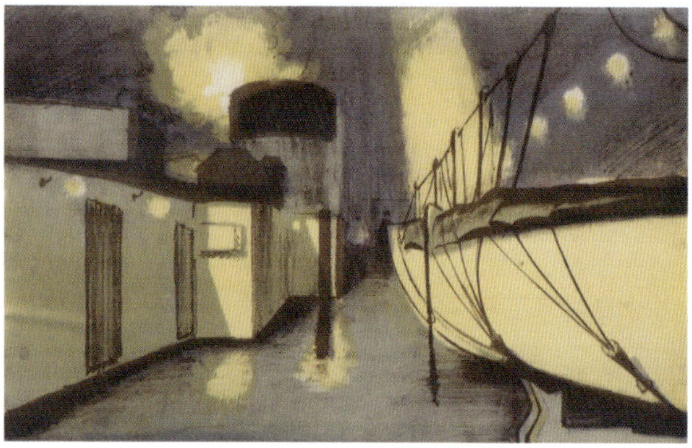
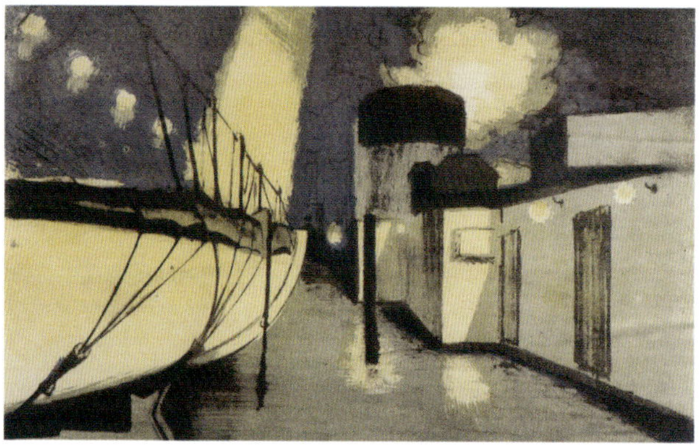
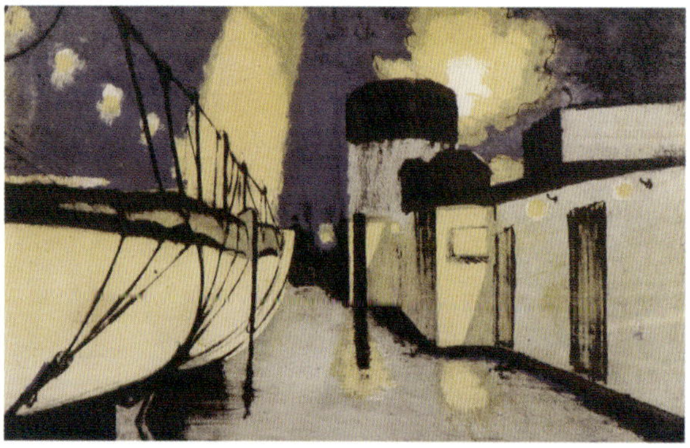
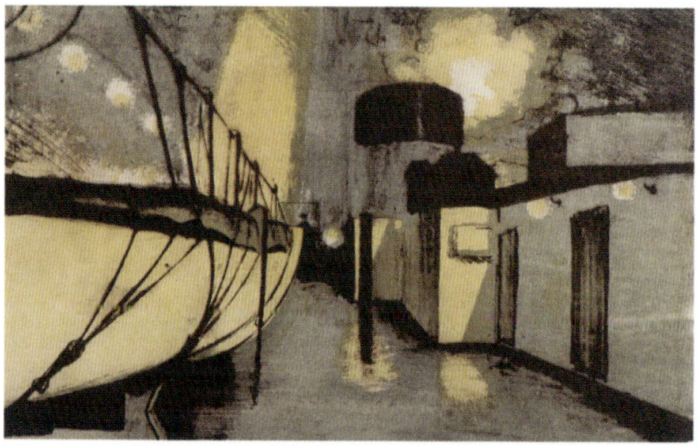
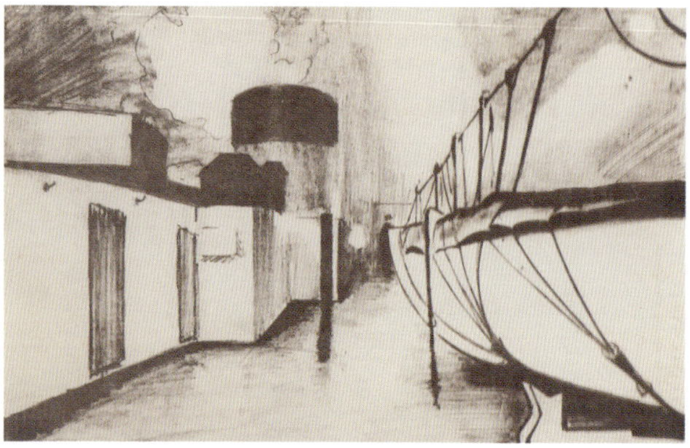
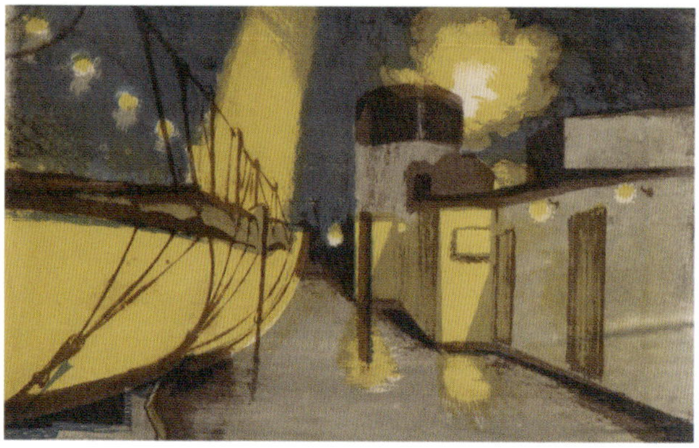
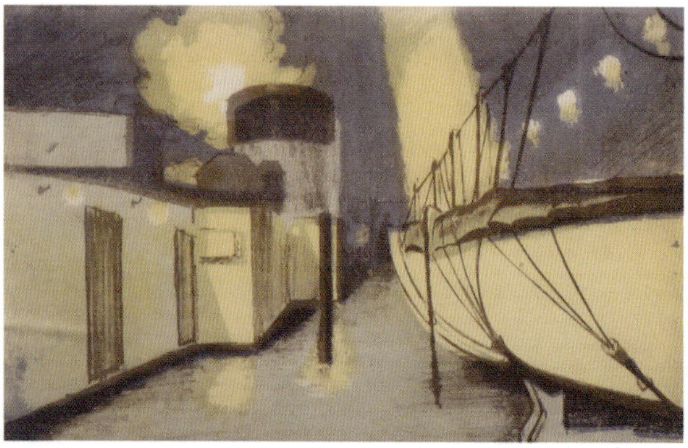
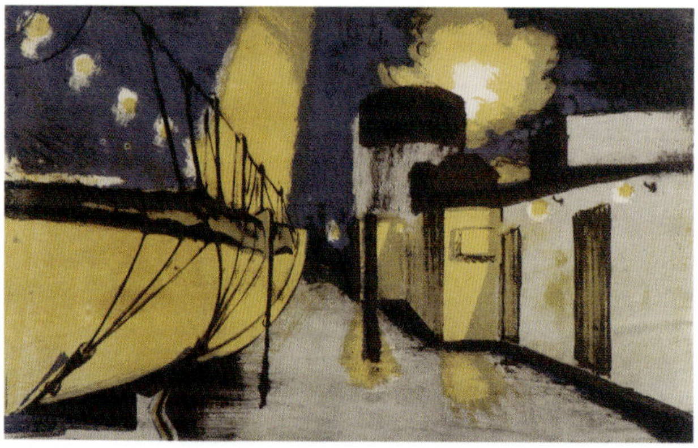

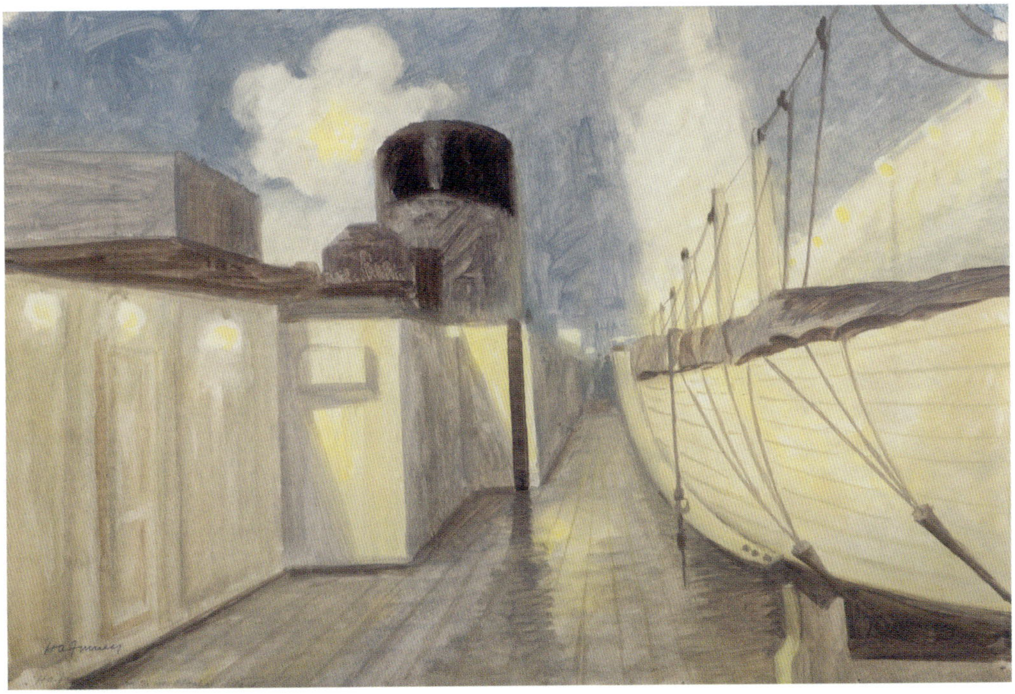

CAT. 89 – *On the Boat to the Hook of Holland*, signed, thinned oil on paper, 15 x 22 in. (38 x 55.5 cm).

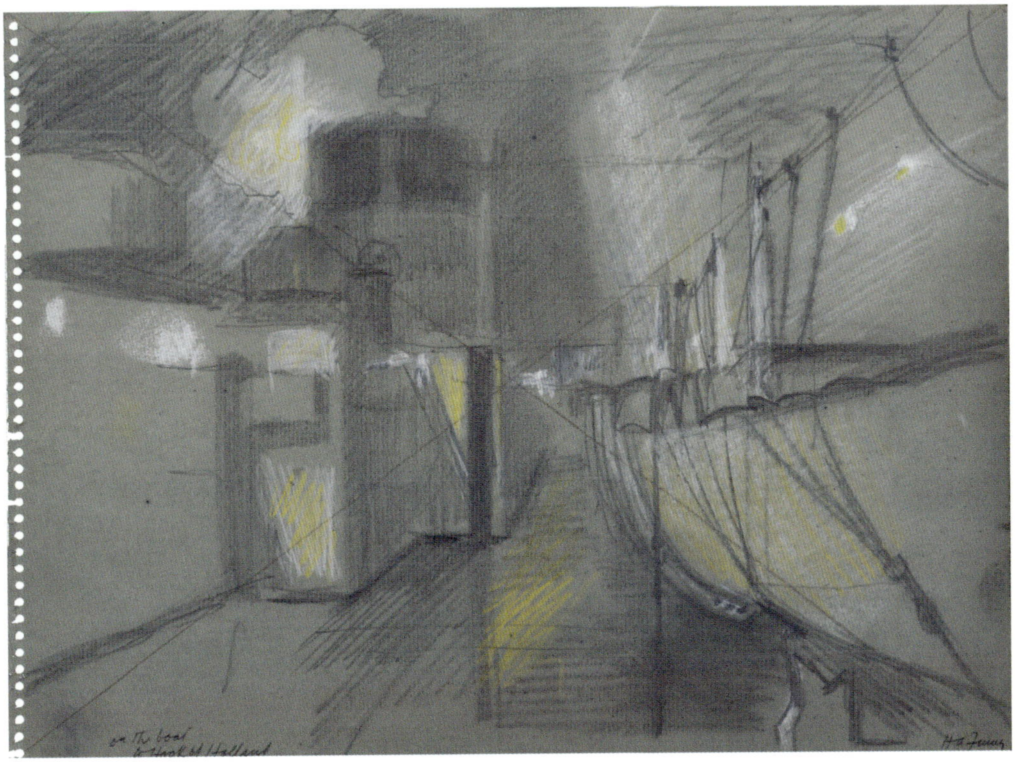

CAT. 90 – *On the Boat to the Hook of Holland*, signed and inscribed 'On the boat to Hook of Holland', pencil and white & yellow chalk on paper, 9 x 12 in. (22.5 x 30.3 cm).

CAT. 88 – *Life boats and deck at night*, set of 8 lithographs, individually framed 9 ½ x 14 ¼ in. (24.2 x 36 cm).

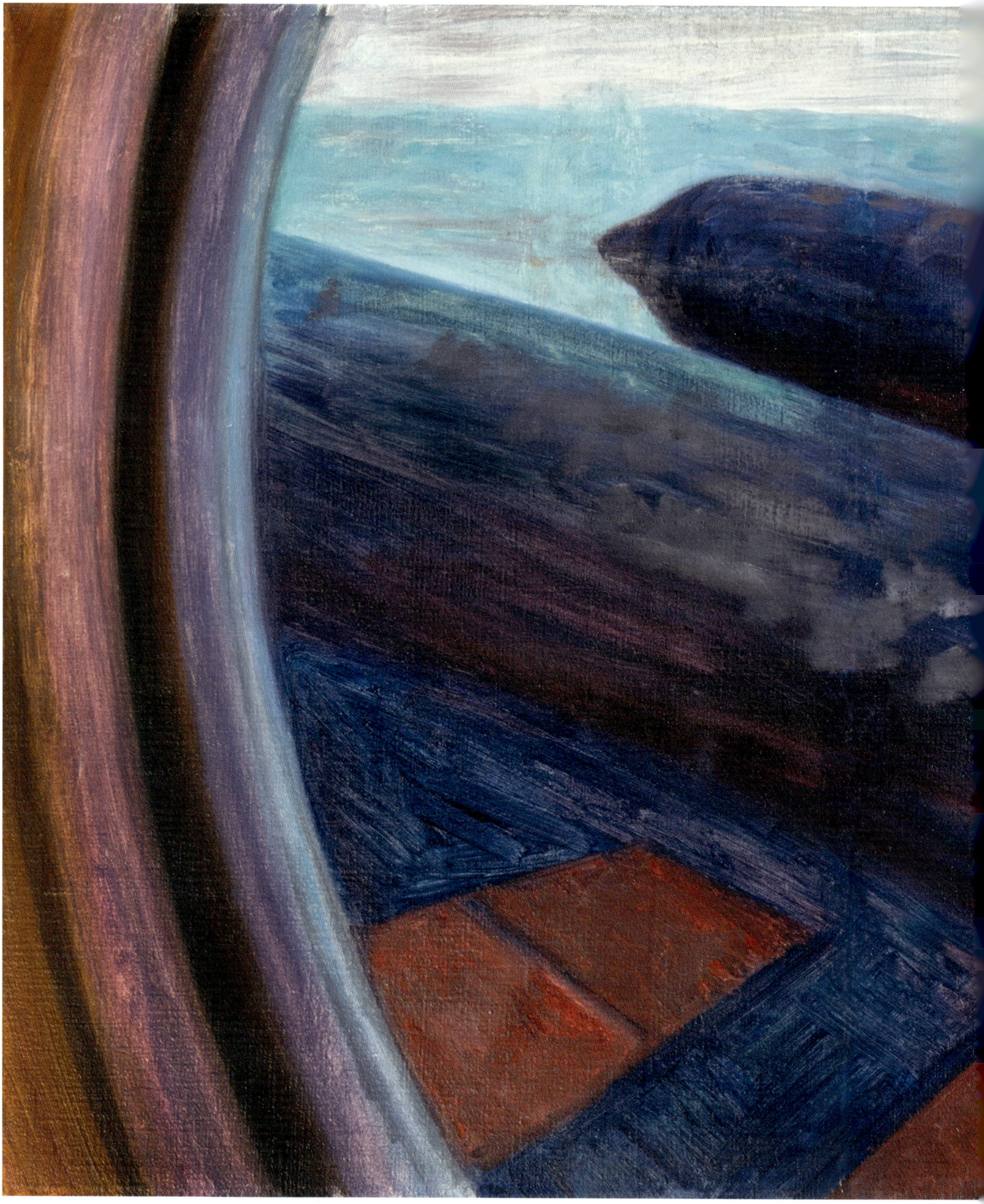

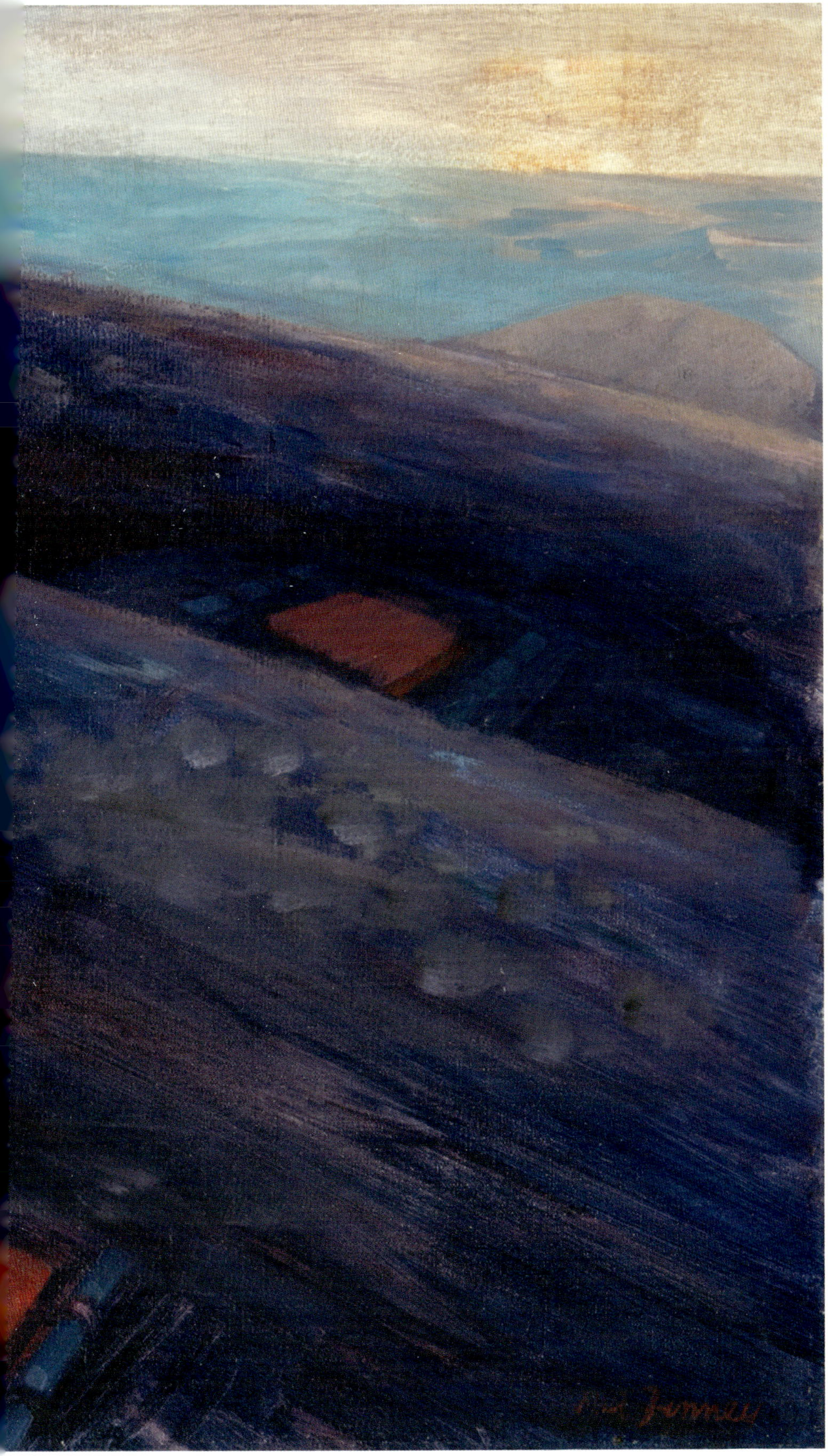

CAT. 91 – *Setting Sun*,
oil on canvas,
22 ½ x 32 ¼ in. (57 x 82 cm).

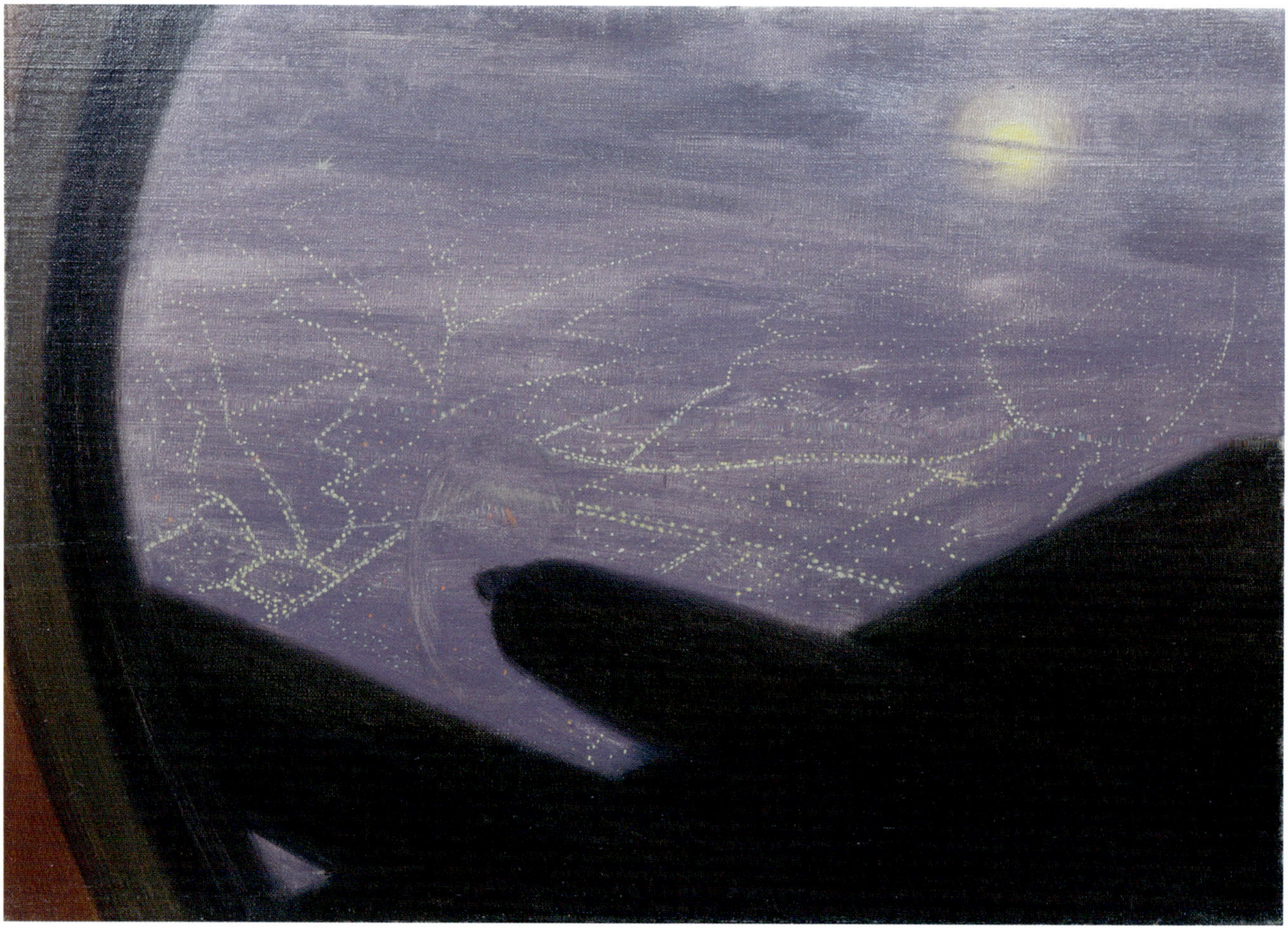

CAT. 92 – *Dusk*, oil on canvas, 16 ¾ x 23 in. (42.5 x 58.3 cm).

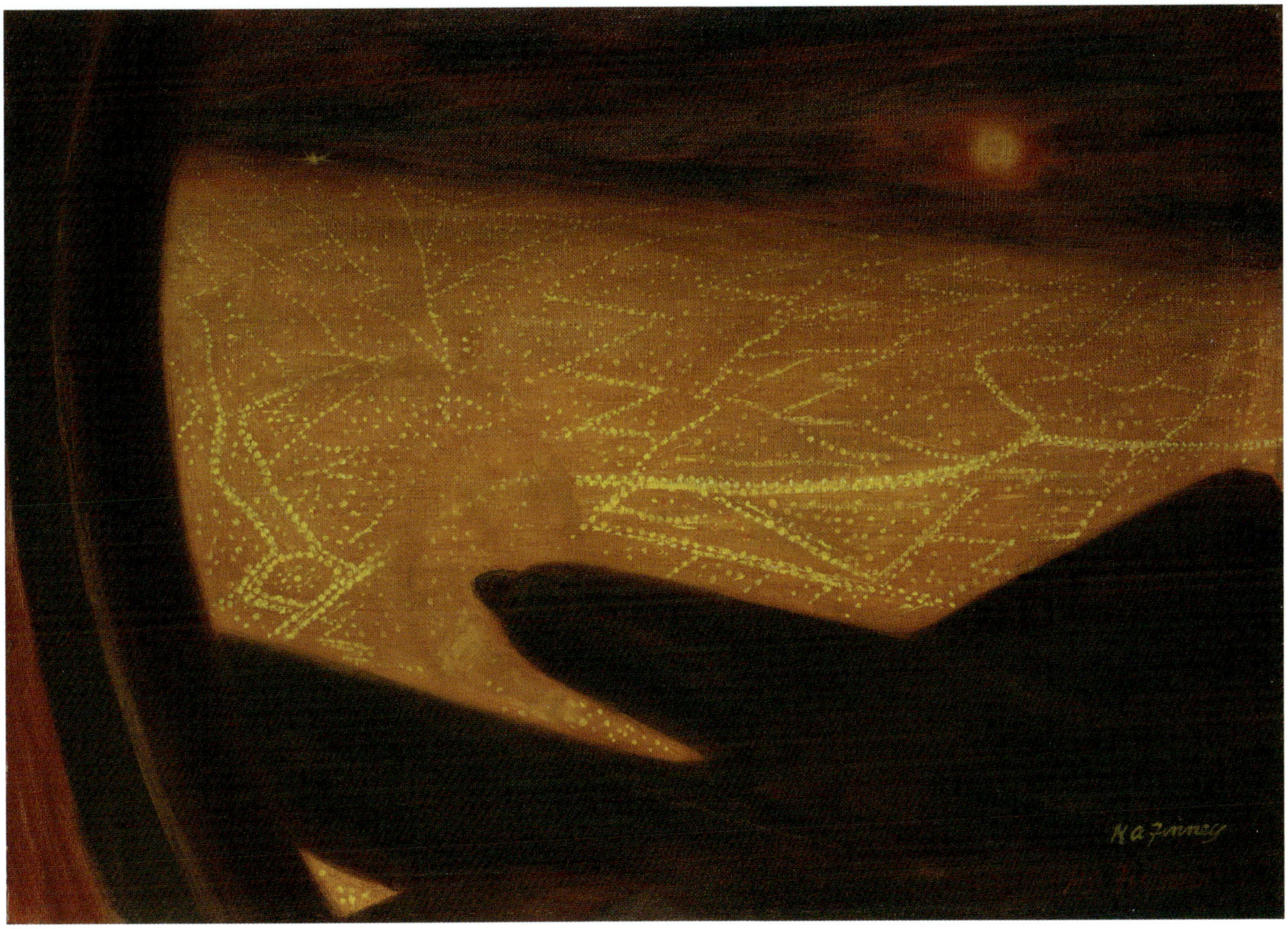

CAT. 93 – *Dawn*, signed, oil on canvas, 16 ¾ x 23 in. (42.5 x 58.3 cm).

"Life is not chaos, there is an order behind this universe. That belief has never left me."

'By this time Amy was seeking a divorce which was successful, but it was a very unpleasant experience for me. I felt sullied and dirtied after the court case, but the two children were given to the custody of the father. So here was I plunging into a complicated situation which was to develop still more, because after obtaining a teaching post at Sutton school of art, after six months I became very ill and developed wet pleurisy and had to have a pint of fluid removed from my lung which eventually collapsed. This must've been a great blow to Amy, whom I remember said to me at the beginning of our friendship, "I long for someone to take the responsibilities which I have had to bear off my shoulders, so I want someone strong and not being ill." Fate decided otherwise and her tremendous energy, optimism helped her through this difficult period of our relationship and Nita was fully aware of this new relationship with Amy, and at the beginning if she had really wanted to, could have pulled me away had she offered to share a home for Brian and myself, but no, she had set her mind on living in Europe and obtained a post in France with the American administrative forces. So the new pattern of my life was set.

After the armistice Amy's mother died and her father went back to live in the London house. Although Amy's children Christopher and David were in the custody of her father, they lived with their mother and myself for a year or two until the father took them away to live with him. The war was now at an end and we all had to make new adjustments to our lives, and find new ways of earning a living.

Amy attended a design and drawing class at Reading University, and knew Professor Betts who was the head of the Fine Art Department. He knew me as a student of the Royal College of art, and Amy mentioned to him that I was looking for a part-time teaching post, which encouraged him to offer me one in his department now I was recovering from my serious illness. A new pattern now began to develop in my life and as Amy was teaching part time, we were able to live without too much financial pressure and to plan a continual holiday each year. . . .'

CAT. 94 – *Venus*, oil on paper, 20 x 15 in. (51 x 38 cm).

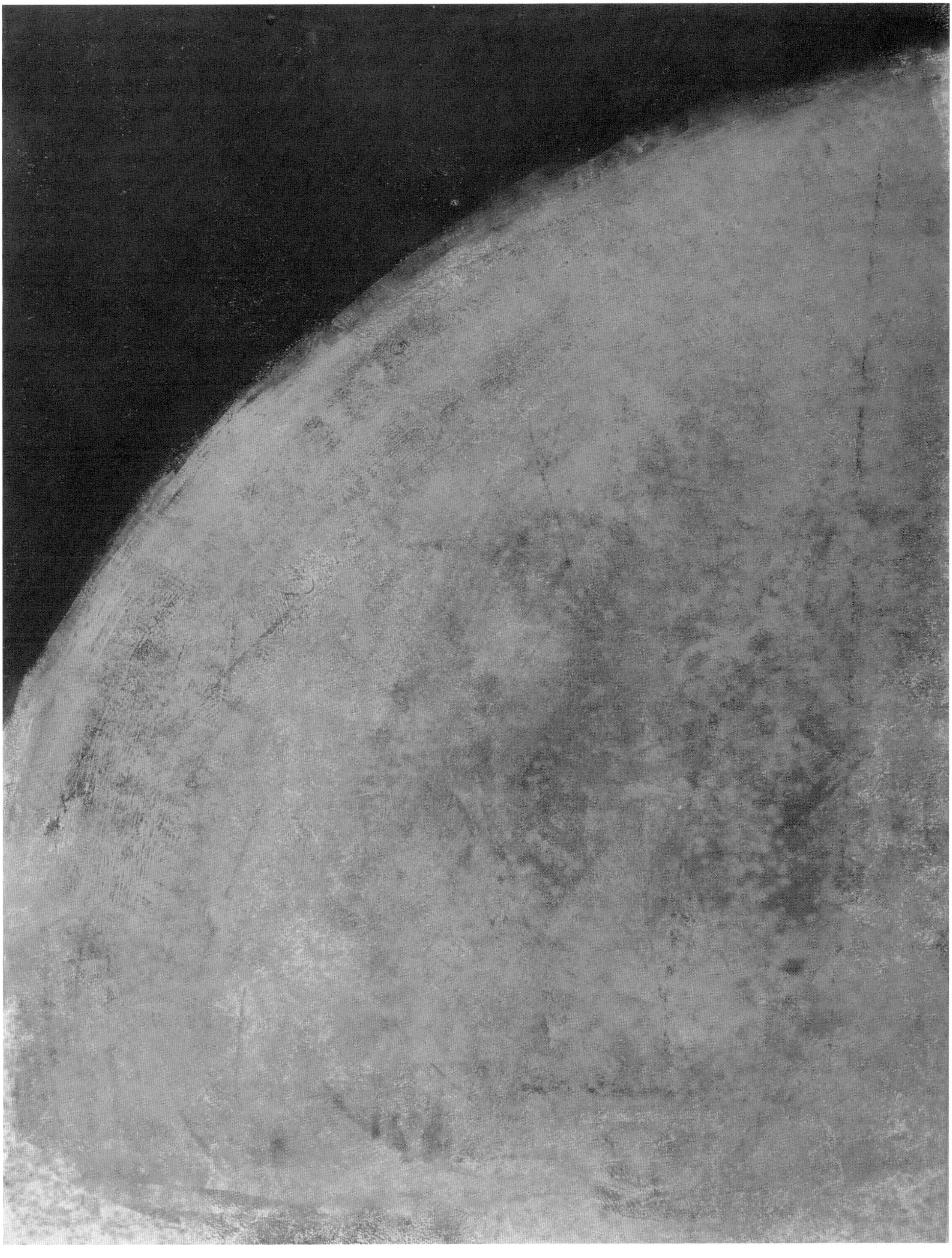

CHRONOLOGY

1905 1st February; born Hubert Arthur Finney.

1915 Aged ten invited to attend evening classes at the Bromley School of Art.

1918 Wins a Trade scholarship to the Beckenham School of Art. Meets and befriends Charles Mahoney and Gerald Gardiner. Studies under Amy Katherine Browning (1881-1978) then P H Jowett. His magnum opus from this period was *Three Marys at the Sepulchre*, (stored with Percy Horton until WW2, destroyed or lost). Taught etching by Eric Gill.

1926 Wins a £90 a year Royal Exhibitioners Scholarship to the Royal College of Art. Studies under Sir William Rothenstein who mentors him. (CAT. 95)
Shares studio with Mahoney, who introduces him to Barnett Freedman, Gerald Ososki, Albert Houthnesen, Perry Horton, Mollo Kestelman. Mahoney introduces Finney to socialism and encourages him to attend Socialist Sunday school.

1929 Gains degree and wins the travelling scholarship awarded by RCA each year. Set subject: 'Supper at Emmaus'.
Visits Paris, Florence, Arezzo, Siena, Orvieto, Ravenna, Venice, and Rome.
Befriends 1929 Rome Scholar for Engraving Eric Jones. On return to the England attends evening classes at the working men's club at Camden town for drawing, where Percy Horton taught and meets and befriends Edward Le Bas.

1930 Gets post as part time teacher at the Chelsea School of Art under P H Jowett, who is soon superseded by H.S. Williamson. Befriends Raymond Coxon and Edna Ginesi, who were on the teaching staff, and becomes an acquaintance of Henry Moore who was in charge of the Sculpture Department and Graham Sutherland, who ran the department of Design.

1934 Meets and marries Nita Patti Hayes. (CAT. 96)

1935 Birth of his first son, Brian. (FIG. 4)

1936 Carlisle Art Gallery (through the influence of Sir William Rothenstein) acquire large oil *Mother and Child*. First one man show at Cooling Gallery.

1938 In an effort to try and earn more money completes commercial work for large posters, of the Kent land-scape and Shell hoping to sell one of them to the southern Railway; in a mood of despair applies for a

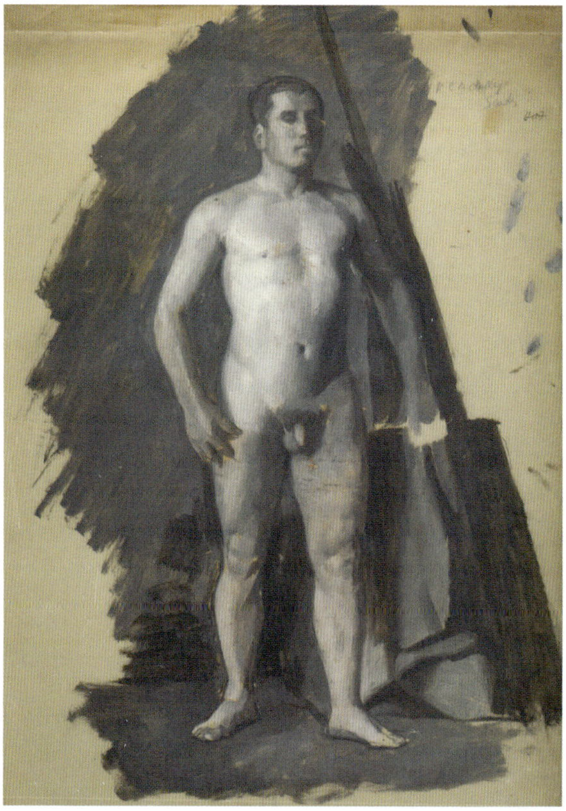

CAT 95 – Life study, Royal College of Art,
oil on tracing paper, 19 ¼ x 14 ¼ in. (49 x 36 cm).

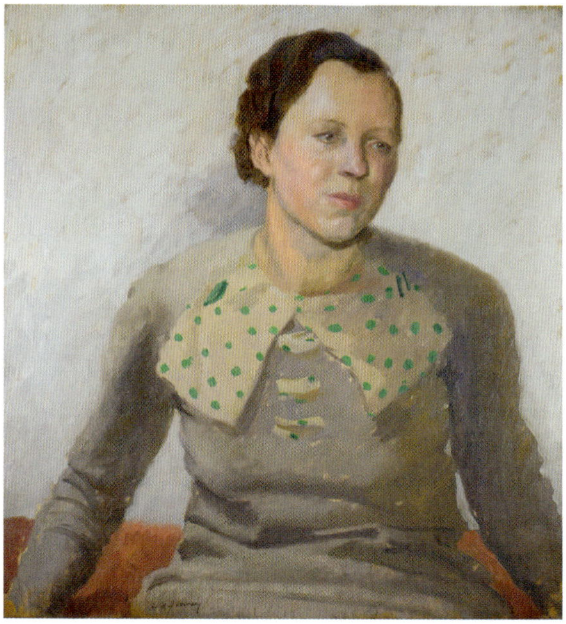

CAT. 96 – *Nita (one sitting sketch)*, 1935,
oil on panel, 21 x 19 in. (53.2 x 48.3 cm).

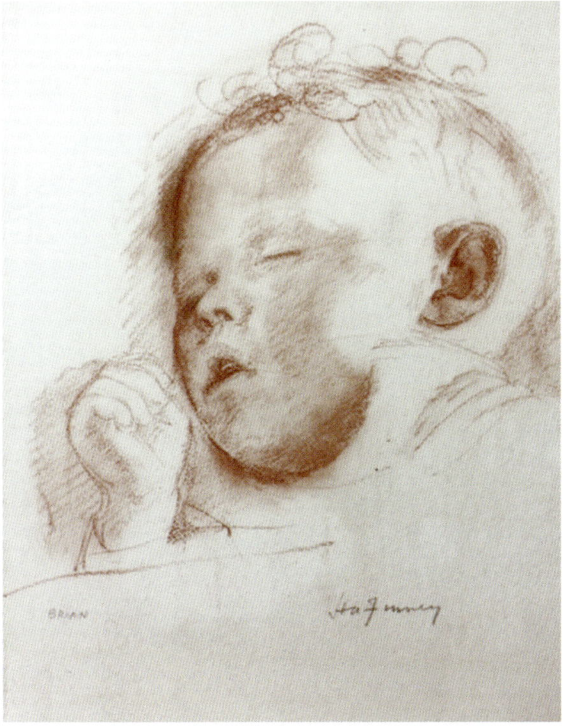

FIG. 4 – Portrait of Brian Finney.

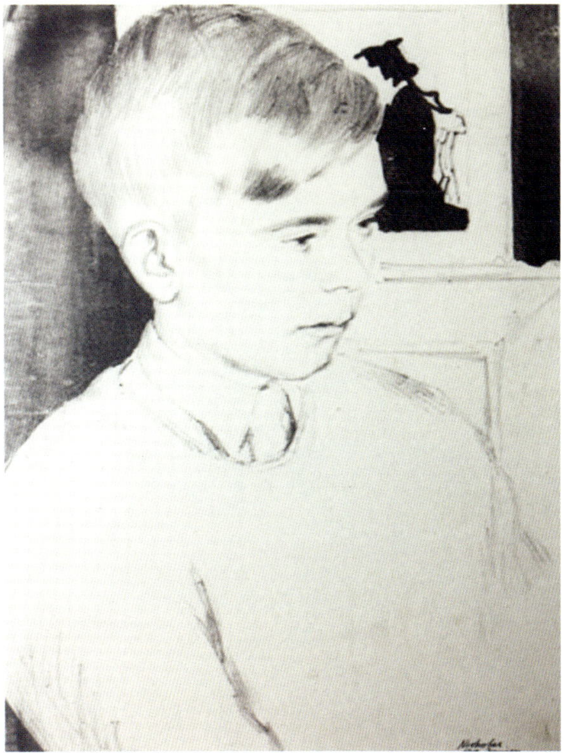

FIG. 5 – Portrait of Nicholas Finney.

Steward job on board a ship at Liverpool.

1939 Joins the Light Rescue Service of the Civil Defence.

1940 Chiswick studio bombed resulting in the loss of most of his pre-war work.

1943 Joins Communist Party.

1944 Obtains a teaching post at the Sutton School of Art but falls ill.

1945 Meets Amy Dyer, 'a lovely intelligent woman with gifts in the visual arts as a designer', who had attended design and drawing classes at Reading University, and knew Professor Betts who was the head of the Fine Art Department. Secures a part-time teaching post which resulted in Finney being put in charge of life drawing, a position he holds until his retirement in 1970.

1946 Birth of his second son, Nicholas. (FIG. 5)

1950 *An Austrian Woman* (wash study) is exhibited at the Royal Academy [No. 1047].

1954 Buys White Cottage in Winnersh Berkshire which becomes his home for the next two decades.
The First Fall of Snow is exhibited by the Pastel Society for their touring exhibition.
Mrs Margaret Sylvester [No. 13] and *Master Nicholas Finney* [No. 19] are exhibited in the 59th and 60th Royal Society of Portrait Painters touring exhibitions of 1953 and 1954.

1955 *A Portrait of Mademoiselle Alix* is exhibited in the Salon in Paris. The same painting was exhibited at the Royal Academy in 1954 [3381].

1964 Exhibition of drawings and paintings at the University of Oxford's Institute of Education (80 works).

1966 Spends a year in America (on an exchange program) at the University of Wisconsin; living in Milwaukee during Which he produced a distinctive body of new work inspired by friendships with celebrated American artists such as Joe Freibert and Danny Pierce.

1967 Betts retires from Reading University and is replaced by Professor Claude Rogers. Support for life drawing begins to wane.

1970 Retires from Reading University Art School as Head of life drawing. Moves to Barrington, near Ilminster, Somerset.

1991 January, Hubert Arthur Finney dies, aged 85.

30TH ANNIVERSARY

LISS LLEWELLYN

Founded in 1991 by Paul Liss and Sacha Llewellyn, LISS LLEWELLYN are exhibition organisers, publishers and Fine Art dealers specialising in the unsung heroines and heroes of British art from 1880 to 1980. During the last thirty years LISS LLEWELLYN have worked in association with museums and cultural institutions in the United Kingdom and abroad to develop a series of in-depth exhibitions to encourage the reappraisal of some of the lesser-known figures of twentieth century British art.

EXHIBITIONS

LISS LLEWELLYN exhibitions have been staged at Sir John Soane's Museum (London) / Pallant House Gallery (Chichester) / Cecil Higgins Gallery (Bedford) / Harris Museum (Preston) / Alfred East Gallery (Kettering) / Young Gallery (Salisbury) / Royal Albert Memorial Museum (Exeter) / Royal Museum and Art Gallery (Canterbury) / Fry Art Gallery (Saffron Walden) / Beecroft Art Gallery (Southend) / The Church of England / The British School at Rome.

PUBLICATIONS

LISS LLEWELLYN have published over twenty books on British Art and Artists. Our last four publications have all been longlisted for the Berger Art History Prize. *Alan Sorrell – The Life & Works of an English Neo-Romantic Artist* was chosen as one of the best art books of 2013 by Brian Sewell. *Evelyn Dunbar – The Lost Works* was chosen as one of the best books of 2015 by *The Guardian*.

MUSEUMS

LISS LLEWELLYN sells to museums throughout the UK, in Europe, America, Canada, Australia, Japan and New Zealand. Our clients include:

Tate / The Victoria & Albert Museum / The permanent collection of the House of Commons / The Imperial War Museum / The Science Museum / The British Museum / The National Portrait Gallery / The Fitzwilliam / The Ashmolean / Leeds City Art Gallery / Jerwood Gallery / Southampton Art Gallery / Wolverhampton Art Gallery / Cheltenham Art Gallery / The Ferens City Art Gallery / Scottish National Gallery of Modern Art / Garden Museum (London) / The Courtauld Institute, London / The Hull University Art Collection (Hull) / Williamson Art Gallery and Museum (Birkenhead) / The Bowes Museum (Co. Durham) / Central St. Martins Museum and Study Collection / Geffrye Museum (London) / The Whitworth Art Gallery (Manchester) / Metropolitan Museum of New York / Yale Center for British Art / National Gallery of Canada / Le Musée National du Moyen Âge (Paris) / Palazzo Strozzi (Florence) / Art Institute (Chicago) / Wolfsonian Museum (Miami Beach, Florida) / Musée Cluny (Paris) / The Frick Library (New York) / The Museum für Kunst und Gewerbe (Hambourg) / The Gates Foundation / The National Museum of Western Art, Tokyo.

We have gifted work to the following museums:

V&A, British Museum, UCL Art Museum, National Maritime Museum, Ben Uri, Tate Archive, Imperial War Museum, The Garden Museum and The Wolfsonian, Miami. The collection that we created for Laporte in 2000 was the winner of the Corporate Collection of The Year Award.

LISS LLEWELLYN

Adam House, 7-10 Adam Street, London WC2N 6AA

T: + 44 (0)207 520 9225 PAUL@LISSLLEWELLYN.COM SACHA@LISSLLEWELLYN.COM

www.LISSLLEWELLYN.COM